The
Successful
Paralegal

Job Search Guide

The Successful Paralegal

Job Search Guide

Chere B. Estrin Ph.D
Stacey Hunt

Foreword By
Richard Shaffran, Esq. Director,
UCLA Extension Attorney Assistant Training Program

WEST

THOMSON LEARNING ™

Australia   Canada   Mexico   Singapore   Spain   United Kingdom   United States

WEST

™

THOMSON LEARNING

WEST LEGAL STUDIES

The Successful Paralegal Job Search Guide

Chere B. Estrin Ph.D and Stacey Hunt

Business Unit Director:
Susan L. Simpfenderfer

Executive Editor:
Marlene McHugh Pratt

Acquisitions Editor:
Joan M. Gill

Editorial Assistant:
Lisa Flatley

Executive Marketing Manager:
Donna J. Lewis

Channel Manager:
Wendy E. Mapstone

Executive Production Manager:
Wendy A. Troeger

Production Editor:
Betty L. Dickson

Cover Designer:
Dutton & Sherman Design

Library of Congress Cataloging-in-Publication Data

Estrin, Chere B.
   The successful paralegal job search guide / Chere B. Estrin, Stacey Hunt.
     p.cm.
   Includes index.
   ISBN 0-7668-3025-X
   1.Legal assistants–Vocational guidance–United States.
   I.Hunt, Stacey. II. Title.

KF320.L4 E773 2000
340′.023′73—dc21
                                                                00-049789

NOTICE TO THE READER

Publisher does not warrant or guarantee any of the products described herein or perform any independent analysis in connection with any of the product information contained herein. Publisher does not assume, and expressly disclaims, any obligation to obtain and include information other than that provided to it by the manufacturer.

The reader is notified that this text is an educational tool, not a practice book. Since the law is in constant change, no rule or statement of law in this book should be relied upon for any service to any client. The reader should always refer to standard legal sources for the current rule or law. If legal advice or other expert assistance is required, the services of the appropriate professional should be sought.

The Publisher makes no representation or warranties of any kind, including but not limited to, the warranties of fitness for particular purpose or merchantability, nor are any such representations implied with respect to the material set forth herein, and the publisher takes no responsibility with respect to such material. The publisher shall not be liable for any special, consequential, or exemplary damages resulting, in whole or part, from the readers' use of, or reliance upon, this material.

Dedication

To Andrew, Kevin, Letty, Ric, and Joel
All things are possible.

C.B.E.

I dedicate this book to the past, present, and future directors of the California Alliance of Paralegal Associations. Through their single-minded dedication to the paralegal profession, they have inspired me, taught me, and encouraged me to stretch my wings.

S.H.

Foreword

The professional paralegal is a creation of the later twentieth century. Yet, in one of the fastest-changing and fastest-growing professions today, a paralegal career in the 21st century looks very different than that same career looked only 25 years ago, when the idea of the paralegal as an important professional member of the legal service team was almost unknown. Today, the paralegal is integral to the provision of high-quality, efficient legal service in law firms, corporate legal departments, nonprofit organizations, and all levels of government.

Not only is the number of paralegals growing, and likely to continue growing well into the twenty-first century, but the scope, complexity, and sophistication of the projects undertaken by paralegals are growing also. Paralegals are involved in virtually every area of the law, from entertainment to litigation, securities to probate, immigration to corporate. Smart, dynamic, energetic, and creative paralegals are building a highly respected and recognized profession.

In the early days of the profession, the typical paralegal had been a secretary in the same firm where she—almost all paralegals were women in the beginning—was then a paralegal, often working as a paralegal for the same attorney for whom she had worked as a secretary. One firm's practice and procedure, and, often, the practice of one individual attorney, represented the breadth and depth of the paralegal's experience. Formal educational, training, and sophisticated job search and professional advancement techniques and strategies were virtually nonexistent.

From a cottage industry, the paralegal profession has grown explosively. Paralegals today must have a wide-ranging base of substantive knowledge, far beyond the practice of one individual attorney. Thoughtful and sophisticated personal presentation, job search, and professional advancement skills are essential, as the typical career path often involves a multiplicity of different jobs in a variety of practice areas, organizational types, and locations.

What do these changes in the profession mean to you? First, formal education, almost unknown 25 years ago, is a virtual necessity for the individual wanting to enter or advance in the paralegal field. A range of certificate, two-year degree, and four-year degree programs, approved by the American Bar Association, provide a theoretical and practical base for effective paralegal performance. Second, every paralegal, from the entry-level beginner to the seasoned veteran, must understand and utilize a conscious and organized process to secure the most interesting and challenging position available, and to progress in skill and reward in the series of individual positions which make up the span of a paralegal career. The demands on today's paralegal are far greater than before, but so are the rewards, both intellectually and economically.

What traits make for a successful modern paralegal? Certainly we would have to list intelligence, flexibility, energy, commitment, and creativity (and probably endurance as well). But without the skills and strategies necessary for successfully navigating the job search and job advancement complexities of today's profession, even a paralegal with all of those qualities is likely to experience frustration and burnout. Conscious career self-management is essential.

Competition for high-quality paralegal positions is increasingly intense. More people, with better credentials and better experience, are applying for each job, and competing for advancement and promotion once hired. Multiple jobs in the course of a career are today's standard. In this arena, getting ahead and staying ahead means that at every step—resume, networking, interviewing, advancing—you must have an effective plan. So where do you look for the practical, creative, and up-to-date information you need to start and maintain a satisfying and rewarding career as a paralegal? There are probably a variety of good answers, but one of the very best is also one of the very simplest: buy this book, read this book, and incorporate the skills and insights Chere Estrin and Stacey Hunt provide to you in this book into your daily life as a professional paralegal.

No one in the paralegal field knows more about these issues than does Chere Estrin. From her earliest days as a temporary secretary (where I first met and was impressed by her) to her current position as founder and head of a nationally recognized legal staffing and litigation support firm, Chere has focused on what you really need to know to successfully compete in the paralegal world. So whether you are looking for an entry-level or an advanced position, the same rule applies. Buy this book. Read this book. Use this book. You and your career will be happy you did.

Richard S. Shaffran, Esq. Director,
UCLA Extension Attorney Assistant Training Program

Preface

With today's push for lower-cost legal fees, paralegals have established themselves as an integral part of the legal system. But competition for the good jobs is fierce! In this market, whether jobs are plentiful or jobs are scarce, you'd better know how to compete like a first-rate athlete! It doesn't matter whether you are just entering this field or have been in it for quite some time; the more closely you reflect the "true you," the better the results in your job search.

Why? Because today's hiring authorities are trained to spot just the right candidates and to spot them quickly and efficiently. Maybe your resume doesn't read quite right. Maybe your interview style leaves something to be desired. Maybe you are so new to this market, you just don't know quite what to say! Some power-hungry human resources types take delight in the equivalent of pulling wings off butterflies—spotting innocent errors that can determine whether or not you get the job of your dreams. We have put together this book to assist you in getting past the naysayers and put you in the hands of the people who get the message of what a great candidate you are.

Because your job search process involves lots of self-marketing, you need to make yourself look as though no other candidate can top you (within the boundaries of common sense, honesty and skill level, of course). You can make your job-hunting adventure a very rewarding experience.

The bottom line is, attorneys are very picky. How you present yourself is how an attorney perceives you will present your work product and professionalism to the attorney's client. You represent the firm's paralegals and are an indicator to clients of the quality of services that the firm provides. You need to present a professional and realistic picture of yourself. That's why Stacey and I wrote this book. After years in the paralegal field and legal staffing field, respectively, we know what it takes to get you a great job.

This is not just another job-hunting guide filled with resumes. It's a complete how-to manual. It's chock-full of resumes, cover and follow-up letters, 275+ questions you might be asked in the interview, tips on how to overcome objections, recommendations on how to evaluate a job offer, and more.

An added bonus to this book is the one-on-one feedback you need. We'll make sure your resume is reviewed by an expert in the field. Here's how it works: Once your resume is finished, send it with the form in the back of this book and a self-addressed, stamped envelope or e-mail it to:

Resume Critique
The Estrin Organization
1901 Avenue of the Stars, Suite 350
Los Angeles, CA 90067[1]
estrin@estrin.com

We'll have it back to you in about 3 weeks. Unfortunately, we will not be able to take phone calls or give phone consultations. However, feel free to ask questions via our Web site at www.estrin.com or E-mail us at estrin@estrin.com. We want to express how sincerely we wish to assist each and every candidate who desires to get into, continue in, or move up in this terrific field. The possibilities are endless, the opportunities yours to behold.

Best of luck to you in your new endeavors. We wish you outrageous success!

Chere B. Estrin
Stacey Hunt

---

[1]You must send a self-addressed, stamped envelope in order for your resume to be reviewed and returned.

Acknowledgments

You can't write a book without publicly acknowledging those around you who helped you. You just can't. As Stacy and I finish each book, we are acutely aware of the assistance necessary to complete these massive projects. To those around us who heard our pleas for help, our whining, our sighs of relief, thank you. Now, we get a chance to give you our gratitude.

Joan Gill, Acquisitions Editor, West Legal Studies

Lisa Flatley, Editorial Assistant, West Legal Studies

Betty Dickson, Production Editor, West Legal Studies

Marge Dover, Executive Director of NALA, for continued support.

Laurie Roselle, Past-President, Legal Assistant Management Association (LAMA), whose letters of encouragement are so appreciated.

Angelo Capora, Director of Paralegal Studies, Palomar College, San Diego, who bought this book sight unseen. Thank you, Angelo.

Clark Moscrip, Past President of American Association for Paralegal Educators (AAfPE) and Director of St. Mary's Paralegal Program, whose support is never ending.

George Mulqueen, the staffing mentor, who gives unfailing support always.

Danny Litt, Professor, UCLA Anderson School, who let us hire the professor.

Katie Thoma, Paralegal Administrator, Loeb & Loeb, for supporting us with an honest, insightful chapter.

Kevin Behan, Vice President, The Estrin Organization, for his very fine chapters.

Eleanor Kendall, who creatively refused to allow writer's block.

My partners and staff at The Estrin Organization for understanding and giving much appreciated support:

Andrew Spathis, Letty Marquez, Kevin Behan, Lupe Ramirez, and Mimi Belous, for pushing and pulling us in the right direction.

Bridgett Brooks, Bill MacMillen, Judi Behan, Mary Bishop, Mike Decano, Kathy Fry-Watson; Dr. Jay Pooler who told me I could do it.

Los Angeles, California   *Chere B. Estrin*
                                                                    October, 2000

I would like most to thank Chere Estrin not only for giving me the opportunity to work with her on this book but for opening many other doors for me in the profession as well. I also thank Sandra Sabanske and the American Association for Paralegal Education, Lu Hangley and the National Federation of Paralegal Associations, Inc., and Marge Dover and the National Association of Legal Assistants for providing information used in this book. And finally, I would like to express my appreciation to my family, Don, Derek, and Erin, who only saw my silhouette at the computer for several months.

Los Osos, California   *Stacey Hunt*
                                                                                   October, 2000

About the Authors

Chere B. Estrin, Ph.D., A well-known legal staffing trailblazer, Ms. Estrin demonstrates a solid range of expertise: from CEO of **The Estrin Organization,** a Los Angeles-based legal and financial staffing organization, to senior executive in a four billion dollar staffing conglomerate; to president of a legal staffing division in one of the country's top three international litigation support companies; to successful entrepreneur building one of the largest paralegal temporary staffing organizations in the country. Her history as an administrator in two Top Ten law firms allowed her access into this niche field.

Ms. Estrin founded **C.B. Estrin and Associates** in 1986 which quickly rose as one of the largest multi-office paralegal staffing organizations. The company was acquired by Interim, where Ms. Estrin held a senior management position as head of a $40 million division. She then joined The Quorum/Estrin Group as president of a division of an international litigation support company. She is now CEO of **The Estrin Organization,** a Los Angeles-based professional staffing organization. Ms. Estrin is a well-known national seminar leader and teaches at prestigious universities such as UCLA.

Recently featured in *Newsweek* magazine and *The Los Angeles Times* Business Section as head of a fast-tracking staffing company, her achievements and awards include winner of the Century City (Los Angeles) Chamber of Commerce prestigious "Woman of the Year 2000 Achievement Award"; finalist for *Inc.* magazine's "Entrepreneur of the Year Award" and winner of *California Lawyer Magazine's* LAMMIE award. She was featured on the cover of *Legal Assistant Today* magazine as the legal field's "Career Guru". Ms Estrin is an author of eight career books including *The Paralegal Career Guide Third Edition* (Prentice-Hall) which has sold over 50,000 copies.

In addition to her column in *Legal Assistant Today,* Ms. Estrin has been featured in *Newsweek* magazine, *The Los Angeles Times, The Chicago Tribune, The New York Times, Working Woman, Working Mother, CNBC.com, BusinessWeek Online, Entrepreneur, Frontier, The Daily Journal,* and *Entrepreneurial Edge* magazine.

Her experience as co-founding member of the Legal Assistant Management Association (LAMA); expertise; books; articles; quality reputation; and frequent guest speaking engagements has helped to firmly establish the Estrin name.

The Estrin Organization
1901 Avenue of the Stars Suite 350
Los Angeles, CA 90067
310.284.8585 (e) estrin@estrin.com

Stacey Hunt, CLA, has been a litigation paralegal since 1985. She is the litigation columnist for Legal Assistant Today and coauthored the book *Hot Docs and Smoking Guns: Managing Document Production and Document Organization* (1994) Clark Boardman Callaghan. Stacey is active in the Central Coast Paralegal Association and is a longtime board member of the California Alliance of Paralegal Associations. She serves as CAPA's liaison to the Law Practice Management & Technology Section of the State Bar of California. She earned her Certified Legal Assistant designation in 1995, and chairs the Advisory Committee to the Commission for Advanced California Paralegal Specialization. She is an adjunct instructor in the paralegal programs at Fresno City College (where she earned her paralegal certificate) and San Joaquin College of Law. Stacey lives with her husband and two children in Los Osos, California, and works for Jencks Law Group in San Luis Obispo.

OTHER BOOKS BY ESTRIN AND HUNT:
By Chere Estrin
The Paralegal Career Guide, Third Edition (Prentice-Hall) (2001)

Everything You Ever Wanted to Know about Being a Legal Assistant (West Thomson Learning)

Where Do I Go from Here? Career Paths for the Experienced Legal Assistant (with Andrea Wagner) (Estrin Publishing, out of print)

Everything You Need to Know About Marketing Your Paralegal Program (with Elliot S. Cohen) (Pearson Publications)

By Stacey Hunt
Hot Docs and Smoking Guns: Managing Document Production and Document Organization (with Rhonda Gregory) (Aspen Law & Business)

Contents

1

Batter Up!

"Keep your eyes on the stars and your feet on the ground."

—Theodore Roosevelt

A paralegal job search is a little like a baseball game. You're the batter; the prospective law firm is the pitcher. Each pitch is different; each has a succession of pitches to deliver, depending on the game. You need to be prepared for whatever pitches you receive—fast balls, slow balls, screwballs, even a nice, slow, easy pitch. You can't always know what's going to be thrown next, and you must be ready to hit that ball and get to first base.

But unlike a baseball game, a job search is a contest that both you and your prospective employer can win. You need to concentrate on your homework and preparation to get that home run. Once you know what is expected of you, you will know how to respond. In the job search game, however, your real competition is all the other batters, not the pitcher.

If it's time for you to start your search for a new paralegal job, this book is for you. Whether you are entry level, experienced, or just thinking about getting into the field, you need to know the ins and outs of landing your ideal position. In this book, we will show you how to be the best player possible to beat out the competition, how to understand what is expected of you, and how to respond accordingly. Your game objective is not only to be the best candidate possible but also to get that message across to those hiring authorities who have access to the job that you want.

WHERE ARE THEY?

Paralegals today are everywhere. In a rapidly changing legal environment, paralegals are at the forefront for today's most cost-effective method of delivering legal services. Because of escalating client demands for lower legal costs, lawyers are becoming increasingly aware that the quickest, most efficient manner in which to deliver those low-cost services is to hire and retain good paralegals. Today, according to the Bureau of Labor Statistics (1998), there are more than 136,000 paralegal jobs in the United States. We have reason to believe this is a glaring underestimation of the actual number of paralegal positions in this country. That belief is based upon the reality that innumerable positions do not bear the title paralegal, yet duties and responsibilities are the same. This belief is further evidenced by the many, many paralegal-related titles, such as litigation support manager, case manager, legal assistant, and legal executive that may be unaccounted for in any census or surveys.

Private law firms today employ the vast majority of paralegals; most of the others work for in-house legal departments of corporations, for not-for-profit organizations, and for the various levels of government. You can find paralegals in almost any practice specialty: litigation, corporate, criminal, tax, employee benefits, intellectual property, maritime, high-tech, administrative, real estate, bankruptcy, admiralty, insurance defense, environmental, and personal injury are only a few.

Paralegals are found in nearly every federal government agency. The Departments of Justice, Treasury, Interior, and Health and Human Services, and the General Services Administration are the largest employers. Even the FBI hires paralegals. State and local governments and publicly funded legal service projects employ paralegals as well. Banks, real estate development companies, insurance companies, high-tech companies, entertainment and venture capital companies, and major accounting firms also employ paralegals. You'll find paralegals in not-for-profit organizations such as The Salvation Army. In your job search, you'll discover organizations with political causes that have strong legal departments, such as Greenpeace. Some paralegals own their own businesses, and there are many freelance paralegals contracting their services to attorneys or corporate legal departments.

And that's not to mention the paralegals who have entered "alternative" or nontraditional careers. These paralegals are employed with or own their own companies as vendors to the legal community, are high-ranking corporate secretaries or vice presidents of corporations, have interesting positions with publishers or legal aide agencies, or hold teaching jobs in paralegal schools. The opportunities for paralegals are endless. And that's just the beginning.

Other paralegals have moved up what used to be an invisible career ladder. Some have moved into paralegal or office management, case management, litigation support, training, MIS (manager of information systems), or IT (information technology) positions; others have gone on to be lawyers, and still others have captured new and exciting specialty areas such as Internet Research Specialist, Trial Specialist, Patent Prosecution Specialist, International Business Legal Assistant, and more. Opportunities have even opened up in the military, where paralegals are placed all over the world.

PARALEGAL HIRING WORLD

In the hiring world, there are two overall categories of hires: career paralegals and transitional. Career paralegals are those who have decided to make this field a career and stay in it for some length of time. Mostly, they are those who have chosen to get training either through a paralegal institution or on the job. Transitional paralegals are hired generally by large law firms. These law firms hold to the belief that a paralegal position is more of a transitory: someone who has recently graduated college and within 18 months to two years will be on his or her way to law school or graduate school. This type of hiring is generally found in large metropolitan areas. Presently, the majority of law firms and in-house legal departments are leaning more and more toward the career paralegal. Fewer and fewer firms have the resources or people power to train on the job. They want you to arrive with at least some training.

The job outlook for paralegals is expected to grow much faster than the average for all occupations through the year 2008. These opportunities are expected to expand as employers become aware that paralegals are able to do many legal tasks for lower salaries than lawyers demand and at lower costs to the client. New jobs created by rapid employment growth will create most of the job openings for paralegals in the future. Other job openings will arise as people leave the occupation. More opportunities have been found in the past few years in the in-house legal departments of corporations of all sizes. This change has been welcomed by many paralegals who have been through the billable hours wars in law firms.

Although the number of job openings for paralegals is expected to increase significantly through the year 2008, so will the number of people pursuing this career. Thus, keen competition for jobs should continue as the growing number of graduates from paralegal education programs keeps pace with employment growth. Still, job prospects are expected to be favorable for professionals with bachelor's degrees who graduate from well-regarded paralegal training programs.

The outlook is bright for paralegals seeking to enter the public sector. Community legal service programs that provide assistance to the poor, aged, minorities, and middle-income families operate on limited budgets. They will seek to employ additional paralegals in order to minimize expenses and serve the most people. Federal, state, and local government agencies, consumer organizations, and the courts are also expected to continue to hire paralegals in increasing numbers.

GOOD TIMES AND BAD TIMES

To some extent, paralegals are affected by the economic cycle. In good economic times with a low unemployment rate, job opportunities are in more abundance than are available candidates. This cycle pushes up salaries, particularly for specialty paralegals, resulting in "candidate shortage." In bad times with high unemployment rates, the rule of thumb is more candidates than job opportunities, creating stiffer competition and lower wages for more senior-level professionals. During a recession, demand declines for some discretionary legal services such as estate planning, real estate transactions, and mergers and acquisitions. Corporations are less likely to litigate when they are in the process of downsizing and saving their skins. As a result, full-time paralegals employed in offices adversely affected by a recession may be laid off. During the early nineties, this was the case across the country. On the other hand, the recession plays well for those corporations and individuals with other emerging legal problems such as bankruptcies, foreclosures, and divorces. Furthermore, the continuous emergence of new laws, judicial interpretations of existing ones, and new specialties such as high-tech and the Internet create new business opportunities for lawyers and paralegals regardless of the business cycle.

SO, WHAT ARE THE DOLLARS?

Paralegal salaries have risen over the years. Although the Department of Labor has declared paralegals nonexempt (meaning you earn overtime pay), there are still many firms that do not pay overtime. This issue has been hotly debated for many years and will probably continue for quite some time. Some law firms still offer bonuses, although generally speaking, these bonuses are not as large as seen in years past.

If you are an entry-level paralegal, you may find that your first job consists of routine and repetitious assignments. Hang in there! As a paralegal you will be recognized for the level of assignment you can handle. As you gain more and more substantive experience, your responsibilities will change. You should find yourself with a more rewarding and challenging position as the years go by. This is a different situation than in some other careers. Because the only activities paralegals are prohibited from doing are giving legal advice, negotiating legal fees, and presenting cases in court, rarely can you top out in task level unless you fail to pursue more challenging assignments.

And sometimes, it takes changing jobs to pursue the avenue of more sophisticated work.

There are paralegals who are earning the "big bucks" in the field. These salaries may be a result of total compensation package—that is to say, base salary, overtime, and bonuses. Any paralegal who is in litigation in a major firm is most likely to have faced significant amounts of overtime. And for those of you looking to earn six figures—it does exist in this field. However, before running off in an earnest search of the six-figure position, understand clearly that only a small handful of paralegals, to our knowledge, have reached utopia. These paralegals are generally found in highly specialized areas, such as transactional corporate, entertainment, or real estate practice specialties. Others have hefty bases and lots and lots of overtime pay. Still others may be in alternative careers such as sales to the legal community or own their own companies.

WHY PARALEGALS CHANGE JOBS

We have found in the past that stumbling blocks to moving on may have been a result of overindulgent guilt associated with the job change. "What will the firm do without me?" "How will they survive?" "I couldn't possibly leave now." "We're going to trial in two years." Although you never want to burn bridges, you do have the right to move on!

The issue of loyalty in the general workplace has been at an all-time low in past years as a result of no loyalty from employers when downsizing struck. Bodies were everywhere. Some employees who have survived these massacres have had little trouble moving on. But others will hang on to a job even when it's time to go. Factors such as low self-esteem, few local job opportunities, the appearance of job-hopping, salaries, benefit plans, and more all play an important role in keeping someone on the job. In fact, these considerations are designed to keep you in place.

So why do paralegals move on? Here are the top reasons:

- Salary
- Personality conflict
- Lack of opportunity or challenging work
- Location
- Change in management
- Downsizing
- Excessive billable hourly requirement or unreasonable overtime
- Lack of recognition
- Lack of appreciation
- Lack of feedback or evaluation
- Lack of control over work environment

While we can't as yet rank this next reason for leaving as one of the top ten, our interviews with candidates in the past year or so reveal an awareness previously unheard of in the legal field. And that is, paralegals are leaving jobs because

• The firm lacks the latest or even acceptable technology.

Paralegals have grown to understand just how important it is to stay up-to-date in the latest technology. If they don't, job opportunities at a higher salary level will be almost impossible to find, as computer skills are one of the most sought-after skill sets a paralegal can possess.

IF YOU'RE READY TO MOVE

Changing jobs can be a positive growth experience. If you haven't switched jobs for quite some time, you might find the process somewhat intimidating. We can only tell you that it can be an adventure that can land you a better position or at least one that is more tolerable! There are no guarantees in this world. But if you do your homework and investigate your future employer carefully, you are more likely to choose wisely. And that's what we're here to help you do.

If we were sitting across from you and you were telling us your story, we might be likely to stop and confront you with a "reality check." Because we're not sitting with you, we've chosen to set these reality checks apart from the rest of the text. Pay attention to them. They are designed to force you to think through your job search process, and they are based upon many, many years in this field. Our "cases in point" illustrate examples of paralegals with good intentions. After you become familiar with the positive steps you can take to research job opportunities, write a great cover letter and resume, interview with a bang, and conduct a copious follow-up, you'll realize the only way to get the job you want is to behave as a paralegal: *find the facts, stay organized and detailed, and follow through.*

2

Getting into the Field

"Even if you're on the right track, you'll get run over if you just sit there."

—Will Rogers

Many people who want to become paralegals have little or no idea what it is that paralegals actually do. They know being a paralegal vaguely has something to do with attorneys and the law. Although the information the public has about lawyers has been glamorized to an extent by television shows such as *Law and Order, The Practice,* John Grisham novels, and the movies, at least people have learned something about the nature of the work that lawyers perform. Unfortunately, these shows rarely even mention paralegals, let alone give us any insight into what their role is in the delivery of legal services.

One of the best overall descriptions of a paralegal appears in the *Handbook on Paralegal Utilization,* published by the California Alliance of Paralegal Associations:

A paralegal is a paraprofessional who assists an attorney. A paralegal is distinguished from legal secretaries and other clerical personnel in that more difficult technical duties and responsibilities are assigned to the paralegal. A paralegal must know basic legal concepts, terminology, principles and procedures and have knowledge of legal reference material. A paralegal must have the ability to reason logically, analyze situations accurately, and recommend an effective course of action. Paralegals must possess a high level of communication skills, prepare reports and memoranda based on research which sets forth the statement of facts, applications of relevant law, and conclusions. A paralegal must be able to read and understand statutes, court decisions, legal documents and other similar information. A paralegal must be able to work cooperatively with attorneys, clerical staff, technical staff, clients, experts and the general public.

In trying to describe what paralegals do, it is often easier to describe what they *don't* do. Generally, there are three basic things lawyers are allowed to do that paralegals cannot.

1. Paralegals cannot represent a client in court.
2. Paralegals cannot make the decision to represent a client, and cannot accept fees from clients.
3. Paralegals cannot give legal advice.

Other than that, the sky's almost the limit. What tasks you perform as a paralegal are only limited by what you feel capable of doing, and the level of trust and confidence your employer has in you.

CHOOSING A PRACTICE AREA

If paralegals can do pretty much anything a lawyer can (with the above exceptions), this also means that there are paralegals working in every practice area in which an attorney works. Some practice areas are more suited to paralegal assistance. They are very labor intensive and have tasks that can easily be delegated by the attorneys to paralegals. The litigation field is one such area, and that is why nearly 50 percent of all paralegals work in litigation.

You will be exposed to some of the many practice areas while you are in paralegal school. Most good schools will require that you take classes in several different specialties. Don't balk at taking classes in areas that might not at first interest you. First of all, it gives you a well-rounded education. There are no areas of the law that are isolated unto themselves. Family law practitioners touch on tax issues when structuring divorce settlements. Litigation paralegals need to know something about bankruptcy laws in case a defendant files for protection from his creditors. The more you know about "crossover" areas of the law, the better paralegal you will be. However, the second reason for taking lots of different types of classes is that it exposes you to interesting practice areas that you had no idea you would like. It gives you a veritable smorgasbord from which to choose your future specialty. And like most lawyers, most paralegals need to specialize these days.

When deciding the area of the law in which you would like to work as a paralegal, keep the following things in mind:

- *Take into account your personality.* If you are sociable, outgoing, and a "people" person, you will be absolutely miserable working in the corner of some office, numbering documents, and entering them into computerized databases (complex litigation), but you might enjoy helping people through their personal crises (family law). If you have a low threshold for stress and prefer a more quiet, structured workday, you will probably not survive the daily rigors of the courtroom (litigation/trial work), but instead you might consider choosing an area where you can do more research or drafting of documents (real estate or transactional).

- *Take into account your interests.* If the thought of numbers and math makes your hair stand on end, you should probably steer away from a career in the tax field or as a probate and estate planning paralegal. If the idea of putting bad guys behind bars appeals to you, then you could look at a specialty in criminal law. Perhaps you have a love of protecting the earth or giant redwood groves. If so, an environmental law attorney needs your help.
- *Be realistic.* If you drool at the thought of working in a firm that represents movie stars or sports heroes, you are not going to be able to do so if you live in a small town in Oregon. You are going to have to move to a big city, preferably on the East Coast or West Coast. If maritime law is your main interest, you are going to have to live in the Great Lakes area or on the coast, not in Kansas. If you are not willing to relocate, then you will have to make an assessment of what legal fields are available to you where you live or within reasonable commuting distance.

PRACTICE AREA DESCRIPTIONS

With all those thoughts in mind, the following is a sample of some of the many practice areas that are available to paralegals, a description of what skills are necessary for each area, and a list of the tasks that paralegals who work in those areas commonly perform.[1] The majority of paralegals fall into the litigation specialty practice area because, quite simply, it is the area that has the most openings. Other paralegals are in the corporate specialty area (meaning business practice specialty, not those paralegals who work in corporations) and real estate. Use this information as a guide in narrowing down the areas that seem attractive to you.

Bankruptcy Law Paralegal

Duties and Responsibilities
- Interview client to obtain information in preparation for filing of petition and schedules; familiarize client with procedures
- Compile list of assets

---

[1] Selected portions reprinted with permission from the *Handbook of Paralegal Utilization,* California Alliance of Paralegal Associations, copyright 1997. Available for $15 from the California Alliance of Paralegal Associations, P.O. Box 2234, San Francisco, CA 94126.

- Coordinate appropriate UCC and real property searches, and appraisals
- Draft and file petitions, schedules, and proofs of claim
- Handle routine calls and correspondence to creditors, creditors' committee chairperson and attorney, trustee, and client
- Attend court hearings with attorney and client

Required Skills
- Knowledge of Bankruptcy Code, Bankruptcy Rules, Federal Rules of Civil Procedure, and Local Rules of Court
- Good organizational skills and attention to detail
- Ability to write well
- Ability to work with clients at possibly sensitive and emotional times

Elder Law Paralegal

Duties and Responsibilities
- Locate sources of income and public entitlements (Social Security, pension, disability benefits, food stamps, rent increase exemptions)
- Assist client in preparation of applications for unearned income
- Locate health insurance and benefits, including private Medigap policies, and federal and state medical programs; prepare application and/or claims
- Research housing, home care, or continuing care facilities
- Research availability of funds to meet financial needs (i.e., loans, reverse equity or mortgage plans, annuities) and prepare documentation
- Research methods for dealing with discrimination in admission, payment, resident rights, and transfer and discharge from care facility
- Identify need for crisis intervention (incapacity, abuse, or intensive health care or financial needs)

Required Skills
- Knowledge of employment issues (i.e., age discrimination, insurance benefits, and pension plans)
- Ability to listen and elicit personal information in sensitive situations
- Knowledge of the aging process, myths, and physical limitations and losses that accompany the process
- Familiarity with the codes, rules, and regulations pertaining to Social Security, Medicaid/Medicare, and state medical insurance and benefit programs

- Familiarity with the state and local welfare program services, including the food stamp program
- Counseling training beneficial, but not mandatory

Intellectual Property Law Paralegal

Duties and Responsibilities
- Conduct patent/trademark searches
- Conduct on-line computer information searches of technical literature for patents and trademarks
- Maintain files of new products and invention development
- Review patent filings with engineers
- Draft trademark/service mark registration application, renewal application, and Section 8 and Section 15 affidavits
- Draft response to trademark examining attorney's official action
- Draft licenses and agreement regarding proprietary information/ technology
- Docket and/or maintain docket systems for payment of patent annuities in foreign countries
- Research procedural matters, case law, and unfair competition matters
- Assist in opposition, interference, infringement, and related proceedings

Required Skills
- Familiarity with computerized research programs
- Knowledge of state and federal patent, trademark, and copright law, including forms and procedures for filing

Public Law Paralegal

Duties and Responsibilities
- Review legal documents and appeals for compliance with regulations and/or requirements set forth in codes
- Review for completeness information furnished by program staff in matters referred for legal proceedings
- Draft answers to inquiries regarding legal requirements and procedure
- Perform preliminary analyses of legislative bills
- Organize, summarize, and index prior opinions, testimony, depositions, and documentary material
- Prepare legislative and trial calendar
- Organize trial documents and exhibits

Reality Check

When searching for your first paralegal job, it is best to keep an open mind. You may be offered a position that is not in your chosen specialty. If the job market in your area is tight, you may be best off accepting it. If you dislike the work, you can always search for another position, and, as the saying goes, it is easier to find a job when you have one. And who knows? You may end up loving your new position.

- Research legislative and case histories
- Gather factual information and perform legal research to assist attorney in determining appropriate action
- Draft and serve complaints, petitions, and pleadings
- Prepare correspondence and reports

Required Skills
- Knowledge of principles, concepts, and methodology of legal research
- Knowledge of discovery and fact investigation
- Knowledge of principles of legal writing
- Knowledge of techniques of client and witness interviewing

Of course, there are many other areas of the law in which paralegals may specialize. This list is just the tip of the iceberg. As you read through these job descriptions, some common themes should become apparent. No matter what the practice area, they all require good reading comprehension and writing skills, good researching skills, and good organizational skills. If you do not currently possess all four of these abilities, you must get good instruction on them and polish them if you ever want to become a proficient paralegal.

WHERE DO PARALEGALS WORK?
The majority of paralegals work in the law firm environment. About half of those work in large law firms (fifty or more lawyers in a large metropolitan area), and the other half work either for small or mid-sized firms (between two and fifty lawyers in a large metropolitan area) or for sole practitioners. The balance of paralegals work for corporations or for the government. Which of these environments would be best for you?

The Sole Practitioner
A sole practitioner is an attorney who works alone rather than for a firm. Some sole practitioners are generalists, meaning they have no particular specialty and will take on many different types of cases. Many of these generalists can be found in smaller towns or rural areas, where one lawyer has to meet the needs of many people, or where the scarcity of work forces the lawyer to "do it all." In larger cities, sole practitioners are usually attorneys who have become so expert at a particular area of the law that they are in high demand, and are sought out by the public and other lawyers.

Some sole practitioners keep their own office and staff. Others, in an effort to keep costs down, will share office space, a receptionist, and even a library with other sole practitioners.

The paralegal who works for a sole practitioner will be relied upon heavily and will become the attorney's right-hand person. Besides performing traditional paralegal work, the paralegal may also be asked to perform more "office managerial" duties, such as researching equipment purchases, doing bookkeeping, keeping the library up to date, working with vendors and outside accountants, and helping make personnel decisions.

The upside to working for one lawyer is having a very close working relationship with one person. Because you are so depended upon, you will both feel and know that your work is making a difference to the office. You will probably have very heavy client contact. You will be given a variety of tasks and will wear a variety of "hats," which many people find more stimulating. You will probably be involved in a case all the way through, "from soup to nuts," as it were.

The drawbacks to working with a sole practitioner must also be taken into account. Your employer may not be able to provide you with any health insurance or retirement benefits. You will probably be the only paralegal in the office, which may give you a feeling of isolation. It will also mean there will be no one to back you up during a work crunch or when you are on vacation. Paralegals who work for sole practitioners are much more likely to get stuck performing a lot of clerical work, especially when the attorney cannot afford to hire both a secretary and a paralegal. Finally, if your employer should retire or die unexpectedly, you will be left without a job.

The Small to Mid-Sized Firm

When working in a small to medium-sized firm, you will shed some of the disadvantages of working for a sole practitioner but encounter some new drawbacks. You will probably not have a one-on-one relationship with an attorney, since most paralegals in mid-sized firms are assigned to several (or even all) of the firm's lawyers. Some paralegals look on this as a plus because they get a bigger variety of work in many ways. First, there will probably be several types of specialists in your firm. That means you may be doing corporate work one day, litigation the next, and probate the day after. Second, some attorneys will delegate more readily than others. If you were teamed up solely with one of those attorneys who believes that no one can do the work better than he can, you will get very little in the way of challenging assignments. However, if you have the freedom to go from door to door in the office searching for work, you will quickly learn which attorneys are the best sources of interesting assignments.

Other advantages of working in a small to mid-sized office include the potential for better benefits, more possibility of social interaction, and

extra hands to help you in an emergency. There is usually a lot of camaraderie because the staff is not of an unwieldy size. It is not unusual for
employees of these firms to be involved in coed softball leagues, have company picnics, throw office potlucks, or go as a group to the ballet.

Of course, every situation has its disadvantages. If you are one of those
people who truly hates "office politics," keep in mind that such goings-on
increase exponentially with the size of the firm. Mid-sized firms may have
more rigid rules than do their smaller counterparts. They sometimes
invest more of their time and energy into training new associates and law
clerks than providing training for their paralegals. Small and mid-sized
firms rarely have any defined career paths for paralegals, who can sometimes labor for years doing the same tasks. Because there is not a large
number of paralegals working at a small firm, there will be little opportunity for advancement into management roles.

The Large Firm

These are the mega-firms that sit in the big-city high-rises. There can be
hundreds of attorneys on dozens of floors. Some have branch offices in
multiple cities, even in other countries. If you dream one day of working
in the London or Tokyo office of a big firm for a few years, these are the
firms you need to target in your job search.

Large firms can offer a world of opportunity for paralegals. They often
work for the biggest clients, performing power transactions. The pace is
exciting and fast—sometimes too fast for more laid-back paralegals, who
enjoy having a life outside work. Paralegals in large firms often put in long
hours and may have higher billable-hour requirements than do paralegals
in smaller firms. There is usually little client contact for paralegals in larger
firms, which may be an advantage or a disadvantage, depending on your
personality.

Because of their larger operating budgets, large firms are often the first
to try more cutting-edge technology, such as scanning equipment, Internet capability, or videoconferencing. If you like being on top of the latest
advances, this will be appealing to you. If you resist that sort of constant
change, you may prefer a more relaxed atmosphere.

There is sometimes less variety of work in a large firm. You will probably be assigned to one or more lawyers in a particular department, such as
the firm's bankruptcy department. (See Chapter 3 for more information
on the structure of law firms.) Paralegals in bigger firms often complain
that they work on only "pieces" of a case, never seeing it all the way
through from start to finish.

Despite the large number of people working in the firm, there is often a loss of esprit de corps. There is simply no way to remember the names of several hundred coworkers, let alone get them all together for a firm function. Often, departments will stick together, having their own Christmas parties or remembering each other's birthday.

Some paralegals complain about the sheer size of the large firm. They feel like just a "number" and that none of the firm's movers and shakers even knows who they are. They don't feel like they make a difference to their employer or their cases. Other paralegals thrive on such a structure and enjoy moving up through the ranks from junior to senior paralegal and on up to case manager or other titles bestowed upon big-firm paralegals.

Corporations

Another potential employer of paralegals is the legal department of a corporation. Many larger corporations have an attorney who is employed by the corporation to provide legal advice. In an effort to trim spiraling legal costs, corporations in recent years have been enlarging their in-house legal staff, rather than hiring outside law firms to perform their legal work. And, just as inside the law firm, in-house counsel require the assistance of qualified paralegals. (See Chapter 3 for more information on the structure of in-house legal departments.)

Paralegal employees of corporations report many advantages over their law firm counterparts. Their salaries are often higher, and there are rarely any billable time requirements. There can be less job stress because if a case gets too large or demanding, the corporation's legal department can merely refer it to outside counsel. One of the biggest advantages for paralegals in a corporation is the possibility of moving upward within the company. In a law firm, unless you are a lawyer, there is not much room for upward movement. In corporations, there is no such limitation. Paralegals have been known to be promoted to vice president positions within their departments.

The downside to working in corporations are few, but they do exist. Corporate jobs are few and far between compared to law firm jobs, and it may be difficult to get your foot in the door. Corporate law departments prefer experienced paralegals, who have cut their teeth in law firms and will be able to hit the ground running, with a minimum of supervision. In-house paralegals sometimes complain they are not challenged because the minute a case gets too difficult, it is assigned out to outside counsel. Boredom can be a problem, since there may not be a variety of work to do.

Reality Check

It is possible to get the big-firm benefits while working in a small-firm environment by finding a position with a satellite office of a large firm.

And just what is it that corporations have their paralegals do? They may be assigned to review the hundreds of contracts the corporation is entering into annually. Paralegals may be found in the intellectual property department, making sure that all of the company's patents and trademarks in the United States and other countries are kept up to date. Corporations sometimes have in-house litigation departments, where it is the paralegal's job to coordinate with and oversee outside counsel who is handling a lawsuit against the company. Other corporations use their paralegals to prepare notices of shareholders or board of directors meetings, draft minutes and corporate resolutions, and make sure all permits and business licenses from government agencies are kept current. Some paralegals are assigned to administer their corporations' employee benefits programs. Here are just a few of the types of corporations and companies that hire paralegals:

Agricultural	Investment/financial companies
Airlines	Magazines
Automobile manufacturers	Manufacturers
Banks	Newspapers
Bar associations	Not-for-profit organizations (such as
Big five accounting firms	The Salvation Army)
Bio-tech	Pension
Cable companies	Pharmaceutical
Casinos	Phone companies
Chemical companies	Public utilities
Clothing	Publishers
Computer manufacturers	Real estate
Cosmetics	Religious affiliations/churches/
Dot coms	synagogues
Entertainment	Research and development
Finance	Retailers
Food and beverage	Schools, colleges and universities
conglomerates	Software
Healthcare	Sports teams
High-tech companies	Staffing companies
Hospitality (restaurants,	Start-ups
hotels, resorts)	Telecommunications
Hospitals	Trade associations
Insurance	Transportation
Internet	Venture capital

Government

Paralegals are utilized in all levels of local, state, and federal government and, in this increasing era of budget cutbacks, are often hired in lieu of attorneys. Paralegals can be found in the City Attorney's Office or County Counsel's Office, drafting and reviewing ordinances, working on environmental cleanup matters, and researching legislative and case histories. The court system hires paralegals to assist the judges' research attorneys or work in the clerk's office. The District Attorney's and Public Defender's Offices both employ paralegals to prosecute and defend criminal actions. The U.S. Trustee's Office uses paralegals to work on bankruptcy cases overseen by that office. State and federal agencies employ paralegals in a number of capacities, and in some circumstances, paralegals are actually permitted to represent clients in administrative hearings.

While paralegals in government settings do not generally command salaries as high as their privately employed counterparts, they usually enjoy more generous benefits. Federal employees also have a great deal of mobility, as they can request transfers to offices in other cities. (See Chapter 13 for more information about government positions for paralegals.)

Here are just a few positions you'll find in government (aside from the many, many government agencies):

Attorney General's Office
City Attorney's Office
City Law Departments
Community Colleges
Department of Corporations
Department of Justice
Department of Labor
District Attorney
FDIC (Federal Deposit Insurance Corporation)
FSLIC (Federal Savings and Loan Insurance Corporation)
Federal Bureau of Investigation
Mayor's Office
Police Departments
Public Defender's Office
Secretary of State
State Universities
Trade Councils
Veterans Administration

Military

Believe it or not, you can find a great position in the service, if, of course, you are eligible and wish to enlist. The Army, Marines, Navy, and Air Force all offer paralegal positions and training. Paralegals can be stationed anywhere in the world and work with attorneys who are also enlisted. Military paralegals handle anything from criminal matters to civilian matters such as drafting wills for soldiers who are about to embark on missions. They have been sent to explore environmental events such as volcano explosions and have worked on matters that are highly secret in nature. Contact your local recruiting office for more information.

Matching Your Personality with a Specialty/Working Environment

Use the following checklist to help you brainstorm regarding some possible practice areas based upon your own interests and skills. The third column will tell you where you might find such a position.

Interest/Skill	Area of Law	Possible Employers
Have financial or accounting interests; are good with numbers and calculations; enjoy balancing your checkbook to the last penny	Probate and estate planning; tax; trust administration; bankruptcy	Firms of all sizes have probate and tax attorneys; banks employ trust administrators; firms of all sizes do bankruptcy work; the U.S. Trustee's office hires bankruptcy paralegals.
Want exposure to courtroom work	Litigation; criminal law	Firms of all sizes employ litigation paralegals; if you are interested in criminal defense work, you may be employed by private defense attorneys or the public defender's office; if you prefer prosecution, look for work in the District Attorney's or U.S. Attorney's office.
Interested in how "big deals" are put together; how big corporations operate or are bought and sold	Transactional; mergers and acquisitions; corporate and partnership law	Law firms of all sizes; many corporations

Interest/Skill	Area of Law	Possible Employers
Fascination with finance and the stock market	Securities law; employee benefit law	Larger law firms; corporations
Concern for protecting the rights of others	Plaintiff's personal injury, products liability, or employment/labor law; environmental law	Law firms of all sizes; government agencies
Have a technical background; love inventions and inventors	Intellectual property law	Law firms of all sizes; corporations
Love computer work, such as designing databases, charts, or graphs	Complex litigation	Mid-sized and large law firms, some governmental agencies
Interested in helping people through their personal crises	Family law; adoptions; elder law	Law firms of all sizes; government agencies
Enjoy buying and selling land; real estate deals	Real estate law	Law firms of all sizes; corporations
Interested in the government and how it works	Public law; administrative law	Law firms of all sizes; government agencies
Have medical background or are interested in medical profession	Personal injury or insurance defense litigation; medical malpractice	Law firms of all sizes

3

Structure of Law Firms and In-House Legal Departments

Kevin J. Behan*
Vice President The Estrin 0rganization

"Only a strong tree can stand alone."

—Arnold Glasow

A s a paralegal, you may believe that it is not necessary for you to know how a law firm operates, what the various levels of responsibilities are for the attorneys, or what the functions are of each of the diverse departments that can be found in a large firm. You may want only to be able to come to work, do your job, and go home. Not so! It is very important for you to have an understanding of the mechanics of how your firm operates, how certain management decisions are made, and why. There are several reasons for this:

- It is important for you to establish yourself in the firm "culture." For coworkers to accept you and for management to consider you for promotions, you must learn what the various power structures are.
- If you have a problem with workload or with a coworker, you must know the proper channels where you can air your grievances. Few things make supervisors more angry than if you ignore the chain of command and go over someone's head.

---

*Mr. Behan is Vice President of The Estrin Organization. In a former life, he was Paralegal Coordinator for the Los Angeles office of White & Case. He holds an A.B. degree from Princeton University.

- When you need help with a project, it is useful to know what the resources are in the firm. Must you go to an associate attorney for help with a research project, or is the librarian available to assist you? When you have columns and columns of numbers to add up for a tax return, must you do it yourself, or is there someone in the bookkeeping department who is fast with an adding machine? Why burden your secretary with a large typing job when the word-processing department can get it out faster?
- Perhaps you would like to make a change in an established firm policy, such as to create an annual retreat for paralegals, where none now exists. To whom would you go with such a request? The office manager? The senior partner? Is there a paralegal committee made up of some of the firm's attorneys? If so, who are they?

Most major law firms have structures that are very similar to each other. There is a core of departments that is common to all big firms, but there will be some small differences that are unique to each firm. Large law firms handle most of the typical day-to-day functions of operating a firm by developing or instituting a department or assigning an individual to handle such duties. Medium-sized firms may decide to outsource certain fringe responsibilities while maintaining only core duties in the office. In very small firms, administrative duties may get portioned out to everyone, including the attorneys and paralegals, who will be expected to perform these duties along with their particular billing requirements. As a paralegal, it is important to know where your position falls in the organizational structure of the firm. The hierarchy among employees is nowhere more evident than within the walls of a law office.

THE HIERARCHY OF LAWYERS AND THE LEGAL STAFF

The lawyers within a law firm may typically be segmented into the following three categories: (1) associates, (2) partners, and (3) of counsel. Each of these different categories of lawyers maintains certain responsibilities and duties within the structure of the law firm.

Associates

The least senior attorneys in the law firm are the associates. Associates are recent law school graduates who have convinced the partners of the firm that they are very capable of doing the legal research typically assigned to junior-level lawyers. Most associates take jobs in law firms with lofty aspirations of becoming partner in their firm of choice. The road to partnership is a long and arduous one, with many associates falling by the wayside.

Associates are recruited during the third year of law school. Often, they have worked previously at the firm as law clerks during summer breaks from school. Associates work their way up the associate ladder through a system that requires them to work in conjunction with the partners on many different tasks. The partners will instruct and guide the associate in an attempt to determine whether the associate has the ability to succeed at the firm and become partner. Due to sheer numbers, fewer and fewer associates are making partner every year. Consequently, the pressure on associates to perform, assuming they want to remain with the firm, is high, and competition for plum assignments can be fierce. Associates will normally work anywhere from six to eight years before being considered for partnership. Over the course of that time, they will be tested in every legal and social skill that may affect their involvement with the firm.

Partners

If an associate is one of the chosen few, he or she may be lucky enough to make partner. Also called members of the firm or shareholders, these senior-level lawyers have been elected by their peers to make the important decisions as to how the firm will manage itself. Each partner has a vote with regard to firm policy, opening new offices, election of fellow partners, and any number of decisions that a law firm needs to make. Typically, partners in a large firm will elect committees amongst themselves to administer procedures on myriad items, such as generating new business, overall management, technology, and the like. A partner, unlike other lawyers within the firm, receives a percentage of the firm's net income for the year as his or her compensation, rather than a salary. A partner's income therefore will typically fluctuate depending upon how well the firm is doing. Partners are also the lawyers who are responsible for attracting the bulk of the firm's business. Oftentimes, a prerequisite for becoming partner is the ability to attract new clients or promote business (affectionately known as "rainmaking"). The firm will usually weigh an attorney's business potential very heavily when deciding whether an associate should be made partner.

"Of Counsel"

Some attorneys are put on "of counsel" status. In days gone by, this title was used to designate a partner who had retired from "active duty" but was still available and willing to consult with the firm on difficult management decisions or complicated cases. It also was often used to show the firm had ties to someone with celebrity status, perhaps a powerful congressman or a sitting judge. The fact that the firm had such a respected person available to give advice was an effective marketing tool.

Nowadays, the term "of counsel" is being used to create all sorts of relationships between attorneys and their firms. Some attorneys have gone on to other careers, perhaps teaching or working for not-for-profit community organizations, and do not want to be full-time lawyers. If their firms do not wish to lose their expertise, these part-time lawyers can arrange to be of counsel, allowing them the freedom to pursue other careers but still maintain a contact with their firms. Another use of the of counsel designation is for lateral hiring between firms. For example, suppose your firm learns that a very well-respected and talented attorney is leaving a rival firm. Your firm wants to offer this attorney a carrot but does not want to bestow full partnership status until it knows that this new attorney will work out. Offering this attorney "of counsel" status is a convenient way to test the waters, and is more prestigious for the talented attorney than merely being hired as an associate.

Paralegals

The other members of the legal staff are the paralegals. In many large firms, the paralegals are supervised by a paralegal manager or paralegal coordinator. While the responsibility of the paralegals is to assist the attorneys in the preparation of the clients' work, the paralegal coordinator or manager is responsible for administering paralegal assignments. The coordinator also structures the budget for the department and helps define the direction of the paralegal department.

Some large firms offer career paths for their paralegals, which allows the paralegals a way to advance through the ranks to more and more challenging assignments. Many paralegals in large firms have even worked their way into management positions.

NONLEGAL STAFF

Within every large law firm, there is a considerable amount of nonlegal or support staff. Each member of the support staff plays an important role in the overall effectiveness of the law firm and quality of its work product. Do not be misled because the partners and associates are the big "breadwinners" in the firm. Each department and every employee has a responsibility that, if done well, will separate that particular law firm from its competition.

Secretaries

The most obvious members of the support staff are the secretarial pool. These integral employees are leaned on heavily by the partners, associates, and paralegals. It is true that the lawyers of today have become more computer literate, thereby taking some of the routine typing and word-processing work out of the hands of the secretary. This, however, has not diminished the role of the secretary. In fact, in many situations, it has increased the responsibilities of the secretary by allowing the secretary to have a more varied and diversified role within the firm. It is not unusual for the secretary to assist the paralegal with some of the traditional paralegal responsibilities. In the litigation area, secretaries are becoming more and more familiar with court and filing procedures to the point of handling filings from beginning to end. In the corporate arena, tasks such as blacklining, previously reserved for paralegals, are many times undertaken by a secretary. Some firms have created word-processing departments, which do the bulk of the heavy typing, leaving even more time for secretaries to assist in other projects. These developments have helped many secretaries to increase their skills and enhance their importance within the firm.

Office Services Department

Another example of the importance of support staff can be found in the office services department. In many firms, the office services department's responsibilities include the copy room or department and the mailroom. Depending on the size of the firm, these departments can be one and the same. The functions of these individuals, while most often behind the scenes, are invaluable to the effective lawyering within any law firm. Additionally, the office services manager is responsible for maintenance within the firm. Whenever carpeting needs to be fixed or offices need to be painted, the office services manager is responsible for interacting with the maintenance personnel to ensure that appropriate repairs and renovations are made.

The purpose of the mailroom in most firms is to distribute incoming mail, ensure that outgoing mail is collected and processed, and distribute and transmit facsimiles within the firm. The copy center in a law firm has grown in importance as the utilization of paper has overwhelmed the legal community in the last 30 years. Because many litigation matters nowadays produce hundreds of thousands of pages, and deposition transcripts and trial exhibits can measure into yards and yards of paper, effective and efficient photocopying has become increasingly important within the law firm. Corporate mergers and general agreements have become ever more complex and wordy, requiring revision after revision. This necessitates an abundance of photocopying. The manager of the copy center in a large firm is a valuable member of the law firm staff.

Librarian

Almost all large firms and most medium-sized firms have their own libraries. Depending on the size of the firm, the library may require a full-time librarian. The librarian is responsible for cataloguing and maintaining myriad state and federal statutes, thousands of volumes of case law, treatises, periodicals, and other legal tomes that the management of the firm believes are necessary for effective lawyering. Additionally, the librarian and his or her staff is typically responsible for the coordination of an ever-growing number of electronic databases to which the law firm subscribes, such as LEXIS or Westlaw, to name only two.

Office Administrator

Another member of the law firm staff who bears mentioning is the office manager or office administrator. This is the individual who has day-to-day oversight of the firm. The office administrator has been selected by the partners as the person who has immediate responsibility for overseeing the entire support staff, interacting with building management regarding leasing issues and the like, and imposing office procedures of an administrative nature. The legal staff in the firm leans on the office administrator to handle the daily functioning of the firm. The support staff looks to the office administrator for guidance and assistance in doing their daily activities. A good office administrator is invaluable to a law firm. His or her responsibilities are enormous, and the strength of the firm depends on the quality of the office administrator.

Information Services Director

A relatively new member of the legal community, but an increasingly important member of the staff, is the firm technician. The Information Services Director, as that individual is sometimes called, is responsible for organizing and facilitating the use of the computers within the firm. This individual's function is to ensure that the telephones work, that the personal computers, which are increasingly appearing on each employee's desk, can interface with each other and, in many firms, can talk to satellite offices of the same firm halfway around the world. As these local area networks (also known as LANs) and wide area networks (WANs) are installed in law firms, these firms are hiring the necessary personnel to handle the upkeep of the networks.

Depending on the size of the firm, the number and size of these support staffs will vary. Many firms will have a docketing department that is responsible for maintaining deadlines for cases handled by the firm; other firms shift this responsibility to a paralegal. Some very large firms have their own graphics departments, which create trial exhibits, blowups, and charts. Most firms have runners and file clerks on hand, to run errands and keep the enormous amounts of documents generated or received by the firm filed away in their proper places. Many larger firms have their own accounting departments, while small firms may have bookkeepers who only come in a few days a week. In any event, it is important to be aware of which of these different departments exists within your firm. Their roles will inevitably have an impact on your responsibilities as a paralegal, and your ability to function effectively will, in many instances, depend on your awareness of these individuals and your utilization of their skills. Knowing where to find assistance when you are presented with a task is oftentimes as important as having the answer yourself.

DIVISION OF DUTIES IN MEDIUM AND SMALL-SIZED FIRMS

The general makeup of a medium or small firm is not significantly different from that of a large firm, especially on the legal side. The major difference between the large firms and the smaller firms is in the amount and type of support staff maintained by the firm. Several departments described above may not exist in a smaller environment. Many smaller firms will, for example, share a library with another firm. This will often happen when a smaller firm takes up residence in a building that also has large firms as tenants. Similarly, smaller firms may choose to outsource their Information Services personnel and even their accounting work. Some of the functions may be handled by the lawyers and the paralegals themselves. For instance, in some smaller firms, the hiring, firing, and other personnel duties may be handled by one of the partners, while administration of the firm's web site may be handled by one of the paralegals.

IN-HOUSE LEGAL DEPARTMENTS

Traditionally, the in-house legal department of a corporation is very different from that of the law firm. While law firms will typically have a multitude of attorneys and paralegals available to tackle any case, the in-house department is usually more streamlined. In past years, the in-house attorneys have performed the function of oversight coordinators, primarily responsible for supervising the outside counsel. Over the last several years, due to numerous factors, including spiraling legal costs, in-house legal departments have grown by leaps and bounds, in many cases handling a significant number of their own cases.

Large Firm Organization:

While the organizational structured displayed is not universal, most large firms incorporate the strategy shown here. The management committee is typically made up of only senior partners, but in some firms, a Chief Financial Officer or firm Business Manager may be included on the committee.

Large Firm Organization

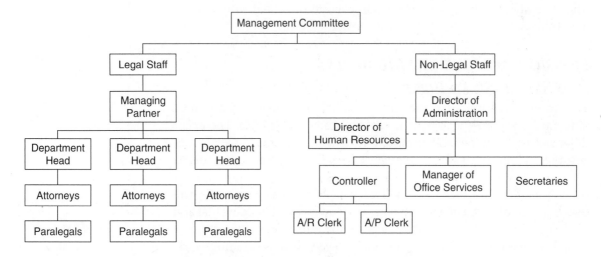

Small Firm Organization:

Most small firms will function with one partner as the firm leader. In some cases, the responsibilities of the Managing Parner will be divided among two or three name partners.

Small Firm Organization

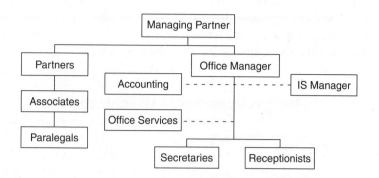

Mid-Sized Organization:

As they grow, many mid-sized firms will begin to develop new departments akin to their larger firm brethren. While there is no specific guidelines for adding these departments, the displayed chart shows a typical mid-sized firm.

Mid-Sized Firm Organization

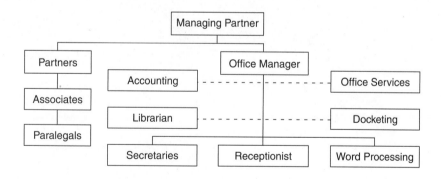

Corporate Legal Departments:

Since a great deal of work is delegated to outside counsel, the size of many corporate legal departments differ depending on their independent corporate culture. Typically, the structure of the department will be as described, but the number of personnel can vary widely.

In-House Department Organization

4

A Top Paralegal Manager Tells You What She Wants

Katie Thoma*
Paralegal Manager, Loeb & Loeb, Los Angeles, California

"We would rather have one man or woman working with us than three merely working for us."

—F.W. Woolworth

Over the years, I have spoken with dozens of paralegal coordinators and paralegal managers and written several articles about their thoughts, wants, hopes, and needs. I have asked them to specify what they look for in a candidate. Their responses to these questions will add some insight into the interviewing process as well as how one should perform on the job. At a minimum, the responses will help you to be better prepared for some of the more commonly asked questions and techniques used by paralegal managers when evaluating a candidate.

WHAT PARALEGAL MANAGERS LOOK FOR

When interviewing for a paralegal position, it is important to have an understanding of what characteristics and qualities are most meaningful to a potential employer. The interview process is difficult enough without having to be in the dark regarding what the interviewer is looking for in a successful candidate. Interviewing is an art form, and being aware of the interviewer's potential mind-set will make the experience all the more palatable. Whether one is an entry-level applicant or an experienced one, employers have a set of criteria that they consider when judging a candidate. These criteria will aid the employer in assessing the candidate's potential success with the organization.

When I, as a paralegal manager, review a candidate's resume, there are certain important factors that will either entice me to interview the candidate or cause me to pass on the candidate. Job stability is

---

*Ms. Thoma is the paralegal manager for Loeb & Loeb, a 300-plus-attorney firm with offices in Los Angeles, New York, and Rome. She has over 15 years experience in major firms and supervises over 55 paralegals.

the first thing I look for on a resume. If a candidate has moved around frequently from job to job, the impression the manager gets is that the candidate, for whatever reason, will not last very long in the new position. Many managers feel that past behavior is indicative of future behavior. On the other hand, if a candidate has remained with the same firm or corporation for many years, the manager feels as though the candidate has a strong commitment to the work and the employer.

Many paralegal managers express an interest in candidates with a solid academic background. At a meeting for paralegal managers, when several were asked if they only wanted to interview and hire individuals from Ivy League schools, the answer was no. Paralegal managers were most interested in people who put forth a considerable effort in attaining a degree. These managers wanted to discuss with the candidate his or her undergraduate education to get a sense for the individual's thought process. A small firm paralegal manager once said, "I want to find out in the interview how articulate a person is. In many instances, asking candidates about their classwork is a good barometer." This particular paralegal manager felt that if a person spent four years at an institution, that person should be able to speak adequately about his or her studies.

Once a candidate has gotten beyond the resume stage and secured an interview, the first thing a paralegal manager notices in a candidate is his or her attire. The paralegal manager wants to know how the candidate will fit into the organization. An applicant's dress is the first indication of compatibility with the firm. If the firm is an old, white-shoe firm (very conservative), and your dress is casual rather than formal with a conservative accent, the interviewer may immediately have reservations about how you would fit into the firm's environment. I have had interviews stop with the candidate's dress. Although one may find this to be rather shallow and unimportant, the nature of law firms and corporations is toward harmony. Employers may not be looking for someone who will stand out, because compatibility with the firm environment requires someone who will fit in. Another factor is that law firms, especially older, larger ones, are very much concerned with "appearances." Their clients tend to be conservative, well-heeled people who expect their attorneys to have a certain image. That image is portrayed in many ways: in the firm's decor, in its stationery, and, most importantly, in the dress and manner of its employees.

The newest trend, however, with intellectual property firms and particularly with entertainment firms is a more dressed-down, informal look. Find out from your network about the firm's culture and image.

Paralegal managers will, in many cases, focus on accoutrements other than whether you are wearing a suit (male or female). Interest in the candidate's dress also shows how the candidate feels about himself or herself. A neatly and appropriately dressed interviewee could very well be someone who takes pride in his or her work. Unshined shoes, wrinkled clothing, ripped pantyhose, and unmatched socks all give the impression to the paralegal manager that the candidate is sloppy. Sloppy dress may give the impression of sloppy work.

Many managers use an interviewing technique that allows them to ascertain how a candidate will handle everyday paralegal responsibilities. These managers ask questions of the candidate that will demonstrate the candidate's aplomb at dealing with certain situations. For example, instead of asking a hypothetical question such as, "How would you handle this problem?" these managers ask, "How have you handled this problem in the past?" The answers to this type of question help the manager determine, with greater likelihood, the overall abilities, common sense, and experience level of the candidate.

Paralegal managers notice whether a paralegal pays attention to detail. One of the overriding tasks of any paralegal is to be responsible for a multitude of documents. Whether you are in litigation, corporate, bankruptcy, intellectual property, or even estate planning, it is the paralegal's goal to organize every document he or she handles. If you are successful in devising systems allowing you to be organized, you will most likely impress your paralegal manager. Another detail-oriented issue is preparation of a finished product having as few mistakes as possible. Your ability to proofread your own work and present a quality product will have a positive effect on your superiors.

Several paralegal managers have pointed to the type of law practiced by the firm as the reason for their particular interest in a candidate's academic record. In firms specializing in corporate law, securities transactions, and the like, several managers felt a strong academic background allows better understanding of documents the paralegal works with on a daily basis and, therefore, supports the individual's ability to succeed. A few managers conceded this is not necessarily the case. Given the limited amount of time a firm has to choose a candidate, demonstrating a strong academic background makes the decision easier, all other factors being equal.

Not all entry-level paralegals are people who come directly out of college or paralegal school. Many paralegals are people who have worked, in many cases for a long time, at another career and have transitioned into

---

Reality Check

We once knew a paralegal manager who, after greeting her candidates, asked them to walk ahead of her toward her office. Contrary to what you think may have been good manners, the manager was checking out the back of the candidate: hair, heels, and hemlines.

the legal field. When hiring an entry-level paralegal from another field, paralegal managers look for candidates who have shown some success in their previous field. While these individuals may have never worked in a law firm before, there is a perception that success breeds success.

It is important to give potential employers a sense that the candidate is hungry for the position. Lack of enthusiasm is one of the first turnoffs for any paralegal manager. Just as a lack of awareness about the firm can be perceived as a negative, a lack of pep or zeal during the interview or on the job gives a bad impression.

Over and over again, managers have expressed their concern about candidates who slumped in the interview chair. Or worse, sometimes the questions asked of the candidate were met with a perceived lack of interest in the entire process.

"Whenever I interview a prospective employee, I want to get the feeling that the candidate is ready to start work immediately." In many law firms, the hours paralegals keep are extensive, and employers want to feel as though the long hours will not be a burden to their staff. An individual who is dragging through a one-hour interview does not have much of a chance of convincing the paralegal manager that long hours would not be a burden.

Interviewers like candidates who ask questions. This is how impressions are formed about one's hunger for a job. Asking questions of your interviewer about the position, the firm's benefits, or the typical paralegal day (if there is such a thing!) gives potential employers a feeling you are someone who is attentive and thinks things through, particularly when confronted with an unknown situation. One of the important characteristics of a successful paralegal is the ability to ensure that assignments are completed as assigned. A candidate who asks questions will be viewed as someone who makes sure the assignment is understood before attempting to complete it.

It always intrigues me when a candidate interviews without knowing anything about our firm. Not having done any homework about the firm prior to the interview gives the impression that the opportunity to work for the firm or corporation is of little importance to the candidate. Questions about the size of the firm, what kind of law the firm practiced, even where the firm had its main office. These types of questions convey a message that the candidate was not overly concerned with making a good impression.

Paralegal managers are similarly impressed when a candidate arrives for an interview and knows the types of practice the firm has or, if a corporation, what sort of businesses or products the corporation is involved in. It is always a good habit to do some research about a firm or corporation prior to your interview. You want to show the interviewer that this firm or corporation is truly of interest to you. The impression you want to relate to the firm or company is that this interview is special to you.

The interview is possibly the most important opportunity an applicant has to convince the paralegal manager of his or her chances of succeeding. It is important to convey to the paralegal manager that you are capable, hungry, and attentive. Conveying these qualities enhances your chances of success as a paralegal. Take the opportunity you are given now—second chances at first impressions are rare.

5

Hi, Ho! Hi, Ho! It's Off to School We Go!

"If you think education is expensive, try ignorance."

—Anonymous

Relatively speaking, a formal paralegal education is a new concept. Before approximately 1970, all paralegals were products of on-the-job training. Gradually, as the need for paralegals rose, more and more schools began offering programs. In 1987, when the U.S. Department of Labor named the paralegal profession as one of the fastest growing in the country, an explosion in paralegal education took place. Some of the fallout was good, and some was bad.

When schools began designing paralegal curricula, they were breaking new ground. The paralegal profession itself was not that old, and there was little guidance offered as far as what a paralegal was expected to know. Some schools leaned too heavily on clerical skills, and others tried to re-create an attorney's first year of law school. Some courses took two years to complete, and others claimed you could earn your paralegal "wings" in six months or less. As recently as 10 years ago, many attorneys sneered when potential paralegal employees proudly produced their school credentials. Because many of the programs were meaningless, the certificates that were earned were meaningless as well.

Today, with the assistance of such approving bodies as the American Bar Association and the guidance of organizations such as the American Association for Paralegal Education, legitimate paralegal programs have made great strides in the quality and relevance of their programs. Today, students can earn master's and bachelor's degrees as well as associate's degrees and certificates in paralegal studies.

If you are thinking about entering this field or if you are an experienced paralegal without a certificate or undergraduate degree, choosing a school or university that meets the demands of today's legal environment is critical. More and more employers across the country now require a B.A. or B.S. degree and a certificate from a reputable school. Your choice of paralegal programs can have a direct impact on what kind of job you land when you've finished.

WHAT TYPES OF COURSES SHOULD BE OFFERED?

In its publication entitled "Core Competencies for Paralegal Programs," the American Association for Paralegal Education (AAfPE) states that

> [i]n order to be a successful paralegal/legal assistant, a person must not only possess a common core of legal knowledge, but also must have acquired vital critical thinking, organizational, communication, and interpersonal skills.

AAfPE recommends that paralegal education programs incorporate courses that develop a student's:

- *Critical thinking skills* (problem analysis, logic, application of relevant legal authority);
- *Organizational skills* (categorizing and prioritizing, efficient use of time);
- *General communication skills* (reading comprehension, effective listening, writing and speaking skills);
- *Interpersonal skills* (establishing rapport, diplomacy and tact, teamwork, ability to work with minimal supervision);
- *Legal research skills* (use of law library, use of computer-assisted legal research, cite checking);
- *Legal writing skills* (reporting results of legal research, use of appropriate citations, proper formats for correspondence and pleadings);
- *Computer skills* (training in word processing, database and spreadsheet programs);
- *Interviewing and investigation skills* (identify witnesses and potential parties, conduct and record interviews, gain access to public and private records);
- *Organization and operation of legal system* (structure of U.S. legal system, source of law and its classification, procedures and functions of state and local courts);
- *Organization and operation of law offices* (practice arrangements, functions of personnel, organizational and administrative procedures);
- *Paralegal profession and ethical obligations* (duties, terms, ethics, prevention of unauthorized practice of law).

AAfPE also recommends that paralegal students are taught a background in four common practices areas: contracts, torts, business organizations, and litigation.

To grasp the above concepts and skills takes time and concentrated study. Some programs, such as the one offered by the UCLA Extension Attorney Assistant Training Program, require students to attend five days per week during the day in a very intense four-month program. The university also offers a night-time program, which continues for one-year. Entrance to the program requires students to take a test equivalent to the GMATS—the evaluation test given to enter graduate school. Graduates from the UCLA program are sought after by the very best firms, and the school has a very high ratio of placements.

Call or write the schools that offer programs in which you are interested and ask them to send you a course catalog. The catalog will give you such information as entrance requirements (if any), the number of units necessary to complete the program, which classes are required and which are electives, and whether an internship must be completed. The school should offer an introductory course, a legal research and writing course, an ethics course, a course in business law or the U.S. legal system, computer labs, and courses in a variety of specialty areas. The more specialty courses offered, the better, as it will give you exposure to a wide variety of practice areas. (See Chapter 2.)

OTHER EARMARKS OF A GOOD PROGRAM
Reputation
When performing your research on a school, there are other particulars to be aware of besides the curriculum. One is the school's reputation in the community. If the quality of the students coming out of the school is not high, attorneys will have very little respect for any certificate or degree you earn there. If you have any friends in the legal community, ask about the reputation of your target school. Word of a poor program gets around quickly. If you don't have anyone you can talk to, examine the school's course catalog. Some schools require a minimum grade point average or a minimum score on an entrance examination. These are good signs that the school is being selective about the caliber of the students who are allowed in.

Director of the Program
Another detail you should check into, if possible, is the background of the individual who is the director or administrator of the paralegal program. This person is responsible for selecting the curriculum, hiring instructors, advising students, choosing library materials, obtaining proper funding so

that the program can have the supplies and support it needs, promoting the program to local attorneys to help with placement of graduates, and keeping on top of changes in the profession. In the best-case scenario, this person should be a full-time employee of the school, whose time is devoted exclusively to the paralegal program. The director should be a former practicing attorney or paralegal, so that he or she will have the background necessary to understand the peculiarities of the legal profession. When a school has such a person administrating its program, it means that the school is treating the program seriously. If, on the other hand, the program director is a part-time attorney, who still has a law practice on the side, or an administrator within the school who is responsible for several different divisions, it is an indication that the school is not completely devoted to turning out the best possible product. To get the information you need to evaluate your potential school's director, make an appointment to see him or her to discuss the program. While you are there, you can ask about the director's background.

Faculty Qualifications

The next bit of research you should do on your paralegal program is to find out the qualifications of the instructors who will be teaching the courses. Are they merely staff teachers at the college, who have no legal background? Are they attorneys? Are they paralegals? How many years of experience do they have? Some schools make the assumption that attorneys are the best instructors for a paralegal program. This may not necessarily be true. Some attorneys teach their courses as though they were re-creating their law school classes. And although paralegals do need to know some of the things attorneys know, the paralegals' education should be more focused on procedures and practicality, rather than legal theory. Because some attorneys have no concept of the paralegal experience in the law firm, they are unable to give their students the special insights that a paralegal instructor can offer.

If the majority of the instructors in your target program are attorneys, at least try to ascertain whether they even utilize paralegals in their practice. Although this may seem elementary, you would be amazed how many attorney instructors are out there teaching future paralegals who themselves have never worked with one!

One of most successful teaching methods is to team an attorney with a paralegal to teach the class. The attorney can talk about the law and what she expects from her paralegal. The paralegal can discuss procedures and how to work smoothly with the attorney to accomplish their common goals of getting the work out and keeping clients happy.

During your meeting with the program director, inquire about the instructors and their backgrounds.

Student Services

Another test of a good program is whether there are adequate services offered for the students in such areas as orientation and counseling. Is there a student paralegal association in place? Is there an alumni association? Such organizations can create and foster a sense of closeness and unity among the paralegal students, both during their schooling and after. They can also promote the paralegal program in the community by organizing and sponsoring public service or charity events. These associations are often charged with the responsibility of providing continuing education to graduates of the program. Truly professional paralegals are willing to keep their skills honed by regularly attending continuing education seminars throughout their careers. Having a paralegal school that offers continuing education seminars for its former students is an enormous convenience.

Placement Assistance

No self-respecting paralegal program will turn you loose at the conclusion of your schooling with a certificate and a handshake. During your meeting with the program director, inquire into the efforts the school makes to help its graduates find positions in law firms, corporations, and government agencies. Ask what percentage of the graduates are hired each year.

Keep in mind that a good program director acts as a "salesman" of sorts, continually championing the program to local attorneys, arranging internships for the students, putting on job fairs, and planning any number of other promotions. Look for a director who is upbeat but realistic about the job market in your area. He or she should be able to give you an idea of your chances of obtaining a position right out of school and of what the expected salary range will be.

ABA APPROVAL—JUST WHAT IS IT ANYWAY?

The American Bar Association (ABA) is a nationwide voluntary organization for lawyers. The ABA has been approving law schools for many years. In 1975, the ABA's Standing Committee on Legal Assistants also began approving paralegal programs throughout the country. The guidelines for program approval are promulgated by the ABA in pursuance of its objective of being "vitally and actively interested in ways and means of extending legal services in the United States."

A paralegal program becomes ABA approved by complying with the ABA's strict guidelines for a number of years, followed by hosting a review team from the ABA, which comes out and inspects the school. Some of the requirements of the ABA include the following:

- Ethics must be taught.
- An advisory committee to the program must be established, consisting of practicing lawyers, legal assistants, legal assistant managers, faculty and school administrators, and at least one member of the general public.
- The program must stress understanding and reasoning rather than rote learning of facts.
- The curriculum must be responsive to the changing needs of the legal community related to the use of paralegals.
- The credits earned by the paralegal students must be transferable to institutions of higher learning.
- The program must have a plan in place for evaluating and reviewing itself.
- Students should be encouraged to acquire computer skills, and instruction in computerized legal research must be available to the students.
- The program must be offered by a school that is institutionally accredited.
- The paralegal program must require at least sixty semester hours, or the equivalent, composed of general education and legal specialty courses.
- The program director and instructors must possess education, knowledge, and experience in the paralegal field.
- The school should use a number of admission criteria for selecting students so that their success as paralegals can be reasonably predicted.
- A well-organized plan for counseling and advising students and assisting graduates in securing employment must be in place.
- Students must be allowed to participate in curriculum review and development and course and faculty evaluation.
- The school shall either have its own library, containing a long list of required books, or access to such a library.

Graduating from an ABA-approved program has its advantages for new paralegals. First of all, as you can see from the preceding list, an institution that meets the ABA's guidelines is pretty serious about its paralegal program and is willing to spend the time and money to do it right. Also today, especially in larger cities, many employers are beginning to require potential paralegal employees to have certificates from ABA-approved programs. There are a few reasons for this: attorneys recognize the ABA name, since many of them graduated from ABA-approved law schools; and because the quality of paralegal programs can vary widely, attorneys have some level of comfort that they will be getting a qualified employee when they hire one from an ABA-approved program.

There is an important thing to keep in mind. Just because a program is not ABA approved does not mean it is not a quality program. The cost for meeting the ABA's requirements and maintaining approval is very, very high. Many schools simply do not have the budgets for it. Instead, using the ABA requirements as a guideline, the school brings itself into what is known as "substantial compliance" with the ABA's rules. In other words, the program meets all the requirements but does not have the expensive approval "sticker." You will get a fine education in a school with a program that is in substantial ABA compliance. Do your homework and make sure the program has the necessary components as described above.

AAfPE Membership

Another item to inquire about is whether the school you are considering attending is a voting member of the American Association for Paralegal Education (AAfPE). AAfPE was formed in 1981, and its members include institutions that offer paralegal programs, paralegal educators, and paralegal administrators.

Unlike the ABA, AAfPE does not approve programs. Instead, AAfPE assists schools by setting forth guidelines for choosing curricula, hiring instructors, maintaining facilities conducive to learning, and other areas for the proper management of the program. AAfPE promotes high standards for paralegal education and offers annual and regional conferences where paralegal educators can meet and learn ways to improve their programs. AAfPE has also established Lambda Epsilon Chi, a national honor society for paralegals and legal assistant students.

Another service provided to paralegal schools by AAfPE is the monitoring of the "real" world—the attorneys, firms, and companies that hire paralegals. Through research, surveys, and other information gathering,

AAfPE keeps up on changes and innovations in the paralegal field and disseminates that information to the educators. In this way, schools can adjust their curricula to keep pace with the changing marketplace. For example, it was AAfPE that first discovered attorneys were searching for paralegals who had more practical training, as opposed to theoretical training.

Only institutions that are ABA approved or in substantial compliance with ABA guidelines may be voting members of AAfPE. Schools that do not qualify as voting members may become associate members. AAfPE maintains a directory of its members. To learn whether the school you are considering attending is an AAfPE voting or associate member, write or call AAfPE at 2965 Flowers Road South, #105, Atlanta, Georgia 30341, (770) 452-9877.

TYPES OF PARALEGAL PROGRAMS

There are several vehicles by which you can obtain a paralegal education. The one you choose will depend on several things:

- Depending on where you live, you may not have much choice; there may be only one program in your area.
- How much college education do you already have?
- How much money can you afford to spend?
- How much time do you have to complete the program?
- What is the job market like where you plan to live and work upon completing your paralegal education?
- What type of position are you hoping to obtain once you graduate?

Certificate Programs

Certificate programs are the most common, and usually the quickest way to obtain a paralegal education. These programs are offered by community colleges, four-year colleges, universities, and private, for-profit schools, such as business colleges. The cost and time of completion of these programs are all over the board. Some programs are as short as six months, and others take two years to complete, if done at night. Public colleges are usually the least expensive, while private schools can cost in the thousands of dollars. The programs offered in private schools and business colleges are often very structured. You must attend classes a certain number of nights per week and take classes in a certain order. Public colleges have a less rigid approach. If you only have the time and money to take one class per semester, you are free to do so. Some people have taken five years to earn their certificates, taking a class here and a class there.

The main reason these certificate programs are so popular is because they are usually offered at night to working people who are in the process of a career change.

Although you may be tempted to find the shortest program so that you can get through your training as soon as possible, in the long run it is best to measure the quality of the program using the steps outlined. Keep in mind that the longer the required course of study, the more information you will absorb and the more skills you will learn. You will be that much more prepared for your first job.

Associate's Degree Programs

Many of the colleges and universities that offer certificate programs will also award a two-year, or associate's degree upon successful completion of the required classes. In addition to the law courses that must be taken to earn a certificate, students must also have taken a certain number of units of general education classes, such as speech, health, English, and math. Because a broader education is required to earn an associate's degree, it is usually considered a step up from a certificate. Because the number of extra classes required for the degree is not onerous, it is well worth the additional time and expense to continue on with your education and earn that degree.

Bachelor's Degree Programs

In the past, few paralegals needed a baccalaureate degree to land an excellent position in a big firm. However, times are changing, and competition for jobs is growing. Many corporations and large firms insist on a four-year degree for new paralegal hires. A growing number of colleges and universities are offering such degrees. Most consist of two years of general education and elective coursework, followed by two years of upper-division courses in the student's major, paralegal studies.

Although the firms where you live may not require a four-year degree, it may be a good idea to plan ahead to what you will be doing 5 or 10 years after you have entered the workplace. Would you like to move up into management? Or maybe enroll in law school? If these possibilities are in the back of your head, a bachelor's degree will open up more doors for you than will a certificate or a two-year degree.

Master's Degree Programs

A very few colleges and universities offer postgraduate master's programs for paralegals. Although not necessary for the general workplace, such a degree would be helpful if you decide you would like to teach paralegal studies at the four-year college or university level.

Reality Check

Once you have completed a certificate program, you are a "Certificated Paralegal/Legal Assistant." Don't make the mistake of calling yourself a "Certified Paralegal" or a "Certified Legal Assistant." The only paralegals who can call themselves "certified" are those who have successfully completed either the Certified Legal Assistant examination, given by the National Association of Legal Assistants or the Pace examination given by the National Federation of Paralegal Associations.

Correspondence Programs

Home study programs in the paralegal field are available. At the time of publication of this book, no such correspondence courses qualified for either ABA approval or AAfPE voting membership. The reason for this is that a good paralegal education requires a lot of "hands on" training and exchanges between students and instructors and between students. Students in a course of home study would not receive the benefit of such communication. Correspondence courses may not give you the breadth and depth of training that you will need to be competitive in today's job market. If at all possible, explore other educational options.

Distance Learning

Along with the surge in use of the Internet, a new phenomenon has emerged: distance learning schools. *Distance learning* is defined as teaching-learning arrangements in which the teacher and student are separated physically. The physical separation of student and teacher requires the instructor to use a medium (usually electronic or satellite) to bridge the distance—using, for example, computers, interactive videos and discs, telephony, instructional television, and cable television.

Today, there are hundreds of correspondence schools in the United States, operating entirely via the mail system or via a hybrid of mail and electronic media. As a result of improvements in educational technology, conventional mail-based correspondence schools will be displaced by Internet-based schools and programs. It is noteworthy that the Accreditation Committee of the American Bar Association approved temporary Distance Education Guidelines in April 1997.

Virtual education encompasses the delivery and acquisition of knowledge and skills through the Internet and the World Wide Web. Virtual education is, simply, education on-line; the broader notion of distance learning includes all learning in which the teacher and learner are separated, including on-line and "off-line" education.

Paralegal programs are only just beginning to find limited application in a small number of distance learning schools and programs. However, some observers predict that on-line or distance learning will hit the education field as hard as the Internet redefined the way we do business today. The International Distance Education Council claims, "There are currently 10 million students around the globe taking degree courses through distance learning." Major universities such as the University of Maryland offer a multitude of courses, including paralegal studies. At this writing, paralegal courses on-line are just emerging. We predict that by the time you are reading this book, on-line courses will have taken hold.

BEWARE THE FLY-BY-NIGHT SCHOOLS

When the explosion in paralegal education took place in the late 1980s, the paralegal profession faced unprecedented popularity. Some people saw this as an opportunity to make a quick buck, training would-be paralegals. You may have seen advertisements for paralegal "schools" in magazines and newspapers that made outrageous claims, such as

"I make over $200,000 a year working at home part-time as a paralegal."

"How you can become a board-certified paralegal in only 8 weeks."

First, there are plenty of attorneys who do not make $200,000 per year. Second, there is no such thing in our knowledge as a "board-certified paralegal." And finally, no one, in our opinion, can obtain an adequate enough education to become a truly professional, legitimate paralegal in only eight weeks.

Being a paralegal is not some sort of get-rich-quick scheme. Assisting attorneys is a demanding, challenging, and extremely rewarding career. It takes a truly professional person to understand the intricacies of the law, remain calm in the face of crushing deadlines, reassure anxious clients, and keep attorneys free from annoying organizational details so that they can practice law.

DECIDING WHICH SCHOOL WILL MEET YOUR GOALS

If you have a choice of paralegal schools to attend, it may be a helpful exercise to think about the type of position you hope to get upon graduation. (See Chapter 1 for more information on what is required in the market today.)

If you dream of working in a large, prestigious firm:

You normally need at least a bachelor's degree and a certificate preferably from an ABA-approved program. There are some regions of the country such as New York and Washington, D.C., that encourage "transition" paralegals—those who eventually will end up in law school or grad school. In these positions, a certificate is generally not required.

If you live in a smaller town or would rather stay with a small firm or sole practitioner:	An associate's degree in paralegal studies or a certificate from a good program is frequently required.
If you plan to get a government job:	You may need a bachelor's degree and a paralegal certificate from a good school.
If you plan to enter the military:	College is preferred. However, find out from each branch what background is necessary. The military offers interesting training once you are in.

6

The Importance of Internships

"The only joy in the world is to begin."

—Cesare Pavese

*I*f you are just starting out in the field and have no paralegal experience, an internship may be just what you need to help you get a job. Internships are generally obtained through the career placement center in your paralegal school. It is the best way for paralegals without any prior legal experience to get firsthand knowledge of their newly chosen career.

Because internships do not usually pay a salary of any sort, students sometimes dismiss the value this program can play in getting your first job. According to Richard Shaffran, Director of the UCLA Attorney Assistant Training Program, "students who demonstrate their willingness to donate their time and efforts to an internship program are the candidates employers generally choose first. These students experience firsthand what is only talked about in class. They come better prepared for the tasks at hand."

An internship may require you to volunteer 4 to 6 hours per week for 6 to 10 weeks in a law firm, in-house legal department, not-for-profit organization or government agency. It is a trainee position, and you could be asked to perform any number of assignments, very much like in an actual job. The advantage to you is that you are a designated trainee, there to learn.

List the internship on your resume even if you are still participating in it. The internship category should be listed directly under education and before prior work history. This shows potential employers that you have some exposure to law office procedures and paralegal assignments. After you have worked for a while as a paralegal, you can either drop the internship on your resume or list it after work experience.

Check with your school to see if internship programs are offered. If not, push your school to implement this excellent approach to gaining experience and job opportunities.

The next resume shows you how to present an internship.

Reality Check

Internships are a win-win situation on two levels: You gain great experience, which puts you in a higher level of probability for getting selected over other candidates; or you may even get asked to stay on as a permanent employee where you are interning!

PARALEGAL RESUME/INTERNSHIP

Nora Tapin
3345 Palms #101
Los Angeles, CA 90034
(t)310.555.4466
(e)Nor@col.com

Profile:
* * Excellent ability to handle multiple assignments
* * Westlaw certified
* * Proficient in Word, WordPerfect and Lotus
* * Graduated with Honors
* * Demonstrated ability to work well with clients

Education:

University of West Los Angeles School of Paralegal Studies   2000
Paralegal Certificate: Litigation Specialty
Graduated with Honors

University of California at Santa Cruz   1999
Bachelor of Arts Degree in Communications

Paralegal Internship:

Department of California Corporations   May–July 2000
Los Angeles, California

Completed 10-week internship. Assignments included preparation of forms for Secretary of State; interfacing with public; answering questions, directing filings.

Work History:

CompUSA   June 1998–Present
Torrance, California

Sales Rep: Assist clients in purchase of computers. Recommend software and hardware choices. Work efficiently in busy store handling several customers at once. Achieved highest award for sales in company.

Computer Skills:

Proficient in Word, WordPerfect 9.0, Lotus, Excel, Microsoft Publisher, Windows '98, ACT, Access

Associations:

Los Angeles Paralegal Association
University of West Los Angeles Alumni Association

7

Entering the Marketplace
and Transferring Your Skills

"How to succeed: try hard enough."

—Malcolm Forbes

TRANSFERRING YOUR EXISTING SKILLS TO A PARALEGAL CAREER

Unless there is a particular area of the law that is calling your name, your wisest course of action may be to choose a specialty that is complementary to the skills and knowledge you already have. Once you are a seasoned paralegal, you can make a switch into a different specialty. The following chart will help you get started in the right direction.

Your Background	Possible Paralegal Position
Accounting	Tax or employee benefits law
Administrative assistant	Litigation or trial specialist
Bank teller or other financial institution work	Banking litigation or trust administration
Computer/MIS	Complex litigation/Internet research
Construction	Construction litigation or real estate law
Counseling/day care center	Family law
Graphics designer	Complex litigation or intellectual property law
Human resources	Employment or labor law
Insurance coverage/adjuster	Medical or professional malpractice; personal injury
Investigator	Criminal law or litigation
Journalism	Legal research and writing in any area of the law that interests you
Law enforcement	Criminal law

Your Background	Possible Paralegal Position
Mechanic/engineer	Products liability
Medical or related field	Personal injury or medical malpractice
Own(ed) business	Corporate or transactional law/franchise law
Radio/television	Constitutional law or entertainment law
Rest home/retirement center	Elder law
Science or lab work	Environmental law
Stockbroker/financial planner	Securities or employee benefits law
Store credit department	Collections
Title or escrow company	Real estate law

There are other talents you may have that at first don't appear to have a direct crossover to a particular legal specialty. That doesn't mean they won't be useful to you in the future. Paralegals, whether they be in large firms or small, are often asked to perform tasks outside the normal purview. For example:

If you have teaching experience:	Paralegals (especially in mid-size and large firms) frequently assist in training new paralegals and secretaries.
If you have worked in marketing or advertising:	You may be able to volunteer to assist your firm with its marketing efforts, or help design a firm brochure.
If you have management experience:	You may be able to work your way up to a position as team leader or paralegal manager; your skills may be tapped to help prepare an employee manual for the firm.
If you have worked in a placement company or temp agency:	Your help may be needed in recruiting new staff employees.
If you have formerly worked as a social director or events coordinator:	Law firms often become involved in community services activities that you could help organize.

If you are a writer or editor:	You may be called upon to help create or contribute to the firm's newsletter.
If you have good computer skills:	Law firms must always be researching the latest software and hardware to stay competitive.
If you have worked in a library:	Paralegals who love books have gone on in their careers to become law librarians in larger firms.
If you used to work in the travel industry:	Attorneys (and occasionally other staff) must often fly to other cities on business. Also, during the recruiting season, many firms bring prospective attorney employees in from other cities across the country to the firm to interview. Paralegals have been put in charge of coordinating all travel plans for the firm.

At this point, you may be saying, "Wait a minute. I'm not going to paralegal school just so I can do all these non-law-related assignments for my employer." However, you must remember that running a law office is just like running any other business. Books must be kept, budgets must be created, employees must be hired and fired, marketing of the firm's resources must be done to keep new business coming in, client relations work is performed constantly to keep the "customer" happy, and someone must be responsible for the care and feeding of the computer network. Most small and mid-sized firms don't have separate departments to do all these jobs. They are divvied up between existing employees, including attorneys, paralegals, and secretaries. As part of the law office team, you may be asked to do your share of administrative work. While some paralegals find this type of assignment boring, others welcome it as a nice break from the endless round of billable hours.

Reality Check

Performing occasional administrative tasks is often viewed as a smart thing to do politically. The more you do, the more privy you become to the inner workings of the firm and the more access you will have to movers and shakers whose clout you may need someday.

8

Unsung Heroes and Rising Stars

"It is not enough to aim—you must hit."

—Italian proverb

*I*f you take a poll in your paralegal classes, you will discover very few students fresh out of high school. The vast majority of new paralegals are individuals who are on their second, and sometimes even their third, careers. Some of them have had law-related careers, such as being legal secretaries or law office receptionists. Others, in their current positions, have worked on various legal matters affecting their companies and have had their interest piqued. Still others have always had a fascination with the law but just never did anything about it until now.

Many of the students in the latter two categories feel intimidated by the legal secretary students in their classes. The secretaries know so much about the law already, while the other students struggle with every new term and concept. Because of this, students with no prior legal knowledge have the misconception that they are at a disadvantage and that their prior skills don't count. *NOTHING COULD BE FURTHER FROM THE TRUTH.*

YOU CAN TAKE IT WITH YOU

People who are making the transition to a paralegal career can take heart in the following two concepts:

1. Much of what a paralegal does has nothing to do with the law.
2. Much of what the law is about is good, old-fashioned common sense.

These theories imply that all of the skills, all of the knowledge, and all of the common sense you have learned, both in your prior career(s) and in your life experiences, will be useful in your new paralegal position.

Sit down and analyze what you have accomplished in all the jobs and positions you have ever had. Did you work in sales at a department store? Then you know what it takes to work with the firm's clients. Have you done any type of bookkeeping tasks? If you become a litigation paralegal, you may be called upon to review the books and records of companies your firm's client is suing. Did you previously work as a carpenter or roofer? An attorney who specializes in construction litigation would be delighted to draw upon your expertise in the industry. Do you have medical office experience? Then you would be in great demand in firms that sue or defend doctors in malpractice cases. People who can decipher a doctor's handwriting in hospital records and know the names of the various procedures and anatomical parts are highly valued.

How about your personal skills and life experiences? Have you ever completed your own tax return? Just by going through that process, you are already a step ahead if you want to work with tax attorneys. Have you ever served as an administrator for a relative's probate? That knowledge and experience will serve you well if you decide to go into the probate specialty. Have you ever owned your own business? Then the law has already touched your life in many ways, from filing a fictitious business name statement, to incorporating, to withholding employees' taxes. Are you a very organized individual who could, within minutes, put your hands on your 1991 tax return, the last repair receipt for your car, or your canceled checks? Those are precisely the skills you need to be a good trial paralegal.

Many people do not realize how much they know. For example, have you ever purchased or sold a house? If so, you know many things. You know that an escrow must be opened. You know that title insurance must be obtained and that you will receive a report showing what sort of liens and encumbrances are of record against the property. You know that the buyer usually must obtain a loan and that certain things must be done to satisfy the lender. A pest report must usually be obtained. An inspection is performed on the house to make sure it is structurally sound. Papers may have to be filed with the county showing that the title to the property is being transferred. A grant deed must be recorded with the county recorder. If you know these things, you already know something of what a real estate paralegal must know. And you don't just know it, *you've been through it.* This is valuable experience in the law office. If you are competing with another person for a position with a real estate attorney and you can say you know what a grant deed looks like and you can read a title report, it may be just the edge you need to get that job.

Of course, you will learn a lot about the law and how to find it while you are in paralegal school. And there will be times that you will apply that knowledge. But the rest of the time, you will be given tasks that merely require a commonsense approach. For instance, suppose an attorney asks you to locate some hospital records for a person who was put into an asylum somewhere in the state of Louisiana in the 1920s (true story!). Here are the steps you will have to take to solve that puzzle:

1. Call the state capital and find the name of the agency in charge of mental hospitals.
2. Call that agency and find out what mental hospitals were open and active in the 1920s.
3. Call each of those hospitals with the name of the patient until you find the one to which that patient was committed.
4. Ask the records department of that hospital what sort of document they need from surviving family members to release the records to you, and what their copying fee is.
5. Draft the necessary document, have a family member sign it, and send it off to the hospital with a check for their fee.

Now of all those steps, only No. 5, the drafting of the release document, needed any sort of legal knowledge at all. The rest just required sitting down, thinking about a plan to get at the information you needed, and then having the patience to wait on the phone while being transferred from department to department until you got the right one.

BEEN THERE—DONE THAT: INTERVIEWS WITH SECOND-CAREER PARALEGALS

Insurance

Rhonda Gregory
Coordinated Legal Technologies

Rhonda was a six-year veteran as an adjuster for an insurance company. Her duties included reviewing property and casualty loss claim reports, interviewing the insured, locating and interviewing witnesses, reviewing police reports, and reviewing policies to determine whether losses were covered. Following all of this investigation, she would work up the files and prepare a report. On small cases, she would decide herself whether a claim would be paid. On larger cases, she would report to her claims manager.

While performing her job duties, Rhonda often had contact with her employer's law firm. The law firm personnel admired Rhonda's thoroughness and good judgment, and asked her occasionally if she ever thought about becoming a paralegal. Rhonda laughed, as nothing was further from her mind.

One day, Rhonda was struck by the dreaded "D" word—downsizing. Her position was eliminated, but she was rescued by the admiring law firm, who gave her a job working up plaintiff personal injury cases. Her responsibilities were very similar to what she had been doing before. She gathered the factual information about the case, interviewed witnesses, and gathered relevant documents. The only work she had not done before was drafting the initial complaint and other legal documents. Recognizing that she needed a better education in the law, Rhonda enrolled in paralegal school at night, and after a few years earned her certificate.

"The best carryover skills I took with me from my insurance career," said Rhonda, "were my ability to read contracts" (i.e., insurance policies) "and to interview witnesses to obtain the facts."

That switch in careers 17 years ago changed Rhonda's life forever. From her start in the personal injury area, she went on to work in other specialties, including tax, ERISA, transactional, corporate, probate, and business litigation. In 1989, she opened her own business as a freelance paralegal, Coordinated Legal Services. Her developing love of and knowledge about computers over the years has led her to embark on her latest business venture. Rhonda is now the proud owner of Coordinated Legal Technologies, specializing in researching and evaluating software for law firms. She develops computer protocols for complex document management and provides law-specific software consulting and training.

Chemistry

Tammy Parubchenko
Rogers & Wells

Tammy was content with her career in the sciences, working for a synthetic chemical research company. Her current assignment was doing pure research to find new insecticides and herbicides. Tammy's first step was to spend a lot of time in the library doing research. Once she had located a compound she wanted to test, she would get approval from the Ph.D. chemist in charge of the lab. It was then her job to order the chemicals, glassware, and any other supplies she needed and start the project. She would perform the analysis of the chemicals and then prepare the analogs (all of the variations of the compound).

After a time, Tammy began feeling very unwell. She was constantly tired and sluggish. After going to several doctors (all of whom told her nothing was wrong with her), she found a bright internist who recognized she was suffering from an allergic reaction to the chemicals she was surrounded by every day. Her doctor advised her to seriously consider changing her career.

Tammy returned to school to get a degree in political science. While in school, she learned of the paralegal profession, which she previously did not even know existed. It sounded interesting to her, so she earned her certificate while finishing her degree.

Around the time Tammy was finishing her schooling, the school received a call from the legal department at DuPont, a huge chemical corporation. DuPont's patent attorney, himself holding a Ph.D. in chemistry, wanted a new graduate with a technical background to help in the intellectual property department. Tammy filled the bill. She was put to work handling DuPont's worldwide patent filings. Later, she was allowed to begin doing patent prosecution at the U.S. Patent Office. This involved a lot of technical research into what is known as "prior art," or inventions that had already been patented that were similar. It was her job to then show the Patent Office how her company's new invention was different from the prior one.

"My research skills from chemistry have been invaluable," says Tammy. "A paralegal needs good organizational skills. You have to be *very* organized in chemistry, or you'd blow yourself up!" she laughs. "One also needs patience and persistence in dealing with the Patent Office. I also learned those skills in the laboratory."

Tammy eventually tired of her long commute to DuPont and took a position in the intellectual property division of a large law firm, where she currently specializes in patent litigation.

Teaching

Darlene Johnson

State Farm Mutual Automobile Insurance Company

Waiting for the telephone to ring was the spark that ignited Darlene Johnson's paralegal career. Darlene had a degree in English and a teaching credential that allowed her to teach any grade from kindergarten all the way through high school. With two small children to raise, she decided to become a substitute teacher, so that she could work when she pleased. The arrangement was working well until one year when six weeks went by without a single call to teach. Darlene had enough of the waiting game and took a part-time job. While there, she learned through a coworker of a position that had opened at a legal publishing company in town. This company published the official Illinois appellate reports, and Darlene saw there the opportunity to use her English major. She was hired and began working in the editorial department, reading, editing, and correcting the legal opinions before they were published. Toward the end of her tenure, she was even writing some of the headnotes.

After five years, Darlene was beginning to get bored. One of her coworkers at the publishing company was a paralegal, and Darlene became intrigued with the idea of becoming a paralegal herself. She went back to school and took some paralegal courses. She was hired by an attorney for whom she was interning and worked for him for the next six years doing family law and criminal work. Darlene enjoyed writing appellate briefs and credits her English background, which gave her confidence in her ability to research, write and edit. "My teaching background was also of great help," says Darlene. "I was used to speaking in front of groups, so I was not intimidated during my interview. Plus, teaching children gives you a great deal of empathy about what other people are going through, and you learn to understand things from other peoples' points of view." Darlene believes this empathy helped her in dealing with clients in such sensitive areas as family law.

Desiring more job security, Darlene left the small law office and took a position with State Farm. She worked for several years for the corporate secretary, researching licensing and corporate issues and preparing databases. She now does research and prepares memos on insurance and coverage issues. Darlene recently completed her master's degree in legal studies at the University of Illinois. She keeps her teaching skills sharp by team teaching "Introduction to Paralegal and Law Office Management" classes with an attorney at Illinois State University.

Banking

Deborah L. Fechik
Ruden, McClosky, Smith, Schuster & Russell

Deborah turned her construction and savings and loan background into a high-level paralegal position without even earning a certificate. After working for a time for the vice president of construction of a development company, Deborah took a position in the construction lending department of a savings and loan company. Following the closing of a loan, Deborah would set up the files for and monitor the construction draws against the loan. Contractors and borrowers would come in with draw requests, and it was her job to make sure they met the S&L's requirements. She also monitored the interest on the outstanding loan and was responsible for analyzing whether the loan was on schedule or whether the funds were being depleted too quickly.

When the savings and loan industry began to get shaky 10 years ago, Deborah decided it was time to move on. A friend in a large law firm told her about a temporary job that was available, and Deborah decided to take it while searching for another position in the banking industry. Once the firm learned of her background and discovered she had a degree in finance, they offered her a position as a real estate paralegal. Although she had no formal paralegal schooling, Deborah was given plenty of on-the-job training.

"My business and finance background really helped me," says Deborah. "I had working experience from both a developer's point of view and a lender's point of view. I was able to compensate for my lack of legal knowledge by putting all that information together and knowing what the steps and mechanics were of that particular area of the law. All I needed to learn was how to actually draft the documents."

Deborah works in the commercial real estate department of her firm. She does title review, research and analysis, survey review and analysis, and document preparation. She is heavily involved in real estate closings.

Medical

Diana Thompson
Dowling, Aaron & Keeler

As a board-certified respiratory therapist, Diana worked in hospital intensive care units, treating people with lung disease, monitoring patients post-surgery, and caring for people on ventilators. She also worked with premature infants, monitoring their blood gases and treating them.

After 12 years of working nights, weekends, holidays, and 12 hour shifts, Diana had enough. Casting around for a new career, Diana considered law school but didn't want to make the necessary time commitment because she had two young children at home. Realizing she always had an interest in the law, Diana decided that a paralegal career would be a good alternative, so she enrolled in a correspondence course.

The course took her a little more than a year to complete. She felt isolated without having any other students with whom she could study, but she stuck with it. After receiving her certificate, Diana took an internship with the local public defender's office. She was interested in criminal law and thought that she would pursue that specialty, but a position opened up with a senior partner in a mid-sized firm doing medical malpractice insurance defense and plaintiff's personal injury work. Diana seized the opportunity.

"It was an easy transition for me," says Diana about her first paralegal job. "A large portion of my work involved obtaining and reviewing medical records and helping the attorney understand what sort of care had been given to the patients." Diana also helped prepare the cases for trial, including working with the firm's consultant and expert witnesses. "They liked working with me," said Diana, "because I could speak their language."

After working several years in a medical/legal setting, Diana decided it was time to broaden her horizons. Now an experienced paralegal, she easily landed a position in her current firm, where she works in business litigation.

9

The Secrets to Creating a Great Resume

"Knowledge doesn't pay—it is what you do with it."

—Arnold Glasow

When a potential employer first meets you, chances are he or she is not looking you in the eye. Ninety-seven times out of a hundred, he or she is looking at a piece of paper known as the resume. Initially, more opportunities are lost because of a poor resume than any other factor known to job seekers.

With so much riding on the appearance and content of the resume, it's amazing half the workforce doesn't just give up in the job search process! More resumes than ever before are rejected—and after someone peruses it for less than five seconds.

Your resume should be a well-constructed, easy-to-read presentation of your capabilities, accomplishments, and skills. It should be reader-friendly and short. Its purpose is clear cut: to entice a prospective employer to the point where she has no other choice except to invite you for an interview. That's all! Interesting then that so many future careers have been aborted all because people don't know how to put together such a simple but crucial document.

Paralegals must remember that people in law firms are all too critical. Because so much is riding on a law firm's product—its people and presentation of legal documents—most potential law firm employers are unforgiving when it comes to a poorly written resume. That resume, they are certain, is indicative of the kind of work product you will produce. And if you can't produce a great looking resume, you surely cannot produce great work product.

Everything counts when writing the resume: from format to paper, from key words to brevity. The result should be one tightly written, perfect portrait of you and your related work accomplishments, education, and skills. This is the first impression you'll usually make on a law firm. And if you want the job, it had better be good.

Every resume received by a potential employer has only three buckets into which it can be placed: "call for interview," "possible," or "reject immediately." While there are no real statistics as to how many resumes get rejected, chances are that it is an overwhelming 90 percent—another argument for why your resume has to be absolutely perfect.

63

Few people actually read a resume thoroughly the first time they pick it up. There are simply too many resumes that hit the interviewer's desk at any given time. Rather, a practiced eye will scan it to see if there are key components that leap out. An employer will check to see if the individual has the qualifications, education, and background that meshes with current job openings. Reviewing resumes from a pile that can number anywhere from 2 to 200 causes the potential employer to call upon his physical being: a jaundiced eye immediately catches a poorly prepared resume. The eye may not have even completed the scanning process when other body parts begin to react. The hand takes over quickly and reaches for the paper. The arm then tosses the rejected resume directly into the round file. And finally, the brain blocks out any memory of ever having seen that particular piece of paper.

Your resume is a reflection of yourself. It can be compared to how you've put yourself together. When you wake in the morning, get dressed and ready for work, chances are you hardly just throw anything on in any which way. Generally, you've given some thought to what you want to wear and for what purpose. Not only is your clothing indicative of where you are going and what you are doing, it is a statement to others about you. The same thinking should be applied to preparing your resume. You don't want to just throw anything into it. Preparation time and thought behind what you are going to say are important. What you don't say is just as powerful as what you do say.

Reality Check

The Golden Rule for preparing any resume: Do not lie—ever.

Your resume is more than just a recitation of where you've worked and what you've done. It is a reflection of your writing skills, thinking pattern, sense of organization, and pride in work product. When you are creating a resume, hoping to attract potential "buyers" of your skills, you are also laying the groundwork for the kinds of positions you are willing to accept. You may want to have two or three different resumes targeted to different industries or jobs. There's nothing wrong with having various formats. Just remember, the resume is a marketing tool that is designed to get you in the door. It cannot get you the job!

PREPARATION FOR WRITING YOUR RESUME

The biggest mistake most candidates make when attempting to construct a resume is to believe they will simply start writing and within an hour or so, a finished, beautiful, flowing product will be ready to go. Please don't shoot the messengers when we tell you that the less thought that goes into your resume, the less effective it is likely to be!

Before you begin to redraft your resume or create one for the first time, consider what your previous job hire experiences have been:

Resume gets few or no responses: While the resume may look right to you, it may be quite wrong for the legal community. You may not see obvious errors, typos, or quality of composition. Your skills may not be in harmony with the positions for which you are applying. On the other hand, you may have a great resume but be using the wrong version of it to fit into positions you are seeking.

Resume gets interviews but no job offers: You may be overselling or underselling your skills on paper. Nothing comes through more loud and clear than a candidate whose skills do not match what was presented in the resume. Review it for false advertising. And while you're at it, check out your interviewing skills, mode of dress, and your perfume.

IF YOUR RESUME ISN'T WORKING, WHY NOT?

Listing resume sins could take up another book. However, the following are the most common mistakes candidates make:

1. *Too long:* ONE page is what employers want. So often, candidates complain that they simply cannot contain themselves. As a result, lengthy, boring, and useless resumes emerge. In today's 15-second sound-byte mentality, less is best. And if you are applying to a firm or organization that scans resumes, most likely anything beyond one or two pages will be rejected.

2. *Too barebones:* Candidates who list "name, rank, and serial numbers" in an attempt to capture brevity are making a mistake. Not enough information does not capture a potential employer's interest.

3. *Too wordy or wrong tense:* Resumes that ramble on and on get chucked. Are your sentences too long? Have you put in too much information? Do your sentences make sense? Keep the resume in the present tense, avoiding the use of the third-person tense "Prepare, monitor" instead of "Prepares, monitors." Always, always avoid the use of the word "I."

4. *Unattractive appearance:* Resumes that are not on quality paper are too hard to read. Ones that use unacceptable fonts, are disorganized with no consistent format, and have an unprofessional appearance give the impression you are sloppy. Sloppy is not listed as one of the ten most desirable skills you'll need to get hired.

Reality Check

One of the most common assignments paralegals are asked to do is to condense material into an easy-to-read, summarized format. If you can't do it with your own resume, employers will assume you can't do it on the job.

5. *Irrelevant information:* Including personal information such as marital status, height, sex, date of birth, race, weight, health status, number of children, political affiliation, hobbies, religion, or your picture indicates you are not up-to-date on current changes in employment law. Employers do not have a right to this information—and as a paralegal you should know this!

6. *Laundry list:* Simply listing every assignment or responsibility you have ever had does not impress employers. You must give some thought to what you will include and in what order. PUT YOUR MOST SUBSTANTIVE DUTIES FIRST. For example, if you draft pleadings and attend depositions, those duties should surely be mentioned before your responsibility to index documents. If one of your duties was to wash the coffee cups each morning upon arrival, by all means leave it out! No one really will consider that a job accomplishment.

7. *Typos:* Without a doubt, besides a resume that is too long, this is the number one reason a resume will make it into the reject pile. There simply is no excuse for not checking your work product.

8. *Lack of integral accomplishments or achievements:* Without quantifiable achievements, you're underselling yourself. So be sure to include them. "Lead paralegal on highly visible tobacco litigation matter," "Dean's List for three semesters," and "created filing system that saved colleagues substantial time," are just a few stellar accomplishments.

9. *Overpackaging:* Resumes that are in presentation folders, have cover pages, are in unusual colors, are velobound, or are three-hole-punched are out of place in the legal community. Stick with a conservative look and proven formats as discussed in this book.

10. *Doesn't fax well:* Because so many employers ask that you fax your resume, it is important that you create a resume that faxes well. Dark paper, black blotches, paper with spots on it all come out the other end looking as though your resume went through a grinder. It does not make a good first impression.

11. *No dates:* The absence of dates of employment on a resume will lead potential employers to believe that the candidate has something to hide. Resumes without dates are among the first resumes to get chucked.

There are two types of resumes: chronological and functional. There is also a hybrid of chronological/functional. Employers today seem to prefer the chronological resume that lists your work history in reverse chronological order. Most employers feel that the chronological resume gives them a better handle on your experience. The functional resume is used for people who have been at one job for a very long time, those who have job-hopped a lot, and those with something to hide.

FORMATS

1. You can choose a paragraph format or use bullet points. Bullets help the reader understand individual subunits of an overall paragraph. If you use a paragraph format, do not create a paragraph longer than eight to ten sentences. If you do use bullet points, make sure that there is enough information to adequately describe what it is that you do. Make sure the key word of each statement is at or near the beginning of the line. Use the strongest one to begin each statement:

• Successfully led a team of litigation paralegals in large-scale insurance defense matter.

2. Make sure all your headlines are consistent. Whether you choose to underline them, use italics, and/or capitalize, they must be positioned the same and use the same method of emphasis.
3. Use proper spacing throughout the entire resume. Make certain dates line up, particularly if you are using a paragraph format.
4. You may want to use a combination of paragraphs and bullets when you have complex phrases. Use action statements, and break them up with subheads:

   Assisted attorneys at trial of $200 million dollar multidistrict environmental case. During eight-month trial, responsibilities included:

   • Preparation of witness files   • Coordination of war room
   • Expert witness coordination   • Set-up of computers in courtroom

5. Use 1 to 1½-inch margins of white space at the top, bottom, and left- and right-hand sides of the page, which creates a balanced look.
6. Use caps sparingly. Do not write your entire resume in caps—it's too hard to read. Don't underline too much either. That's also hard to read.

HEADING
At the very top of the resume goes your name, preferably in all capitals and bolded. You can either place the heading in the right-hand corner or

Reality Check

Don't underestimate the number of copies of the resume you might need to get a job! You may need anywhere from 100–500 copies!

better, center it for fast identification. Never write "resume" on top. It's obvious what this is. Do not use a curriculum vitae in the legal field. It's out of place.

Next, put your street address or P.O. box, followed by city, state, and zip code. After that comes your home telephone number and, if appropriate, your work phone but only if you can receive private calls on a direct line where no one can tap into your voice mail. Otherwise, you may just as well send a memo around to the entire office that you are planning to jump ship.

You might also wish to add your E-mail address if it is a private address and not the one assigned to you at your present place of employment. No sense letting the entire office know your private business.

Make absolutely certain you have voice mail. It sounds much more professional than having your roommate, significant other, spouse, or kids try to take a message. Make certain the voice mail has a businesslike message on it. Leave off cute sayings, music, "God bless you and keep you," the dog singing, and the kids barking. This is the second impression a potential employer will have of you. Let's not lose them now.

Sample Headings

Judi Smith
2040 Elm Place
Los Angeles, CA 90067
(310) 555-1330 (e) Smith@eol.com

Robert Brown
4245 Highland Avenue
Woodbridge, NY 10024
Home: (212) 555-3001
Office: (212) 555-2330

EDUCATION

If you are an entry-level paralegal with no experience in this field, education is the next heading. If you are an experienced paralegal, education is placed *after* work experience. Generally, the more experience in the legal field you have, the less important your degree becomes. But no matter how much experience you have in other fields, you are still considered entry-level if you have held no jobs as a paralegal. If this is your first paralegal position, education is the first thing an employer will look at. If, however, your academic credentials are much more impressive than your work history, it's perfectly OK to list them prior to employment history.

If you have received a paralegal certificate, degree, or education, this designation is placed *before* your undergraduate degrees. It is even placed *before* postgraduate degrees. Indicate coursework only if you are an entry-level paralegal with no prior legal experience.

The most commonly awarded degrees may be abbreviated: B.S., B.A., Ph.D., J.D., M.A., M.B.A., M.F.A. However, if you have a degree in a lesser-known area such as Master of Human Relations, spell it out. NEVER list your high school—ever—even if you have no college or paralegal schooling.

Indicate your grade point average only if you achieved a 3.4 (B+) average or higher (on a 4.0 scale). Be prepared to furnish your transcripts. List any significant academic achievements such as scholarships, Dean's List, Honors, Magna or Summa Cum Laude, Valedictorian, Editor of Newspaper, or more.

Sample Education

B.A., UCLA, Los Angeles, California, 1997
Major: English   Minor: Business

Paralegal Certificate: Litigation/Corporate Specialty
University of Paralegal Studies, Legal Assistant Training Program 1998
Graduated with Honors

M.F.A., University of Michigan, Ann Arbor, Michigan 1996
Dean's List; *Graduated Summa Cum Laude*

B.A., UCLA, Los Angeles, California 1994
Awarded Thespian scholarship

You do not need to put the year that you graduated college. If you leave it off, it is generally an indication that you are over the age of 40. Be aware, however, that you are not hiding your age. You will tip recruiters off that you are over 40. Just how far over 40 is anyone's guess. You should, however, put the year that you received your paralegal certificate. Employers want to get a handle on how recent that education is.

If you have been awarded a Certified Legal Assistant or PACE Registered Paralegal designation, you can either put this after you list the paralegal certificate, above the paralegal certificate, or under a section entitled "Awards, Achievements, Professional Accomplishments."

SKILLS AND ABILITIES

You get your choice. If you are an entry-level paralegal with no work experience, you should put your skills and abilities section right after education. If you are experienced, place it after work history. It's best to bullet-point these areas.

Sample Skills and Abilities
  • Solid interpersonal skills
  • Excellent analytical background, with attention to detail
  • Strong financial and research skills

Generally, information relating to your computer skills, languages, or public speaking follows the employment section.

WORK HISTORY

You can call this section several things: Work (or Employment) History, Work (or Employment) Experience, or even Professional Experience. If you are an experienced paralegal and have related work history in another field, you might divide the work history section into two categories: Legal Experience and Related Experience. Legal experience should always be listed first.

Work history should always be listed in *reverse* chronological order. In other words, start with your present position and work *backward*. It's not enough to simply list every assignment or job duty you have performed. Rather, go back through your experience and determine which assignments and skills sell you the best. Match up your achievements to reflect value-perceived factors such as *ability to work independently, flexible, excellent crisis-manager, team-oriented.* Tie these elements in with your specific duties.

Avoid the use of "I," "me," and "my." Use brief phrases that begin with action-oriented verbs. However, if you are preparing a resume for the Internet, this type of resume requires fewer action-oriented verbs and more emphasis on skills. More on this later.

If you are an experienced paralegal, do not mention the names of cases, clients, or matters in the body of the resume. You may be violating attorney-client confidentiality. If you are working for a law firm that is in-house counsel for a corporation, of course mention that. Stating that you were a paralegal on the *White v. Green* case is not a good idea. Or that you worked on probate matters for clients such as Rock Hudson or Cary Grant. You can, however, state that you were a litigation paralegal on a large-scale insurance defense matter involving more than 300,000 documents or that you handled the estates of very high-profile movie stars.

Sample Work History
Entry-level

American Eagle Land and Development Company
Minneapolis, MN   Nov. 1995–Jan. 2000
Responsible for financial accounting for land and tax credit subsidiaries. Reviewed monthly financial statements; maintained land ledgers, recorded property taxes and assessment district amortization schedules.

Experienced Paralegal

Helland, Marks and Osborn
Lexington, KY   Aug. 1995–Present
Responsibilities include: organize and maintain documents; analyze factual information; construct exhibit list for trial; review, index, and summarize pleadings and correspondence produced by opposing parties; draft legal memorandum to clients regarding case status and preparation; research legal issues and rules; assist in trial preparation; summarize discovery responses.

COMPUTER SKILLS

Because few paralegals without computer skills get jobs anymore, we highly recommend that you entertain another section in order to sell your computer skills. List software, hardware, and unique abilities here. If you are an expert in any one program, say so. If you are "really good," state that you are proficient. If you are somewhat skilled, you may say you are "knowledgeable." If you have little knowledge but have used the programs, state "familiar with."

Sample Computer Skills

    Proficient in Word, WordPerfect 9.0, Access, Excel, Lotus 1-2-3
    Excellent PC and MAC background
    Familiar with LAN/WAN
    Extensive experience with PageMaker, Adobe Illustrator

SPECIAL SKILLS AND ABILITIES

Here is where you'll list special skills and abilities. If you used a skills and abilities section above, you may want to call this section "Additional Skills." This section is for language skills, technical skills, public speaking skills, writing skills, and the like.

Sample Special Skills and Abilities
- Fluent in Mandarin Chinese
- Notary Public
- Excellent Public Speaker

ORGANIZATIONS AND AFFILIATIONS

If you are a member of a paralegal association or other business-related organization, this is the section to list it. It is not a wise idea to list political or religious affiliations. Keep it to business.

SAMPLE ORGANIZATIONS AND AFFILIATIONS

- Member, Los Angeles Paralegal Association
- Member, Toastmasters International

REFERENCES

Do *not* include the names of references on your resume. It is not professional. You may add a line at the bottom of the page that states, "Professional references furnished upon request." However, even that line is not used too often. Most employers understand that you will provide a list of references. Have a separate sheet of references handy to take with you on the interview. The paper should match your stationery and resume. List three professional references, preferably those with whom you have worked.

If you are relying upon a colleague or past or present employer to vouch for you, be sure they know about it ahead of time. Employers will check references, and we cannot emphasize how important it is that you list people who know your work, skills, and abilities. Send your references a copy of your resume. Make sure you provide current phone numbers. Giving a prospective employer a former work number indicates you are not too detail oriented—a faux pas for paralegals.

THE "OLDER" WORKFORCE

It seems absurd to address the "older" workforce as those over 40 when the average age of paralegals is 38. Still, there's no denying that age discrimination does exist. Fortunately, for paralegals, it appears to exist less in this field than perhaps in others.

Anyone with highly specialized technical skills is highly in demand. Registered nurses, real estate specialists, and those with a securities background are also in demand in the legal field as of this writing. Hardly anyone cares about age when specialty professionals are so hot. But even if no one in the entire world ever expressed a single discriminatory thought, you might be sensitive about your age and not want to broadcast it to the world.

As an older candidate, there are some guidelines you might want to follow if you are sensitive about the issue. If you're not, by all means go for it! It's really your choice. Experience is wonderful, and every kind of background is useful in the paralegal field.

If you are sensitive about age, leave off the year you graduated college. You do not have to list every job you've ever held. And you do not have to account for gaps in the resume, particularly if you were a homemaker. Typically, you don't have to go back any farther than 10 or 15 years at the most. You can leave off the date you received your paralegal certificate if it was more than 15 years ago. However, many employers will want to know.

The reverse chronological resume is still a good resume for the "older" candidate. You can use the functional resume to focus on specific expertise. By focusing on achievements and skills related to the paralegal field, you may make the resume stronger.

JOB-HOPPERS

The functional resume is frequently used for those who have jumped around in their careers or for longtime contract employees. During the recession of the early and mid-'90s, so many people were merged, purged, or otherwise scourged that job-hopping became routine. Now that the economy has straightened out somewhat, it may not be as readily accepted. High turnover is a negative in the minds of many employers, who tend to shy away from job-hoppers who may contribute to the trend.

THE FUNCTIONAL RESUME

A functional resume has been the subject of a lot of controversy for quite some time. Some employers believe that the functional resume is used to hide information, while others believe that it is a good way to demonstrate long-term achievements. Although most employers prefer to see a chronological development, there are a few instances when a functional resume is useful:

- When you have a long work history that doesn't always relate to the position you are seeking
- When you are reentering the job market after a long absence
- When you've job-hopped for quite some time
- When you are a long-term or contract employee

It's not advisable to use the functional resume when:

- You are an experienced paralegal with a number of prestigious firms behind you.
- You want to show a progression in your career.
- You really have very little experience.

Sometimes it is advisable to use a functional resume if you have a variety of practice specialties that you want to highlight. You can structure the resume to use a variety of paragraph categories. For example, you might include headings such as:

LITIGATION	MANAGEMENT
CORPORATE	ADMINISTRATIVE
REAL ESTATE	TRAINING

THE TARGETED RESUME

For those of you, such as experienced paralegals, who are seeking to move up the career ladder, now anxious to get into management, you may want to use a targeted resume. It focuses your search, and because of its specificity, it is often called the "Achievement Resume." It reflects the language of a single job range—even when you have a multitude of experiences.

You can have several targeted resumes. In fact, you should. If you were an experienced litigation paralegal with supervisory experience, seeking to become a paralegal manager, you might want to highlight all of your administrative, human resources, staffing, training, and supervisory experience.

Sample Targeted Paragraph for Move to Paralegal Administrator
Supervised team of twenty paralegals. Coordinated work assignments. Staffed litigation teams with temporary personnel. Evaluated work product. Recommended salary increases. Trained coders in Concordance, and designed accompanying training manual.

TEN COMMANDMENTS OF RESUME WRITING

1. Never handwrite anything on the resume, including strikeovers or cross-outs. For example, if your phone number has changed, change the resume.
2. Don't state current salary. If you are asked to provide salary history upon submitting the resume, follow directions but do so in your cover letter.

3. Don't list references. Provide a separate sheet of paper.
4. Don't include the names of supervisors and phone numbers under work history or anywhere else on the resume.
5. Don't enclose a photo or attach a copy of the ad.
6. Don't try humor or sarcasm. You have no idea what the reader's sense of humor is like. Don't do anything cute such as write the resume in the form of a brief, send a shoe with the note saying, "I'm trying to get my foot in the door," or send a nut that opens up with a note saying, "I'm nuts about this firm." *Don't even think about it.*
7. Don't mention on the resume that you were fired or laid-off.
8. Don't exaggerate or mislead. For example, don't foster the belief that you have a degree when you don't.
9. Don't send a writing sample with the resume unless requested.
10. Stick to one page—two at the most.

TEN GREAT RESUME WRITING TIPS

Your resume is an introduction to a potential employer. Although it does not get you the job, it does serve as the tool that can open the door for you. The resume is an indicator of your key skills and characteristics of your qualifications. It can also give an indication of your personality, writing skills, ability to pay attention to detail, organizational skills, goals, stability, and level of training. Here are just a few tips that can help you get past the gatekeeper and onto the next step, the interview:

1. *Resume appearance:* Never underestimate the importance of first impressions. Keep resumes aimed toward law firms and in-house legal departments in a conservative format. Follow the following guidelines for a clean and organized resume:
   A. Use white or buff-color paper only. Bright colors (even a soft blue) are considered gauche in the legal field. (Keep those for advertising agency or entertainment-related jobs.) Darker colors such as gray or blue will not scan or fax well. Be sure you use a quality bond.
   B. Stay away from textured or parchment paper.
   C. Keep at least a one-inch margin all the way around the resume.
   D. Use only 8½ × 11″ paper. Do not use 8½ × 14″ in an effort to fit everything in. And don't fold over an 8½ × 17″ piece of paper.
   E. Use a conservative font such as Times New Roman, Century Schoolbook, Helvetica, Arial, Optima, or Palatino. Stay away from Courier. It's out of date. Don't use script fonts at all. They

are either too avant-garde or too hard to read. Stay away from Comic Sans—it's not serious enough. Use 12 or 10 point only.

 F. Use only black ink. The legal field is not quite ready for the beautiful colors of ink available today.

 G. Use a laser printer. It's really the only way to go. Many jet printers just don't have laser quality. By all means, do NOT use an old dot matrix printer.

 H. Do not use computer paper.

 I. If you are using two pages, do not print on the front and back of the paper. Use two sheets of paper.

 J. Use at least 24-pound quality bond paper, preferably with a cotton rag content. Do not use a cardboard or cover stock. It's too heavy. Get matching blank stock to use for the cover letter and references along with matching envelopes. You may need to make as many as 500 copies of your resume. Be prepared!

2. *Keep the resume to one page:* This rule *does* apply to you. Employers no longer have the time to wade through pages and pages. On the average, employers will spend 10 to 20 seconds eyeballing the resume first to see if you are the ideal candidate. Many corporations today will scan the resume into a software package that is designed to accept only one page of your resume. Don't get ruled out.

3. *Put dates of employment on the resume:* Resumes without dates of employment look as though you have something to hide.

4. *Education:* If you are an entry-level paralegal, put your education first. If you are an experienced paralegal, your work history is first and education is last.

5. *No personal information:* Do not put personal information on the resume such as marital status, age, number of children, or health. Do not attach a picture or put salary history on the resume. Address salary history, if asked, in the cover letter.

6. *References:* Take a list of professional references with you to the interview. Make sure it is on paper that matches your resume and that your name is on the reference list. Bring at least three references and be sure you have called them to let them know someone may be calling.

7. *Job descriptions:* Describe your job with the most substantive duties first. Don't just prepare a laundry list of duties. Prepare each job description so that it substantiates why you can move up the ladder.

8. *Skills and abilities:* List computer skills under a separate category titled "Computer Skills." Unless you want a secretarial job, do not

put how fast you type or include office machine skills, such as adding machine, photocopier, or fax. It is assumed you know how to use these.

9. *Cover letters:* Here is the first test of whether you can write. Use your imagination. Tailor each letter so that the employers know you are interested in their firm. Be sure the letters are personally signed and addressed to a specific individual. Nothing is less impressive than to receive a photocopied bulk-mailed cover letter.

10. *Never lie:* Although you do not have to list every job you have ever had, do not fudge on dates, work history, skills and abilities, job descriptions, education, or anything else on your resume. Remember: your work history, education, and salary can all be verified. If you exaggerate your skills and get hired, most likely your skill gap will be discovered once you start. Keep the process honest.

THE EVERY RESUME WRITING BOOK ACTION WORD LIST

A	appropriated	budgeted	compiled
abbreviated	approved	built	computerized
abstracted	approximated		conceived
accessed	arbitrated	C	conceptualized
accommodated	arranged	calendared	condensed
accounted	aspired	carried out	conducted
achieved	assessed	cataloged	confirmed
acquired	assigned	centralized	consolidated
acquisitioned	assisted	certified	constructed
acted	attached	changed	consulted
administered	attained	checked	contacted
adapted	attended	cite-checked	contained
adopted	attracted	claimed	contracted
advised	audited	cleared	contributed
advanced	augmented	clerked	controlled
affected	authorized	closed	coordinated
aided		coded	copyrighted
allocated	B	collaborated	correlated
analyze	Bates stamped	collected	counseled
answered	benefited	communicated	created
applied	briefed	commuted	crisis-managed

D

decentralized

decreased

dedicated

defined

delayed

delegated

demonstrated

deposed

designated

designed

detailed

determined

developed

diminished

directed

disclosed

discovered

dispensed

displayed

disseminated

distinguished

distributed

docketed

documented

downsized

drafted

drove

E

earned

economized

edited

educated

elevated

employed

empowered

enforced

enhanced

ensured

entered

established

estimated

evaluated

examined

exceeded

excelled

executed

expected

explored

expressed

extended

F

facilitated

familiarized

filed

filled

finalized

fixed

focused

followed up

forecasted

formalized

formatted

formulated

founded

functioned

funded

furnished

G

gathered

generated

grew

guided

H

handled

headed

highlighted

hired

I

identified

illustrated

imaged

implemented

imposed

improved

increased

indexed

informed

initiated

input

inquired

instigated

instituted

instructed

integrated

interfaced

interned

interviewed

invented

investigated

involved

issued

J

judged

L

led

legitimized

liaised

linked

listened

located

logged

M

maintained

managed

marketed

marshaled

mediated

memorialized

merged

monitored

motivated

N

negotiated

noted

notified

O

operated

ordered

organized

oversaw

P

performed

persuaded

phased

photocopied

placed

planned

positioned

practiced

prepared

presented

prevented
prioritized
problem solved
proceeded
processed
produced
profiled
profited
programmed
projected
promoted
protected
provided
publicized
published
purchased
purged

Q
qualified
quantified

R
rated
readied
received
recognized
recommended
reconciled
recorded
recruited

redacted
reduced
referred
registered
regulated
related
relayed
relied
relieved
relocated
rendered
reorganized
reported
represented
requested
required
researched
responded
restricted
retrieved
reviewed
revised
right-sized

S
saved
scanned
scheduled
screened
searched
selected

served
serviced
set up
Shepardized
showed
signed
simplified
solicited
solved
specialized
specified
spotted
spun off
staffed
steered
stored
streamlined
strengthened
structured
studied
submitted
substantiated
summarized
supervised
supplied
supported
systematized

T
tabbed
tallied

targeted
taught
telecommunicated
televised
terminated
tracked
trained
transacted
transferred
translated
transmitted
traveled
treated
triggered
turned around

U
updated
utilized

V
validated
verified
videoconferenced
videotaped
volunteered

W
wrote

PRETTY DARN GOOD PHRASES TO USE . . .

Accurately and clearly
   communicate . . .
Action oriented . . .
Addressed the strengths . . .

Adept at . . .
Appraise and recommend . . .
Assisted in reducing legal costs to
   clients . . .

Assisted winning trial team . . .

Assisted with ongoing
    projects . . .

Attracting media attention . . .

Bottom-line oriented . . .

Closely monitored . . .

Collaborated with . . .

Complete fluency in . . .

Computer information systems
    knowledge includes . . .

Created profitable programs . . .

Demonstrated strengths in . . .

Directed team/staff . . .

Disseminated mountains of
    paperwork quickly . . .

Enthusiastically contributed . . .

Enthusiastically maintained . . .

Established new measures of
    accountability . . .

Excellent knowledge of . . .

Excellent multitasking
    capabilities . . .

Exercised multitalents . . .

Extremely strong . . .

Fast-growth . . .

Fast learner . . .

Fast-tracking . . .

Four completed semesters of . . .

Functional responsibilities
    include . . .

Handled sophisticated
    assignments . . .

Heightened public awareness . . .

High energy . . .

Highly specialized . . .

Initiated projects . . .

Initiated the use of . . .

Introduced employee
    participation program . . .

Knowledge based . . .

Labor intensive . . .

Led project in . . .

Led trial team . . .

Major accomplishments . . .

Met continuous deadlines . . .

Met enormous challenges . . .

Met the current needs . . .

Multifaceted, detail-oriented . . .

Oversaw hiring
and terminations . . .

Personally changed . . .

Plan and direct . . .

Provided detailed
    information . . .

Provided specialized
    assistance . . .

Ready to move up to
    management . . .

Results oriented . . .

Self-motivated and
    well-organized . . .

Skillful problem solver . . .

Strong foundation in . . .

Strongly supported the firm's
    mission . . .

Tackled challenging projects . . .

Tenacious dedication to . . .

Traveled extensively . . .

Well-versed in . . .

Worked in a team effort . . .

SAMPLE RESUMES

ANNIE OAKLEY

1898 Wild West Avenue   Tucson, AR 97654   602.555.1212

OBJECTIVE

To find a challenging and high-powered paralegal position

EDUCATION

THE WILD WEST INSTITUTE FOR PARALEGAL TRAINING AT TUCSON   2000
An ABA approved paralegal program
Certificate in Litigation
Honors Graduate; Dean's List

UNIVERSITY OF ARIZONA   1998
B.A. Degree in Political Science
President of Student Lawyers Association

EXPERIENCE

WILLIAM HITCHCOCK & ASSOCIATES   1998–Present
Marketing Assistant
Responsibilities include promotion of Wild West Show; coordination of experts and talent; scheduling of show dates; preparation of correspondence; training of temporary employees.

CAFE BUFFALO BILL   1995–1998
Waitress while attending college
Responsibilities included the provision of service with a smile. Caught, hog-tied, and prepared meals on wood-burning stove; interfaced with Endangered Species Society.

SKILLS AND ABILITIES

- Excellent creative and graphics abilities
- Ability to prepare presentations for trial and depositions
- Attention to detail
- Excellent writing and drafting skills
- Proficient in legal and factual research
- Ability to learn new software packages quickly

COMPUTER SKILLS

- Proficient in MS Word; WordPerfect 9.0 for Windows; Excel; Lotus 1-2-3; FoxPro; Harvard Graphics; Microsoft Works; PowerPoint; SharpShooter

JACK BENNY
2020 Vaudeville Road East #200
New York, New York 10002
(212) 555-1212

Education
INSTITUTE FOR PARALEGAL STUDIES
New York, New York
ABA approved program
Corporate Paralegal Certificate awarded 2000
Received "Outstanding Paralegal Student" Designation

Livingstone College
Waukegon, Illinois
B.S. Degree in Financial Management

Employment
ORPHEUM CORPORATION, NEW YORK, NEW YORK
Financial Manager   *December 1995–Present*
Responsibilities include preparation of loan documents for stage,
television, and film industry; prepare information regarding demographics;
answer inquiries; research data and prepare reports for accountants;
monitor stock market trends; draft and prepare client newsletter.

NEDERLANDER ORGANIZATION, NEW YORK, NEW YORK
Sales Assistant   *March 1992–November 1995*
Assistant to Director of Sales. Coordinated schedules; set up meetings
and conventions; interfaced with clients; prepared correspondence;
maintained and purchased mailing lists; reviewed daily trades; assisted
accounting manager with accounts receivable; edited telemarketing
scripts; monitored reviews; tallied and distributed sales reports.

Computer Skills
- Extensive knowledge of MS Word; familiarity with Excel
- Experience with LAN/WAN and Windows NT

Community Achievements and Interests
- Past Vice President of The Historical Film Association
- Voted "Best Overachiever" of The Golden Days of Radio Society
- Concert violinist

Jane Smith

123 Main Street
Newport, Rhode Island 12001
(H) 217-555-1212
(e) smith@mol.com

Summary of Qualifications

- Professional, well-organized, detail oriented
- Outstanding communication, analytical and presentation skills
- Demonstrated ability to tackle difficult projects successfully

Paralegal Internship

Paralegal Intern   March–June 2000
LAW OFFICES OF WOODS & WOODS   Boston, Massachusetts

Summarized interrogatory responses; indexed documents; prepared witness binders. Received excellent evaluations.

Employment History

Case Clerk   January 1998–March 1999
ACME, ACME & ACME   Boston, Massachusetts

Organized legal files; handled general office duties; prepared closing binders; prepared exhibits for depositions and trial; filed UCCs; organized loan documents; prepared transmittal letters; Bates-stamped and input data.

Related Employment

Administrative Assistant   March 1997–December 1998
Barnum & Bailey   Concord, New Hampshire

Prepared contracts and lease agreements for real estate transactions; maintained daily reports; interfaced with insurance companies; handled correspondence; answered telephones; prepared faxes and transmittal letters.

Human Resources Assistant   December 1989–March 1993
IPG Corporation   Concord, New Hampshire

Recruited, screened, and interviewed candidates; administered insurance and benefit plans; scheduled training seminars; prepared reports and spreadsheets; monitored worker's compensation claims; placed recruiting ads.

Education

University of New Hampshire   1987
Bachelor of Arts Degree in Education
Volunteer for Special Education Summer School Program

Computer Skills

- Microsoft Word; Paradox; Q & A; Pro Forma; TimeSlips; Concordance
- Ability to use IBM PC and MAC

Sally Jones
1415 Elm Street, Edina, MN 85421
Home: (612) 555-1212 Office: (612) 555-1221
(e) sal@hotmail.net

Objective

To transition to the paralegal field from financial accounting, utilizing my abilities to investigate, analyze, and organize highly detailed information.

Summary of Accomplishments

- Researched and prepared thesis on Reporting Requirements for Oil Companies
- Prepared and analyzed budgets, forecasts, and profit reports prior to presentation to stockholders
- Prepared manuals and provided training for tax credit investments
- Proven team player with ability to interface with all levels of personnel

Education

UNIVERSITY OF MINNEAPOLIS
Legal Assistant Certificate to be awarded in 2002
Program approved by the American Bar Association

MIDWEST COLLEGE, MINNEAPOLIS, MINNESOTA
Master's of Business Administration Degree; Specialty in Accounting 1987
GPA 3.8

THE CITY COLLEGE OF NEW YORK
B.A. Degree; Political Science/American History

Employment

AMERICAN EAGLE LAND & DEVELOPMENT CO., MINNEAPOLIS, MN 1989–1997
Financial Accountant
Responsible for financial accounting for AEL's land and tax credit subsidiaries. Duties included reviewing monthly financial statements, maintaining land ledgers, recording property taxes and assessment district amortization schedules, preparing quarterly bank financials, monitoring international management reports, preparing manuals, and providing training to Accounting Assistant.

IMPORT AMERICA, Bloomington, MN   1985–1989
Import Manager
Responsible for all functions of commercial import operation, including assignment of dutiable values and U.S. Customs tariff classifications.

Computer Skills

- Microsoft Word; Excel; PowerPoint; MS Access; Lotus 1-2-3; Quicken Professional; Quick Books; Accountancy Pro; FoxPro; LEXIS/NEXIS; Westlaw

Louisa M. Alcott

123 West Main Street, Germantown, PA 12345

(215) 555-1212 (e) books@bol.com

SUMMARY OF QUALIFICATIONS

- Diversified experience in legal field
- Demonstrated expertise in civil litigation
- Extensive knowledge of Municipal Court system

EDUCATION

CAMBRIDGE COMMUNITY COLLEGE

Associate in Arts Degree in Paralegal Studies 2000
An ABA-approved program

Courses included legal theory and practice; property; torts; contracts; legal research and writing; remedies and judgments; computers and the law; wills, trusts, and estate planning; family law; bankruptcy law and procedure; criminal law; business litigation; accounting; U.S. government; English composition; and physical and life sciences.

BOSTON STATE UNIVERSITY 1996–1997
Coursework in Cultural Studies

EXPERIENCE

HARBOR CITY MUNICIPAL COURT   1996–PRESENT
Harbor City, Pennsylvania
Deputy Clerk II (Civil/Small Claims)

- Prepare and issue claims, writs, abstracts, motions, subpoenas, and civil bench warrants
- Verify and enter court-ordered judgments; maintain small claims trial calendar
- Assist in training of coworkers regarding policy, procedures, and preparation of documents
- Prepare notices to parties regarding continuances, venue, and court orders

WEST APPLE COUNTY MUNICIPAL COURT   1990–1996
Harbor City, Pennsylvania
Deputy Clerk I (Public Offenses)

- Reviewed and entered proofs of service, satisfactions of judgment and dismissals
- Assisted public with forms and procedural information, e.g., court costs
- Referred matters to government agencies, social services, and higher courts
- Coordinated training of legal specialists
- Managed public information monthly seminars

Louisa M. Alcott
Page Two

THE PETITE WOMAN   1988–1989
Concord, Massachusetts
Manager
Responsibilities included managing a family-owned shop. Oversaw development of family business; created marketing and advertisements; prepared daily cash receipts.

SKILLS

- Excellent written and verbal communication skills
- Demonstrated strength in interpersonal skills handling a variety of public inquiries
- Highly competent analytical ability to assess problems and provide solutions
- Ability to coordinate and produce large volumes of data
- Strong administrative background with more than 10 years' experience

COMPUTER SKILLS

- WordPerfect for Windows; CAT-Links; Quattro Pro; ATMS (text management); STAIRS; On-line research; Pro Forma; Access; Word

LANGUAGE SKILLS

- Fluent in Spanish
- Knowledgeable of French

INTERESTS

- Gardening, theatre, traveling, genealogy, reading, writing fiction and poems

References available upon request.

John Adams
321 East Ocean Avenue # 14
Long Beach, CA 90270
(H) 310-555-1212 (O) 310-555-2112 (E) John@bel.rom

Employment

Jan. 1999– Present:	Litigation Legal Assistant Brown, Goldstein & Whitmann Los Angeles, California

Prepare discovery documents, motions, Points and Authorities, interrogatories, stipulations, orders, notices, applications, and subpoenas. Research factual information. Prepare for trial, set up war room, arrange depositions. Responsible for all phases of deposition preparation, including issuing subpoena and attending deposition. Experience in preparation of trial pleadings and notices to attend trial. Draft designation of expert witnesses, joint statement of the case, joint witness and exhibit lists. Prepare trial exhibits and notebooks. Organize and maintain more than 525 exhibits.

June, 1996– Dec. 1999	Litigation Legal Assistant Lewis & Clark Beverly Hills, California

Preparation of complex commercial litigation cases for trial. Duties included research of database of more than 250,000 documents. Assisted attorneys with drafting of motions for Summary Judgment. Reviewed and organized medical records. Summarized depositions. Corresponded with clients and courts.

Skills and Abilities

Computer Skills: Concordance, Summation, Litigator's Notebook, Pro Forma, ISYS, Word, WordPerfect for Windows, and LEXIS/NEXIS. Abilities: Work well independently and as a team member; excellent focus on detail; excel under pressure.

Education

1996	University of California, Irvine *Certificate in Legal Assistantship (ABA-approved program)* GPA: 3.68
1995	University of California, Los Angeles *Bachelor of Arts, Social Science*

Professional
Associations   Los Angeles Paralegal Association

FUNCTIONAL RESUME
Toni Polk
1275 West Maple Street
Cleveland, Ohio 65231
(Office) 333-555-7777 (Home) 333-555-6565 (E) polk@eed.com

Objective
To obtain an entry-level paralegal position in a law firm or in-house legal department where I can make a significant contribution to the legal team.

Highlights of Qualifications
- Extensive experience in research, contract drafting and negotiation of oil, gas, and other land-related contracts for Fortune 500 Company. Excellent analytical, problem-solving, and communication skills. Known for ability to conduct complex title searches. Technology skills include WordPerfect 9.0 for Windows and Word for Windows.

Research
- Researched internal company files and public records to determine property rights; advised exploration, production, pipeline, and Telecommunications companies regarding operating rights and obligations enabling management to determine land use options.
- Investigated and explained company rights to buyers, increasing buyer understanding and facilitating the sale of $95 million property.
- Researched records on contract rights and advised company regarding title clearances for drilling more than twenty-seven oil wells, enabling production engineers and geologists to determine oil wells to be drilled.

Contracts
- Drafted, prepared, and negotiated oil and gas lease provisions, right-of-way grants, pipeline relocation and joint use agreements, ground leases, and other land-related contracts under attorney supervision.
- Assisted in preparation and escrow for $95 million property.

Employment History

AMERICAN OIL USA INC., Cleveland, Ohio Land Use Consultant	1997–2001
SUPERIOR LAKES CORPORATION, Chicago, Illinois Land Use and Environmental Agent	1996–1997
CHICAGO MIDWEST TITLE AND TRUST COMPANY, Chicago, Illinois Title Officer and Researcher	1992–1996

Education
FARLEIGH DICKINSON UNIVERSITY
Madison, New Jersey
B.A., Education, June 1991

Sample Functional Resume:
Experienced Corporate Paralegal

Susan Miller
1000 Cherry Street
Dallas, Texas 75201
(214) 555.4546

PROFESSIONAL EXPERIENCE:

Corporate Securities Paralegal: Involved in all aspects of transactional corporate department, including preparation of public offerings; real estate syndications; mergers and acquisitions; preparation of S-8 registration statements; proxy statements and private placement memoranda for Regulation D and Regulation S offerings; handle Blue Sky matters; prepare securities purchase agreements, stock option agreements, and licensing agreements. Maintain corporate minute books for 75 clients; draft bylaws, corporate resolutions, and minutes.

EMPLOYMENT:

July 1999–Present	Trafford, Muller, Cofern and Weitz Dallas, Texas
October 1997–June 1999	Stevens, Jones & Silverstein Dallas, Texas

EDUCATION:

University of Michigan Law School
Ann Arbor, Michigan
J.D., 1997
University of California at Los Angeles
Los Angeles, California
B.A. *cum laude,* Political Science, 1994

SPECIAL SKILLS:

Proficient in LAN/WAN, Word, WordPerfect 9.0, Windows 2000, Excel, the Internet
Fluent in Italian

PROFESSIONAL ASSOCIATIONS:

Member, Dallas Association of Legal Assistants

PERSONAL INTERESTS:

Asian travel, poetry, skiing, foreign films

SAMPLE RESUME:
Experienced Entertainment Paralegal

MARCI RAYBUILT
3498 Rosebush Avenue
North Hollywood, California 91601
(t) 818-555-6767 (e) Marci@eol.com

EMPLOYMENT:

September 1999– Present	Boel & Boel Los Angeles, California *Entertainment Legal Assistant.* Prepare agreements and amendments to contracts. Research licensing and distribution deals. Prepare loan documents. Oversee distribution of music royalties. Prepare and negotiate location agreements. Work directly with producers, directors and actors.
July 1997– September 1999	Rosenfeld, Troop & Bloom Beverly Hills, California *Entertainment Legal Assistant.* Worked with Motion Picture Association regarding credits, copyright infringement and unfair competition matters. Prepared pleadings. Summarized depositions and contracts. Prepped witnesses.

RELATED EMPLOYMENT:

June 1995– July 1997	Fox Studios Los Angeles, California *Executive Assistant, Business Affairs Dept.* Worked with vice president. Prepared correspondence; weekly logs; gathered ratings information; scheduled appointments; handled finance data.

EDUCATION:

1993	Associate in Arts Degree Santa Monica City College, Santa Monica, California

SAMPLE RESUME:
Experienced Environmental Compliance Paralegal

EDDIE HARRIS
90566 East DuPont Circle
Washington, DC 20036
(202) 555-9887

EDUCATION:

Yale University
New Haven, Connecticut
B.A., *cum laude,* Economics, 1991
G.P.A.: 3.85/4.0

EMPLOYMENT:

Environmental Compliance Paralegal   March 1998 to Present
Monroe, Taft & Dewey
Washington, DC

Responsibilities include research of regulatory matters in connection
with CERCLA private-party litigation; work with government agencies
regarding Superfund, pollution, and oil spills; prepare and distribute
updates regarding Superfund sites; work with co-counsel researching
hazardous waste regulations and water quality issues.

Environmental Compliance Paralegal   January 1996 to March 1998
United States Environmental Protection Agency
Washington, DC

Responsibilities included filing Superfund liens on property subject to
action under CERCLA; assisting Department of Justice regarding
CERCLA cost recovery actions; preparing costs memorandum; working
with outside counsel regarding underground storage tanks; preparing
agreements for remediation of petroleum contamination.

COMPUTER SKILLS:

Quattro Pro, Word, Excel, Access, Concordance, Summation

LANGUAGES:

Fluent in Spanish, Portuguese, and Italian

SAMPLE RESUME:
Estate Planning and Probate Paralegal

WILLIE SUTTON
555 NORTH BEACH BLVD. APT. 302
PHOENIX, AZ 85005
(602) 555-3939
(e) willie@aob.com

WORK HISTORY:

Brown and Brown   June 1999–Present
Phoenix, Arizona

Estate Planning and Probate Paralegal:
Prepare tax returns; draft wills, revocable trusts, irrevocable trusts;
prepare estate and gift tax returns; prepare conservatorship actions;
prepare 706s; assist lawyers in negotiation of estate tax audits; prepare
charitable trusts; meet with clients.

Johnson and Johnson   June 1997–May 1999
Phoenix, Arizona

Legal Secretary
Prepared correspondence to IRS; assisted attorneys and paralegals in
preparation of tax returns; filed wills with State offices; scheduled
appointments and heavy travel agenda; assisted in preparation of wills
(written and videotaped); prepared correspondence.

EDUCATION:

University of Phoenix
Entered in B.A. program. Expected graduation date: June 2002.

COMPUTER SKILLS:

Proficient in Word, Excel, Lotus, and Quattro Pro, Powerpoint. Familiar
with WordPerfect.

AFFILIATIONS:

Notary Public

MARY KAYE

123 East Walnut Avenue, Houston, TX 85432 (713) 555-1212

OBJECTIVE

To prove my potential in my first professional position and utilize my education in a law firm or corporation where a hard-working, eager entry-level person can make a difference.

EDUCATION

UNIVERSITY OF WEST LOS ANGELES
Los Angeles, California 2001
An ABA-approved Paralegal Program
Certificate in Paralegal Studies; Litigation/Corporate Specialties
Magna Cum Laude Graduate; Dean's List; GPA 3.84
Awarded the Leslie Ridley-Tree Scholarship; Alumni Association
President; Editor, Student Newsletter

Courses include Legal Theory and Practice; Property; Torts; Contracts; Legal Research and Writing; Litigation Specialization; Remedies and Judgments; Probate Administration; Corporations; Real Estate; Criminal Law; Computers and the Law; Wills and Trusts; Bankruptcy Law and Procedure.

UNIVERSITY OF WASHINGTON
Seattle, Washington 1997
Bachelor of Arts—Business Administration; Emphasis in International
Marketing; GPA 3.60
Student Director for Work/Study Clinic

PROFESSIONAL DEVELOPMENT

"Hot Docs and Smoking Guns"
Litigation Paralegal Seminar by The Estrin Organization 2001

"What You Need to Know about Imaging and Scanning"
Litigation Support Seminar by the National Association for Paralegals Seminars 1999

LEXIS Certification Seminar
Legal Research Seminar for Legal Assistants 1998

Coursework in American Sign Language 1997
American Red Cross Water Safety Instructor Certificate 1995–96

SKILLS AND ABILITIES

- Computer Skills: WordPerfect; LEXIS/NEXIS and Westlaw; ExpressFile; PFS:File; PC/Soft Bankruptcy; ExpressCalc; Excel; CDB Infotek; Dataquick
- Fluent in Japanese
- Notary Public

Professional Activities

Member, Los Angeles Paralegal Association
Member, Action Committee for Education

William Shakespeare
2040 Berkshire Lane
Stratford-on-Avon, CA 90067
(310) 555-6699

OBJECTIVE

To obtain a challenging and demanding paralegal position within a firm or corporation.

EDUCATION

INSTITUTE FOR PARALEGAL STUDIES	Seattle, WA
Paralegal Certificate in Litigation; Honors Graduate	2001
UNIVERSITY OF MICHIGAN AT ANN ARBOR	Ann Arbor, MI
Bachelor of Arts Degree	1989

Major:	Political Science
Minor:	Art History
Activities:	Varsity Hockey Team; Debate Team; Drama Club

EMPLOYMENT HISTORY

Researcher	1996–Present
THE MERCER CORPORATION	Seattle, WA

Responsibilities include supervision of market researchers; oversee production of routine reports; prepare analysis of market trends; manage day-to-day operations.

Administrative Assistant	1994–1996
OHBOY CORPORATION	Seattle, WA

Responsibilities included handling heavy volume of phone calls; directing inquiries to proper authorities; meeting and greeting clients and candidates; preparing daily attendance reports; overseeing training of temporary employees.

SKILLS and ABILITIES

- Excellent communication and writing skills
- Ability to follow directions thoroughly
- Fast learner
- Ability to handle high-profile clients
- Proficient in drafting proposals
- Reliable researcher

COMPUTER SKILLS

- Proficient in MS Word; WordPerfect; Microsoft Works
- Excellent skills in Excel and Lotus 1-2-3
- Knowledge of Harvard Graphics and PageMaker
- Internet Expert

ANDREW S. THURSTON

2040 Avenue of the Oaks # 400 · St. Louis, MO · 315-555-6699

PARALEGAL-RELATED SKILLS AND CAPABILITIES

- Trust Administration
- Knowledge of M&I and SEI Trust software
- Financial and Auditing experience
- Technologically proficient
- Personnel and Operations Administration
- Excellent client relations skills and ability to work under pressure

PROFESSIONAL EXPERIENCE

QUINN BANK & TRUST   July 1999–Present
St. Louis, MO

Trust Operations Officer
Responsible for administration of assets totaling $25 million. Account load includes managed agency, non-managed agency, and custodial accounts. Experience in trust administration. Coordinate account activities with each department for clients. Anticipate potential obstacles with key accounts. Provide technical, operational, and administrative support. Assist department with development of office procedures, forms, checklists, and filing system. Prepare synopsis of new accounts. Review and analyze monthly revenue and expense reports.

SANWA TRUST DEPARTMENT   August 1997–June 1999
St. Louis, Mo.

Personal Trust Assistant
Assisted in managing personal trust relationships. Prepared and researched files for committee matters, handled client and attorney inquiries, set up new accounts, prepared synopsis and account reviews. Prepared account compliance reports according to State, Federal, and Bank regulations.

MAIN STREET BANK AND TRUST   May 1993–June 1997
Kansas City, Mo.

Corporate Trust Officer
Oversaw administration of 134 trust accounts with assets totaling more than $75 million. Reviewed bond indentures, escrow agreements, and other fiduciary agreements to ensure compliance with State, Federal, and Bank policy with regard to trustee's responsibilities. Set up new accounts, prepared synopsis, and completed all checklist requirements. Reviewed daily cash sheets and invested and reinvested funds in accordance with governing document(s) and written instructions.

EDUCATION

UNIVERSITY OF MICHIGAN, ANN ARBOR, MI
English and American Literature major with a Business (Accounting) minor

COMPUTER SKILLS

- Word, WordPerfect, Excel, Lotus 1-2-3, FoxPro, SEI—Trust 3000, M&I Trust, Microsoft Works, ACT, Microsoft Publisher, PowerPoint
- IBM and Macintosh proficient

AFFILIATIONS

Gateway Paralegal Association
University of Michigan Alumni Association
Trust Administrators Association

INTERESTS AND OUTSIDE ACTIVITIES

Biking, hiking, theatre, music, book clubs
Member of Big Brothers Association
Member, "IKE," Intercity Kids for Education

KEVIN JOHNS

123 Willow Street, Louisville, Kentucky 40202
(502) 555-1212 (home) (502) 555-2112 (office) kewy@hotmail.com

EDUCATION:

Institute for Paralegal Education
Louisville, Kentucky
ABA-approved program
Certificate in Paralegal Studies Corporate/Real Estate Specialization, 2001

Coursework:
Legal Theory; Property; Contracts; Corporations; Remedies and
Judgments; Business Writing; Legal Research; Computers and the Law
Firm; Accounting; Torts; Law Office Administration; Entertainment Law;
Bankruptcy Law; American Government; English Composition.

University of Kentucky
Lexington, Kentucky
B.A. Degree, History, 1988
GPA: 3.5/4.0

PARALEGAL SKILLS:

Well-versed in factual investigation; proficient in Microsoft Word for
Windows, Excel, PowerPoint, WordPerfect, Internet; excellent writing
and problem-solving skills; ability to interface with all levels of staff.

EMPLOYMENT:

Writer/Researcher
Westbrook Hospital for Special Surgery
Louisville, Kentucky
1992–Present

Research and develop material for grant proposals to corporations and
foundations, coordinate grant sources, interview scientists and doctors
for new techniques, create monthly spreadsheets to track budgets, set
up confidential administrative and legal files.

Assistant to Executive Director, Development
St. Luke's Hospital, Louisville, Kentucky
1988–1992

Identified and researched individual, corporate, and foundation
prospective donors of $500,000+. Set up appointments, wrote trip
briefings, trained new staff in computerized research methodologies,
tracked administrative matters for Executive Director in charge of $100
million capital campaign.

LANGUAGES:

French, German, Spanish, Italian, and Portuguese

PROFESSIONAL AFFILIATIONS:

Louisville Paralegal Association

CINDY SMITH
10608 Euclid Avenue
Nashville, TN 37215
(615) 555-1212

EDUCATION
2001

University of Paralegal Studies
Nashville, Tennessee
Certificate in Litigation/Corporations

Coursework included:
Trial rules; civil procedure; business organizations; probate;
real property law; bankruptcy; family law

1999

University of Tennessee
Memphis, Tennessee
Master of Business Administration

Coursework included:
Financial and managerial accounting; finance; business
economics; statistics

1998

University of California
Irvine, California
Bachelor of Arts Degree in Social Ecology
GPA: 3.3/4.0

EXPERIENCE
May 2001–
Present

Paralegal Intern
Legal Aid Society of Nashville
Nashville, TN

Responsibilities:
Client intake; case evaluation; prepare form pleadings in
bankruptcy and family law matters; index documents; meet
with clients; file court documents.

1997–1998

Customer Service
Snow Summit Ski Resort, Big Bear Lake, California

Responsibilities:
Trained new personnel; extensive client interaction; delegated
tasks to work teams; taught clients to ski.

1994–1996

Customer Service Representative
Thrifty Drug Stores, Irvine, California

Responsibilities:
Handled cash register and cash reconciliations; controlled and monitored inventory; dealt with customer returns.

COMPUTER SKILLS
WordPerfect; Excel; Westlaw; Internet Expert; Lexis/Westlaw

PROFESSIONAL AFFILIATIONS
Nashville Legal Assistant Association
Big Sisters of America

INTERESTS
Skiing, Russian literature and French cooking.

Tricia Toyota
5000 Woodman Avenue
Phoenix, AZ 95432
(t) (602) 555-1212

OBJECTIVE

To find a challenging full-time position enabling me to demonstrate excellent paralegal skills in a firm offering an opportunity for growth and long-term employment.

EMPLOYMENT

PARALEGAL   Jan. 2000–Present
Contract Positions   *Los Angeles, California*
The Estrin Organization; Five Star Paralegals; Special Counsel;
Capstone

Responsibilities: organized and maintained documents; analyzed factual information; constructed exhibit lists for trial; reviewed, indexed, and summarized pleadings and correspondence produced by opposing parties; drafted legal memorandum to clients regarding case status and preparation; researched legal issues and rules; assisted in trial preparation; established d/b/a's for senior partner; data entry and retrieval; summarized discovery responses; prepared witness books; prepared deposition summaries for the following firms:

- Gibson, Dunn & Crutcher
- Latham & Watkins
- O'Melveny & Myers
- Dickson, Carlson & Campillo
- Riordan & McKinzie
- Arter & Hadden
- White & Case
- Shapiro, Rosenfeld & Close

RELATED EMPLOYMENT

Sales Representative   JAN. 1997–JUNE 1999
Fry's Electronics; Select Copy Systems; Rent-A-Center

Account Executive/Collections   JUNE 1995–OCT. 1996
Robinson's-May

Loan Collections Officer   OCT. 1989–MAY 1995
Security Pacific Bank

EDUCATION

UNIVERSITY OF WEST LOS ANGELES SCHOOL OF PARALEGAL STUDIES
Litigation Specialist Certificate: Dean's List; ABA-approved program

CALIFORNIA STATE UNIVERSITY NORTHRIDGE
Bachelor of Arts in Communications

SKILLS

- Proficient in MS Word; WordPerfect; Excel; Access; Concordance; Paradox; Windows 98
- Bilingual in Spanish: oral and written
- Excellent research, organizational, oral, and written communication skills
- Strong problem solving and analytical skills
- Ability to draft pleadings, legal memoranda, and motions

ANA MARTINEZ

2040 Avenue of the Elms, #400, Madison, WI 55432   *(715) 555-1212*
(e) anabanana@coldmail.com

OBJECTIVE

A paralegal position within a distinguished law firm promoting the effective utilization of paralegals.

EDUCATION

MADISON COMMUNITY COLLEGE
Associate of Science degree in Paralegal Studies to be awarded 2002

MINNEAPOLIS COMMUNITY COLLEGE
Office Administration

EXPERIENCE

INSIGNIA COMMERCIAL CORPORATION   MARCH 1998–AUGUST 2000
Madison, WI
Office Coordinator
On-line support for WordPerfect clients. Prepared bids and followed through on sales calls. Purchased hardware and software after comprehensive evaluation. Prepared deposits, transfers, and cash receipts. Supported graphic artists. Procured and maintained insurance certificates. Assisted sales team with backup materials.

HILTON HOTELS   MAY 1996–MARCH 1998
Madison, WI
Executive Assistant
Composed correspondence for executives in English and Swedish. Proofread, edited, and translated letters. Supported staff on phones. Scheduled and maintained meeting log. Compiled advertising information for promotional campaigns. Served as liaison between advertising representatives and Vice President of Marketing.

SUNLIGHT SOFTWARE   JUNE 1994–MAY 1996
Minneapolis, MN
Property Manager
Supervised and coordinated engineering, security, and janitorial services. Assisted in publication of monthly newsletter. Implemented and executed Tenant Retention program. Promoted tenant parties and functions. Prepared and maintained accounts.

Michael Jones
123 Flag Street
Washington, D.C. 20001
(202) 555-1212 or (202) 555-1331 (e) mike@coc.com

Objective
To contribute to a law firm or corporate legal department as a paralegal dedicated to excellent work product and maintenance of the organization's high expectations.

Employment
THE CONSUMER PRODUCT ADVOCATE MAGAZINE, WASHINGTON, D.C.
Legal Intern, June–September 2001
- Performed research for arguments and licensing agreements
- Assisted with ongoing products liability negotiations for litigation department
- Performed analysis of, and drafted memoranda for, various pleadings and actions, including contract negotiations, copyright and trademark infringements and product liability cases.

CONTINUING MEDICAL EDUCATION, WASHINGTON, D.C
Assistant Course Coordinator, November 1994–January 2000
- Designed course curriculum for medical doctors' continuing education needs. Analyzed and interpreted course effectiveness and managed continuous improvement process.

Education
GEORGETOWN UNIVERSITY SCHOOL OF LAW, WASHINGTON, D.C.
- Four completed semesters of law school
- Awarded the PILF Public Service Award and Outstanding Service Achievement Award
- Member, Black American Law Student Association. Conducted fund-raisers for student programs, scholarships, supplies, and resources for the local Adopt-a-School program.
- Special Events Volunteer Coordinator for Pediatric AIDS Benefit.

GEORGETOWN UNIVERSITY, WASHINGTON, D.C.
Bachelor of Science in Business Administration and Finance, May 1992
- Co-Chairman and Teacher, "I Have a Dream" Tutoring Program. Adapted curriculum for low-achiever and gifted student needs. Taught English and advanced mathematics.
- Photographer for Georgetown University Yearbook.

Skills
- Basic Spanish and French language skills, including reading, writing, and speaking
- Excellent client relations abilities
- Strong communication skills
- Quick learner and excellent teacher

Computer skills
- Word Processing, spreadsheet building, presentation, and database management program abilities includes Word, Excel, PowerPoint, Persuasion, Approach, Quattro Pro. FileMaker Pro, Lotus 123, and Harvard Graphics.

Cary Grant

2040 Ave. of the Stars Suite 400
Los Angeles, CA 90067
310.555.1212
(e) grant@coldmail.com

OBJECTIVE

Temporary Paralegal Positions: Long- and short-term assignments

EMPLOYMENT

Contract Litigation Paralegal   1998–Present
The Estrin Organization   Los Angeles, CA

Responsibilities include trial preparation; prepare exhibits for pleadings and into trial notebooks; attend document productions; prepare indexes; prepare witness notebooks; draft Temporary Restraining Orders and Notices of Continuances; enter privileged documents into database; redact documents for privilege; summarize documents and depositions.

Assignments at:

Latham & Bell	Gibson, Dune	Jones, Smith & Day
Orrick, Reavis	Alston Oil Corp.	Lewis, Harrison & Fields
Atlantic Oil Corp.	First Bank	Cooper & Klein

Civil Litigation Paralegal   Jan. 1991–June 1998
Freshman, Senior and Junior   Newport Beach, CA

Responsibilities: Supervised 5–20 paralegals for complex litigation matter. Interfaced with corporate clients regarding exhibits, depositions, and trial; prepared documentation regarding document productions; researched L.A. County Superior Court files; conducted legal research at county law libraries; reviewed files for privileged and work product documents; attended document productions; designed database for 2000 witnesses.

COMPUTER SKILLS

- WordPerfect; Word
- LEXIS/NEXIS; Westlaw
- Leading Edge, Concordance, Summation, Inmagic, dBase IV, CatLinks
- Lotus 123, Excel
- Avery List, MAIL
- Harvard Graphics, Microsoft Publisher

EDUCATION

Paralegal Certificate   1987–1990
Pasadena City College   Pasadena, CA
Dean's list

Bachelor of Arts   1978–1982
Holy Cross College   Seattle, WA

Antoinette King
266 East Lily Lane
New York, New York 10011
(212) 555-1212

SUMMARY OF QUALIFICATIONS

- Ten years of highly responsible and challenging employment experience in fast-paced environments
- Experienced in complex patent litigation matters
- Excellent mathematical, analytical, and computer knowledge
- Demonstrated ability to work independently and as a team player

EMPLOYMENT EXPERIENCE

Delmonico Bank & Co.   *February 2001 to Present*
New York, New York
Legal Secretary

Assist attorneys in a fast-paced legal environment to meet continuous deadlines. Heavy typing of legal documents, transcribe complex documents, prepare detailed patent applications, train new employees, assist with Help Desk, schedule meetings and conferences, prepare monthly billing reports, interface with high-profile clients, assist with all duties from basic to complex administrative tasks. Utilize opportunities to learn responsibilities outside designated duties to better support the department.

Christie, Perkins & Hall   *August 1997 to January 2001*
New York, New York
Legal Secretary

Assisted attorneys and paralegals in meeting crucial deadlines. Heavy typing of various legal documents and correspondence, data entry, transcription duties, and file maintenance. Scheduled depositions, conferences, arbitrations, and court reporters. Trained new secretaries on word-processing system. Handled new associate orientation scheduling. Assisted in preparation of employee manuals.

Herald Federal Bank, F.S.B.   *March 1993 to August 1997*
New York, New York
Junior Analyst/Administrative Assistant

Assisted three vice presidents in a busy investment department with various challenging special projects. Assisted in the trading desk as backup to senior analyst, heavy phone interaction with business clients and personnel, prepared detailed weekly and monthly reports using spreadsheet programs, ordered office supplies, scheduled meetings, ensured that department deadlines were met, prepared expense reports, heavy typing of various documents such as proposals, tables, and correspondence, scheduled and arranged meetings.

New York Life Insurance   *September 1991 to October 1993*
New York, New York
Administrative Assistant

Assisted in accounting department with general ledger entry, heavy data entry.
Assisted clients via phone, E-mail, and correspondence. Handled cash desk,
assisted with payroll, trained new employees, and handled all aspects of
administrative duties.

SKILLS

Computers: WEBS System; Microsoft Word; Excel; PowerPoint; Access; E-Mail;
WordPerfect
Office Systems: Proficient with most word-processing, mailroom, and phone
systems

EDUCATION

Mt. St. Mary's College
Business courses

William Gates
2100 Seatac Lane
Seattle, WA 91234
(206) 555-1212 (e) Bill@Micro.com

PROFESSIONAL WORK HISTORY:

Lucas, Kaemippfer, Bonner & Tierney
Seattle, WA   October 2000–present

Director of Litigation Support Services for major firm. Train attorneys and staff on software applications for litigation projects. Coordination and implementation of coding projects. Responsible for recruitment, screening, training, evaluation of qualified personnel on large litigation projects.

The Whaler Corporation
Seattle, WA   June 1998–October 2000

Senior Paralegal and Case Manager for Fortune 500 Corporation. Supervised paralegals on large complex litigation cases. Specialized in creation and development of litigation databases using imaging technologies and document coding. Solicited proposals and supervised vendors who imaged and indexed documents. Responsible for staffing and review of temporary staff in litigation support. Supervised discovery phase and provided overall trial support. Served as in-house expert on imaging systems and ensured system performance throughout discovery and trial. Worked closely with Litigation, Healthcare, and Intellectual Property departments.

Hewlett-Packard & Gateway
Seattle, WA   November 1996–May 1998

Litigation Legal Assistant for intellectual property firm. Duties included large antitrust cases involving the telecommunications industry. Researched, analyzed, and prepared damage studies. Developed databases for document organization and retrieval. Coordinated litigation support services. Assisted in automated litigation support services including document analysis, quality control. Trained groups on software packages.

COMPUTER TECHNOLOGIES:

Westlaw, LEXIS, Microsoft Word for Windows, Windows 98, Word 97, Access, Concordance, Summation, Doculux, Excel, Folio Views, PowerPoint

TEACHING BACKGROUND:

Instructor, Seattle Community College   1995–Present

Conduct classes for Legal Assistant Certificate Program. Specializing in computerization of litigation projects from discovery through trial. Evaluation and review of student performance.

EDUCATION:

Bachelor of Science Degree/Computer Sciences   1994
University of Washington
Summa Cum Laude

HOBBIES:

Accomplished Pianist, Sailor, Photographer, and Chef.

Abraham Lincoln

1901 Avenue of the Stars Suite 350 • Los Angeles, CA 90067 •
310-555-6699 (e) abbie@smile.com

OBJECTIVE

Seeking a challenging and rewarding entry-level paralegal position that utilizes mathematical, interpersonal, and writing skills.

WORK HISTORY

LEE, GRANT & GETTYSBURG
Paralegal   *March 1996—Present*
Prepare document summaries; index documents; prepare closing binders and witness notebooks; prepare exhibits for trial; summarize depositions.

STATE OF ILLINOIS
Chief Investigator   *April 1992–March 1996*
Investigated domestic violence complaints; referred clients to proper agencies; documented files; prepared detailed reports; ghostwriter for Sr. Chief Investigator speeches; prepared correspondence; handled inquiries.

EDUCATION

INSTITUTE FOR LEGAL ASSISTANT STUDIES
B.S. Degree in Paralegal Studies 1992
Outstanding Student of the Year Award

BOOTH COLLEGE
A.A. Degree in Business
Student Body President—two semesters

SKILLS

- Have given more than 100 speeches related to new business techniques
- Experienced factual researcher

COMPUTER SKILLS

- Windows 98; NT; Word; WordPerfect
- IBM PC and MAC
- Excel; Lotus 1-2-3; Concordance; Summation

LAURA INGERS
400 South Euclid Avenue
Delray Beach, Florida 33445-4696
(H) 305-555-1212 (W) 305-555-1313 (e) lingers@smile.net

EXPERIENCE

8/95–Present   Southwestern Bell Services, *Agent Compensation Specialist*
- Responsible for tracking sales of services by region
- Prepare reports for sales revenue
- Develop commission reports
- Develop specialized reports as needed

4/93–7/95   Team One Staffing, *Temporary Accounting Assistant*
- Worked in various accounting departments such as Prudential Securities; H&R Block; Merrill Lynch
- Assisted in administrative capacity

2/91–3/93   Latin American Stock Exchange, *Trading Assistant*
- Reconciled security holdings to internal accounting department
- Updated databases to reflect corporate actions, security changes, settlement instructions, and price changes
- Developed reports regarding new issues and allocation by Fund
- Coordinated confirmations of all trade details and revisions with traders

6/89–12/90   Auntie Pasto's Italian Restaurant, *Office Manager*
- Responsible for accounting, personnel, and inventory
- Processed payroll and personnel forms for forty employees
- Coordinated special events such as caterings, wine tastings, and holiday events

SPECIAL SKILLS
- Native fluency in Spanish, oral and written
- Advanced proficiency in MS Excel, MS Access, MS Word
- Proficient in Lotus 1-2-3, Quattro Pro, WordPerfect

EDUCATION

8/88–9/92   University of Texas, Journalism Major

MEI HUANG

1855 Carnation Avenue
Los Angeles, CA 90067
(310) 555-1212 (e) Huang@nwl.com

OBJECTIVE

Seeking part-time employment as a legal assistant/secretary in a law firm while attending Loyola Law School part time in the evenings.

EXPERIENCE

LEGAL ASSISTANT   FEBRUARY 1998 TO PRESENT
Law Offices of George Burns   *Los Angeles, CA*
- Interview clients to collect necessary information regarding cases
- Draft and file petitions and applications for various immigration cases
- Research immigration laws to gather evidence in support of clients' cases
- Correspond with the Immigration and Naturalization Service and the Department of Labor in all phases of the immigration application process

COMPUTER CONSULTANT   OCTOBER 1996 TO MAY 1998
Rutgers University   *Rutgers University, New Jersey*
Computing Center

- Instructed users on the usage of software available in the computing center
- Reconstructed incapacitated computers
- Edited user manuals for students
- Prepared charts for teachers' instructional usage

EDUCATION

LOYOLA LAW SCHOOL   FALL 1998–PRESENT
Presently attending

B.S. DEGREE IN ADMINISTRATION OF JUSTICE   SEPTEMBER 1994–MAY 1997
Rutgers, the State University of New Jersey

Graduated with Honors
Selected Member of National Golden Key Honor Society
Dean's List Fall 1994, Spring 1996, Fall 1996, Spring 1997

SKILLS

- Proficient in Word, WordPerfect, Lotus, Excel, Summation
- Excellent writing skills
- Fluent in Mandarin

ACTIVITIES

- Volunteer—Women's Job Center   Sept. 1996 to January 1997
- Taught job search skills to homemakers reentering the job market
- Volunteer—Presidential/Senate Campaign Center
  July 1996 to November 1996

GLORIA HERRERA
2040 Ave. of the Glens # 400
Omaha, Nebraska 55555
(W) 402-553-6699 (H) 402-555-1212 (e) glow@smile.com

EMPLOYMENT

Real Estate Legal Assistant   December 1993 to Present
AMRESCO RESIDENTIAL MORTGAGE COMPANY   OMAHA, NEBRASKA

Responsibilities include retrieval of public records regarding property and owners; conduct title searches and research building permits in the Records Office; check and review zoning regulations; review land surveys, parcel maps, and plots; supervise up to 10 staff members; create and maintain database for special projects.

Appraisal Clerk   August 1990 to May 1993
BANC ONE   OMAHA, NEBRASKA

Responsibilities included preparation of appraisals for staff appraisers; data retrieval; office purchase orders; phone verification of building permits and title searches; interface with DRE.

EDUCATION

University of Omaha   Presently Attending
OMAHA, NEBRASKA

Courses completed: Basic Real Estate, Real Estate Law, Real Estate Construction, Real Estate Appraising 1 & 2 and Appraisal Ethics

Paralegal Certificate   1998
UNIVERSITY OF NEBRASKA   OMAHA, NEBRASKA

Dean's List; President of University of Nebraska Paralegal Alumni Association; Winner Estrin Scholarship; Editor of Case in Point Newsletter.

SKILLS
- Knowledge of IAMB-compatible and Macintosh computer systems
- Windows; Mac OS 8; Microsoft Excel 97; Word; PowerPoint
- Familiar with Westlaw and LEXIS

ASSOCIATIONS
- Member of Omaha Paralegal Association
- Member of National Association of Legal Assistants
- Member of National Federation of Paralegal Associations
- Member of American Association for Paralegal Education

BEFORE

HENRY BARNEY   Phone: 310-555-1212
555 West Palm Avenue Apt. 101   E-mail: hnrybney@nsm.com
Los Angeles, CA 90024

OBJECTIVE: A full-time, permanent or temp permanent paralegal position in Litigation

EDUCATION
UCLA Extension, Los Angeles, CA Paralegal Certificate   07/97–11/97

Whittier Law School, Los Angeles, CA and Irvine, CA   09/95–12/95

Teachers College, New York City, M.A., Ed.M.   10/12/85

Whitmore College, Boston, Mass. B.A.   05/24/84

LITIGATION SUPPORT TRAINING
S.M.A.R.T.—Systems Management and Retrieval Training   09/98
Workshop in Document Coding

LEGAL EXPERIENCE (Professional and Volunteer)
CourtAdvocate   Los Angeles, CA 01/97–Present
Litigation Paralegal for lower income and welfare recipients.
Teachers Union   Los Angeles, CA 07/95–08/96
Grievance Specialist for Community Adult School

REGISTERED WITH THE FOLLOWING LEGAL PLACEMENT FIRMS: LawDate,
Jones Placement Agency, Permanent Solutions, Law Professionals

ADDITIONAL EXPERIENCE (Professional)
Orange County Unified School District   03/93–06/95

AWARDS AND SPECIAL RECOGNITIONS
Civil Rights Activist, Irvine, CA   President's Certificate 05/94

COMPUTER EXPERIENCE
Competent in Windows 95, Windows 98, Office 97, Excel, WordPerfect, Word for Windows

REFERENCES FURNISHED UPON REQUEST

AFTER

HENRY BARNEY   Phone: 310-555-1212
555 West Palm Avenue #101   E-mail: hnrybrny@nsm.com
Los Angeles, CA 90024

EDUCATION
University of California, Los Angeles Extension
Attorney Assistant Training Program, offered in cooperation with UCLA
School of Law, accredited by the American Bar Association
Certificate in Litigation, December 1997

Teachers College/Columbia University, New York City   1986
Master of Education in Counseling Psychology, emphasis on
counseling

Whitmore College, Boston, MA   1985
B.A. Degree/Writing and Literature

EXPERIENCE (Professional and Volunteer)
CourtAdvocate, Los Angeles, CA   Jan. 1997 to Present
Litigation Paralegal
Responsibilities: Interviewed clients, prepared intake, drafted complaints,
assisted CourtAdvocate in child custody cases, attended hearings,
drafted memos, prepared pleadings, reviewed documents, prepared
reports highlighting areas for judicial reform.

Teachers Union, Los Angeles, CA   July 1995 to Aug. 1996
Union Representative
Represented all teachers at main school and branch sites in contract
negotiations and grievance proceedings. Gained familiarity with
collective bargaining.

Orange County Unified School District, Irvine, CA   March 1993 to
                                                      June 1995
Teacher of Adult English as a Second Language. Taught ESL to more than
700 students from many different countries and cultures.

ADDITIONAL TRAINING
S.M.A.R.T—Systems Management and Retrieval Training   1998
Workshop in Document Coding and Electronic Litigation Support

COMPUTER SKILLS
Competent in MS Windows 95, Windows 98, Office 97, Excel,
WordPerfect, Word for Windows

AWARDS AND SPECIAL RECOGNITIONS
Civil Rights Activist—President's Award   1993

Resume Nightmare

Jane Doe
123 South Oak Street
City, State 34567
(616) 555-1212

EDUCATION:	Certified Legal Assistant:	UCLA 1990

Law classes: WCCL : 1983–1986
BA 1983; CSSB

Experience:	E.L. Bond, attorney at law	August, 1992–1997
	425 So. Michigan, San Francisco	

I was a paralegal/secretary responsible for all the factest of the operation. I was the only employee. I managed the law library, did legal research. Filed court documents, answered the telephone, transcribed dictations, was allowed to generate my own correspondence with government agencies, stock ocmpanies etc. I was also responsible for maintaining the office supply inventory. I am proficient in WP5.1 and in the process of learning Lotus 123.4 and Word & Works for Windows.

PERSONAL DATA: *Divorced (but still interviewing)*
In 1993, through the community college, I attended a comparative criminal law class at Worcester College in Oxford.

My other "life" is that of a textile designer. I have an extensive textile library and weaving studio.

ADDITIONAL
References: *John M. Jones, Attorney at Law*

SALARY: *My monthly salary in July, 1997 was $1600 per month.*

I would prefer a location north of the boulevard.

WHAT'S WRONG WITH THIS PICTURE?
(OR I'VE SENT OUT 500 RESUMES.
NO ONE MUST BE HIRING.)

The resume on the preceding page is not a joke. It was an actual resume that was submitted for a paralegal position. Needless to say, this candidate barely received a rejection letter. It is unusual to see quite so many mistakes on any one resume. In that light, we've tackled the most obvious "no-no's" and left the rest to your common sense.

FORMAT	See examples. Unfortunately, there is no format here. Be consistent in spacing and capitalization.
EDUCATION	
"Certified":	Did this person pass the CLA or PACE exam? Or does she mean she has a certificate? There's no indication.
Law classes:	List the school and years attended. It's not necessary to say "law classes."
WCCL:	Spell out the names of schools. Not everyone is familiar with acronyms. Watch for typos. There are three spaces between WCCL and the colon. And that's just a start.
B.A. degree?	What major? Where? The B.A. becomes highly suspect with no additional information.
EXPERIENCE	
Attorney at Law:	This should be capitalized.
Dates of employment:	If using months, be consistent throughout: August 1990–September 1997. Most employers prefer to see months in addition to years listed.
Addresses:	Do not put the address of a firm other than city and state.
Fonts:	Do not change fonts unless you are emphasizing sections.
Tense:	Do not use "I"—ever. Do not use a narrative.
Correct grammar:	Always use correct grammar: "did . . . legal research" is incorrect.

Spelling and typos:	Use correct spelling: "factest," "dictations," "govenment," and "ocmpanies" are incorrect.
Choose phrasing:	Never state "was allowed." It sounds too subservient.
Know what you're talking about:	Be sure to get names of software correct: Lotus 123.4?
Spell out "and":	Don't use ampersand "&" unless it is in the name of a company.

PERSONAL DATA

Personal information:	Doesn't belong in a resume—ever.
Related work history:	State positions and employment. Do not state "other life."

ADDITIONAL REFERENCES

Do not put references on the resume. References belong on a separate piece of paper along with correct address and phone numbers. We question the candidate's thinking. "Additional" was used here but has no merit. There was only one reference listed.

SALARY

Do not list salary on the resume. If requested in an ad, list in the cover letter unless you are specifically asked to list it on your resume.

COMMENTS

A comment section is not appropriate. Do not put additional comments on the resume. State your comments in your cover letter.

10

Your Resume Is Hereby Rejected. Most Sincerely, MAC 9000

COMPUTER PROCESSING OF RESUMES

*I*t used to be that writing your resume was pretty routine: use "action" words, white or buff paper, keep it to one or two pages, chronological or functional, easy-to-read font. Well, folks, say good-bye to the good ole days.

Litigation support, meet human resources. Or, inhuman resources, we should say. Today, in many of the major corporations, your resume is most likely to encounter a computer long before it is scanned by good old-fashioned eyeballs. That is because, at many of the large corporations, computers are taking the first crack at accepting or rejecting the ongoing flood of resumes. What the legal community was first introduced to as litigation support through scanning of documents has now entered the human resources department. In the new era of rejection, resumes are scanned and entered into the computer long before a warm, friendly, hiring authority has placed human hands on them.

Many job candidates never know that their resumes have been scanned by a computer or by human eyes, particularly if they have applied to a major corporation. According to an article in the *Wall Street Journal,* hundreds of large companies—Sony Corporation, Coca-Cola Company, International Business Machines Corporation, Paine Webber, NationsBank Corporation, Avis Rent A Car, Microsoft Corporation, Pfizer Inc., Shell Oil, Staples, to name just a few—use types of text searching or artificial-intelligence software to track resumes. Mid-sized companies are also starting to use the software as vendors start marketing cheaper Web-based versions.

And for those of you who are snickering as you recall that the legal field was the very last to get on the technology express, woe be unto you who firmly believe that scanning resumes will never catch on in the legal field. A simple set up of Opticon and Concordance should do the trick. But enough soothsaying.

These resume-scanning systems make a lot of sense from an employer's perspective. Employers are being bombarded by resumes from all directions—mail, fax, E-mail. And in this candidate-tight market, employers need all the help they can get to quickly identify and court the right candidate. According to the *Wall Street Journal,* Allied Signal filled more than 30 percent of approximately 2,500 job openings from a computerized resume pool, in the first half of one year. The company estimates it can prune the time it takes to fill an opening by at least a month.

From a candidate's point of view, resume scanning is another chink in the armor of job search success. This new phenomenon might seem innocuous if it weren't for the fact that the consequences were so potentially damaging to a person's chances of having a resume end up on the desk of a living, breathing hiring partner. Typically, an administrator, paralegal coordinator, human resources director, or general counsel sets up a search request and asks the computer for specific qualifications. Then many of the resume-scanning systems rank the candidates they pluck out of the system.

Staffing organizations also use scanning systems. The more popular ones, like Resumix, specialize in recruiting systems that place a number or percentage next to a candidate's name indicating how much of a hiring manager's wish list is reflected in the resume. So if you have 87 percent and ten others have 95 percent, you may be out of luck if the manager has no desire to plow through all available resumes before coffee. The systems scan on key words, which makes everybody the same. A computer cannot tell whether the resume reflects a "warm and friendly" person as opposed to a "highly professional" individual. It also protects against discrimination. It doesn't care whether the candidate is an Asian-American or an American with disabilities. It may, however, want to know if the candidate went to an acceptable undergrad university and has a paralegal certificate from an ABA-approved school. If a candidate went to Princeton, has one year of experience with a major firm, but went to a paralegal school that is too new to receive ABA approval, she may get the Big R (for rejection) letter.

Without knowledge as to how a description is typed into the computer, many candidates are at the software program's mercy. Some candidates try to list every conceivable skill in an effort to determine which words the computer is looking for. Others use buzzwords and industry-speak as they try to describe their experience.

According to Yana Parker, author of *Damn Good Resume Guide* (Ten Speed Press 1996), a tracking system can identify behavioral traits—dependability, responsibility, a high energy level—as easily as it can technical skills. "Be enthusiastic," she says. "Let your passion show. Don't use tired language." Hmmm. We wonder if she knows another way to say "drafted pleadings."

But resumes do eventually get read by real human beings—on a computer screen. Although we used to write volumes and volumes of articles that said you have about three seconds to catch an interviewer's eye, we now say you have about twenty lines to grab their attention. If they're interested, they will keep scrolling. So don't waste precious real estate. Lead with your technical skills and personal qualities. Identify yourself as a solution to someone's problem.

Scanning systems comb through resumes for words that signal job titles, technical skills, and levels of education or experience. And most of those words are nouns. Where we used to say use lots and lots of action words, we now say use lots of nouns. Employers are now looking for software programs you can use, what practice specialties you know, what assignments you can perform. Preparing a scannable resume is much like preparing the traditional-style resume in terms of focusing on format and content. The more skills and facts you provide, the more opportunities you'll have for your skills to match available positions.

Some resume-scanning companies and outplacement counselors advise a block of key words at the top of the resume, but this technique doesn't help differentiate you among other candidates. The keyword block can be helpful when comparing apples to apples—a business litigation paralegal searching for a business litigation position. On the other hand, it may backfire if the same business litigation description were written in such a way that a resume reflecting an insurance defense background would get rejected even though the skills were right on point.

A recently published article in a fascinating new magazine, *Fast Company,* states the more buzzwords, the better. Career counselors used to advise clients to avoid buzzwords in their resumes. Today, buzzwords are all the buzz. Because applicant-tracking systems rank resumes by the number of key words, your chances of scoring higher are better when the resume is buzzword loaded. If a firm is seeking a paralegal with experience in LotusNotes, Concordance, and Summation and needs trial prep, bankruptcy and IP background, it can rank resumes according to which ones include all key words. "Turn your experience into keywords," urges Margaret Riley Dikel, coauthor of *The Guide to Internet Job Searching* (VGM Career Horizons 1996), "and maximize the number of them in your resume."

But beware of what buzzwords you use! If your experience is a little old, you might want to watch outdated lingo that wouldn't have registered with computers looking for up-to-date key words. Terminology and technology have changed. You'll need to present yourself with up-to-date skills, or you may not get the hit. Additionally, you don't want to date yourself. So much for eight years' experience as a MagCard operator (the precursor to word processing).

And for those of you who are still not clear on the concept called summarizing, you're in luck! You get to break the one-page rule in this new era of resume writing. One page of paper doesn't mean much in the on-line world because readers scroll. But don't overdo it. Electronic resumes running three pages or more are apt to get bounced. Simply put, you must be able to hold the readers' attention—most of whom only understand 15-second sound bytes.

In the New Do's and Don'ts categories, you get some brand new choices. Scanners work well with these typefaces: Helvetica, Futura, Optima, Palatino, New Century Schoolbook, and Times New Roman. Although some counselors advocate Courier, we feel it looks old-fashioned and is reminiscent of the old IBM Selectric II days. (For those of you who are wondering just what that is, we're sure there's a picture in one of the old encyclopedias on the bookshelf in your grandparents' house.)

If you send your resume as an attachment, rather than paste it into the body of an E-mail message, be aware many employers ignore attachments because they worry about viruses. They don't want to waste time with files that their computers can't translate.

Some career counselors suggest that candidates have two resumes: one for people, and the other for computers. Others think a separate, scannable resume is unnecessary. But advising candidates to write more than one resume is nothing new, particularly if you are emphasizing a different skill set for a variety of jobs. It's hard—if not impossible—to know what will work, particularly since the whole concept of scanning resumes in the legal field is so new. You will, no matter what, still need a hard copy, printed on high-quality paper, to bring with you on the interview and for those companies that use snail mail in lieu of E-mail. Thank God for some traditions. We'd hate to put Kinko's right out of business.

11

How to Write a Revolutionary Cover Letter

"It's a funny thing about life—if you refuse to accept anything but the very best, you very often get it."

—Somerset Maugham

Here's a little known secret: A resume only talks about 20 percent of the information you need to impart in order to get a job. It reveals none of the remaining 80 percent of the information upon which hiring decisions are based. It does not speak to your personality, creativity, work style, work habits, or critical thinking. Rarely will a resume tell a hiring authority you are precisely the right candidate. Only a letter can reveal these things about you—and more.

For all of these reasons, the letter you send along with your resume may be one of the most important letters you'll ever write. To assist you in creating a winning cover letter, let's start with the basics.

TYPICAL NEWSPAPER AD:
Paralegal
Burks, Barks & Sharks seeks an experienced litigation paralegal for our South County offices. The ideal candidate will possess a B.A. degree and a certificate with at least 3–4 years' experience. Must have excellent organizational skills. A team player is a must. Fax resume to Stacey Hunt, Paralegal Coordinator.

A limited number of candidates will submit a resume with no cover letter. These candidates automatically limit their chances of consideration. A larger segment of responding candidates are likely to submit a letter along these lines:

Dear Ms. Hunt:

In response to your ad listed in *The Daily Journal,* please find my resume for the litigation paralegal position with your firm.

I have over 5 years' experience in litigation. I am seeking a challenging position which offers me opportunity for growth and I would be interested in working for your firm.

Thank you for your consideration. I can be reached at (214) 555-1212 during the evenings. I will call you next week in order to schedule an interview. I look forward to meeting with you soon.

Sincerely,

123

We can tell you as employers of paralegals that we receive literally hundreds of letters very close to the one on previous page. In addition to being weak and unappealing, this kind of letter is just plain boring! It tells us nothing about you or why you should be the candidate chosen for the job. As you read the following stronger version of the same letter, you'll see the differences and how much more effective it is.

Dear Ms. Hunt:

Your advertisement in *The Daily Journal* caught my eye immediately as it describes a position that matches my qualifications. Burks, Barks & Sharks is an excellent firm, one of which I would very much enjoy being aboard.

My solid litigation paralegal background has prepared me to apply for a position such as yours. To preview the information enumerated on my resume, let me summarize my background and strengths for you:

- Over 5 years' experience
- B.A. and certificate
- Team player
- Excellent organizational skills

My resume provides further details on my background and accomplishments. Realizing that this data cannot adequately convey my personality, strengths, or work habits, I would appreciate the opportunity to meet with you at your earliest convenience. Thank you for your consideration. I look forward to hearing from you.

Sincerely,

Nora Jones
Work Telephone: (214) 555-1212
Home Telephone: (214) 555-1212
(e) NORA@coldmail.com

Which letter makes a better impression? Which candidate would you be most likely to interview? Employers are just like you. They will choose the candidate who is more convincing and who reflects a more sophisticated, savvy personality.

Cover letters usually follow a standard format. There are three areas you'll want to cover:

Paragraph One:	The position and how you found out about it
Paragraph Two:	How your skills and qualifications fit with the organization
Paragraph Three:	Availability and contact information—when you are available for the interview and how you can be contacted.

THE BASIC AYES AND NAYS FOR
WRITING A KILLER COVER LETTER

1. Write a professional letter addressed to an individual. Do not write a form letter. A handwritten salutation is insulting to the reader. Your reader should not have the impression you are sending the same letter to hundreds and hundreds of employers—even if you are! Create the impression that you are sending an individualized letter created specifically for the reader. Direct your letter to the reader. Using "To whom it may concern" is only appropriate for blind ads. Find out who the proper hiring authority is, get the correct spelling of that person's name and proper title. One quick phone call is all it takes.

2. Don't use standard openings. "In response to your ad in *The Daily Journal*" gets a big ho hum. You want to stand out from the competition, so your letter should be anything but routine and repetitive. Weave information into the opening to suggest that the letter was written specifically for the opening at hand.

3. Don't use legal terminology or try to sound "lawyerly" in an attempt to impress the reader. Using terms such as "The undersigned hereby submits," "this position is not de facto . . . ," "Responsibilities include but are not limited to . . . ," "attached herein or hereto," or "enclosed herewith" is likely to *un*impress the reader. Frankly, the word "tacky" comes to mind.

4. Keep the letter brief. It's not necessary to write your entire life history—or anything close. You should have three to four paragraphs and no more! Explanations as to what has occurred in your career are not necessary. Save that for the interview.

5. Link your strengths and qualifications to the job. Cover letters that do not address the needs of the firm or knowledge of the organization are likely to come across as slightly narcissistic. Me, Me, and more Me. Let the employer know you understand what it takes to fit the bill.

6. Do not use cover letter formats that are designed for industries outside the legal arena. There are some very excellent resume- and cover-letter-writing books on the market. The majority of these books attempt to tackle a multitude of industries and take lots of liberties. But don't be misled that the legal field accepts the same kind of "jazzy" formats acceptable for other industries. It's better to lean toward a more conservative format

for higher acceptance in the legal field. Screaming CAPS and bolded, underlined words are *not* suitable in the legal field.

NO's
- INCREASED sales 87 percent by upgrading services
- I *reduced* bad debts 15 percent within one year.

7. Make your letter visually appealing. The visual appearance of a letter is as essential as its content. Make it easy to skim. (Remember, resume readers may spend as little as three to five seconds. Cover letters often fare no better.) Use stationery that matches your resume. *Stay away from italics; they are very hard to read.* Keep the letter to one page and always, always check for grammatical and typographical errors. Don't forget to sign the letter!

8. Don't exaggerate your skills or experience and never, never lie. End of story. Even if you get hired, dishonesty is grounds for immediate termination. Don't risk your career.

9. Be careful what you fax! Getting your fax numbers mixed up when sending several letters and resumes is a major faux pas. Don't make the mistake of sending a letter addressed to Mrs. Jones at American Express at a fax number for Mr. Smith at Diners Club.

10. If it's broken . . . fix it! *Don't* keep using a letter that's not working. If you've sent out ten or fifteen resumes and haven't heard a thing, haven't scheduled one interview or received one call, it's time to revise your letter or resume. It could be you're perfectly qualified, but your letter or resume is not making the impact you need. It's OK to use the same test marketing techniques direct mail experts have used for years. These companies continually alter their strategies until their goals are achieved. Why shouldn't you?

Reality Check

Don't be afraid to answer ads if you possess most of the qualifications described. Employers will often describe their "ideal" candidate and present a wishlist of qualifications. Your skills and experience may be the best combination potential employers can find. If you don't try, you'll never know!

SALES 101

Any sales training you may take will teach you about features and benefits of the service or product you are trying to sell. There is absolutely no difference in selling a service or product or selling yourself. You will want to alert your reader to your features and benefits.

A feature can be described as a quality, skill, or experience you have to offer. A benefit is what is received by the employer by hiring you. You want to use features and benefits in the second paragraph of your cover letter.

FEATURES AND BENEFITS WORKSHEET
For Use in Your Cover Letter

Sample Feature:
   I am *completing my paralegal certificate* because I *am interested in applying my environmental background to a prestigious firm such as yours*.

Benefit:
   The benefit to you is *a seasoned professional who knows her way around governmental agencies*.

I am _____ because I _____.
The benefit to you is _____.

I am _____ because I _____.
The benefit to you is _____.

I am _____ because I _____.
The benefit to you is _____.

Because I _____, you will benefit because _____.
   Throughout my career, I _____ (achieved/produced/succeeded in). As a result, you _____.

Here are a few examples of the kinds of features and benefits statements you can compose from your worksheets:

- I am an experienced, skilled paralegal because I have worked in a similar firm, Goodman, Moyer & Valery.
- Because I have completed my paralegal certificate with honors at the University of Paralegal Studies, I am knowledgeable in the requirements for this position.
- Because I am experienced in real estate development issues, I achieved excellent results at Raleigh Development Corporation. As a result, you will get a paralegal who can hit the ground running with a minimum of start-up time.
- Because I am well versed in several software programs, I received excellent reviews at Exxon. As a result, you will acquire a paralegal who can minimize unproductive downtime for your clients.

HOW TO RESPOND
Whether you are sending a letter in response to an ad, a networking opportunity, or a blind ad, or the letter is totally unsolicited, the primary

---

Reality Check

Law firms and corporations often run ads for several positions. Use a Re: line to immediately identify the position for which you have applied.

---

purpose of the cover letter is to capture the reader's attention enough to invite you to an interview.

OPENINGS FOR LETTER

There are two ways to open your letter. The first is to promise a benefit to the reader. Describe briefly the advantage you'll bring to the firm. The second is to identify a need that your reader has. Your reader may be searching for someone with a unique specialty. If you are writing to a managing partner, for example, you might open your letter with, "As a managing partner, you know the importance of keeping up to date with current techniques to streamline operations. In my position with the Attorney General's office, I was responsible for creating systems and techniques that accomplished this very task."

HOW YOUR EXPERTISE FITS WITH THE ORGANIZATION

The body of the letter explains why the reader should interview you. If you have completed the Features and Benefits Worksheet, you are already aware of the concepts to present.

First, detail your specific skills or knowledge. If you are just entering the field, explain how your recent education or prior work history relates to your prospective employer. If you are an experienced paralegal, tie in your background to the job skills listed in the ad or to what you've learned about the firm in your research.

- After receiving my certificate from The University of Paralegal Studies, I would like to apply my expertise to the needs of a small firm. I have performed in a frenetically busy environment. As a result, I am expertly capable of managing the demands of a litigation paralegal. I can instantly develop a comforting rapport with attorneys, colleagues, and clients.
- As you'll see on the enclosed resume, I have managed all aspects of pretrial discovery, including complex litigation and database design. Of special value to you, given your need for a litigation case manager, is my expertise in managing all types of business litigation matters, meeting the combined needs of both the trial team and the client.
- After a successful career as a police officer, I was injured on the job. Since my desire was to remain in law, I enthusiastically sought out the paralegal career as a natural alternative to law enforcement. Now, after receiving my degree from Prentice University, I am ready to tackle the challenges this exciting new career will bring. My keen investigative

skills combined with my close attention to detail will be of great value to a law firm such as Hasten and Quicken that specializes in white-collar crime.

DYNAMIC CLOSERS

The next step is to tell the reader how you'll follow up (and make sure you do!). There are examples of this vital step in virtually every sample letter in this book. Here are just a few closers:

- These qualifications, combined with my solid work history, would make me a productive member of your team from my first day on the job. I hope you'll contact me at my home number below as I look forward to meeting with you.
- I would welcome the chance to discuss any openings that may arise. I will contact you next week to explore the possibility of an interview. Or you may reach me at (215) 555-1212.
- I'd like to discuss this opportunity and other ways in which I can bring cost effectiveness to your paralegal program. I will contact you shortly to see when we might meet. I look forward to discovering whether I can assist you and your clients in their legal matters.
- My experience in mergers and acquisitions, securities, and loan agreements equips me to make a significant contribution to your paralegal program. I would be happy to meet with you at your convenience.
- I would welcome the opportunity to discuss with you the numerous benefits my education and background could bring to Acme & Acme. Let's get together to explore these possibilities. You may reach me at (612) 555-1212 any evening after 6:00 p.m.

SAMPLE COVER LETTERS

Cover Letter #1
General

Date

Mr. Bud Rogers, Esq.
Rogers, Johnson & Somers
2345 Natalie Court, Suite 204
San Jose, CA 90803

Re: Litigation Paralegal Position

Dear Mr. Rogers:

   As a litigation paralegal for one of the top U.S. law firms, I have had the opportunity to work with some of the most qualified and respected attorneys in the country. I would like to bring this experience to a growing firm such as yours.

   In return for the opportunity to expand my specialty, I offer expertise in environmental complex litigation and computerized litigation support. I have developed several proven techniques for utilizing paralegals cost-effectively and bring a positive, pleasant manner in my dealings with both high-profile clients and colleagues. I also hold a B.S. degree and certificate from an ABA-approved paralegal institution.

   If you would like to set up a meeting, I can be reached at (408) 555-1212 or you can page me at (408) 555-1313 at any time. I will return your call at once to set up a mutually convenient appointment to discuss this opportunity.

Sincerely,

Sondra Ballantyne

Enclosure (resume)

Cover Letter #2:
To Staffing Organizations

Date

Ms. Mimi Belous
The Estrin Organization
1901 Avenue of the Stars Suite 350
Los Angeles, CA 90067

Re: Full-Time or Temporary Paralegal Positions

Dear Ms. Belous:

The enclosed resume outlines my achievements as an experienced corporate paralegal. Because your organization is one of the premiere staffing agencies in the city, you are certain to be interested in these achievements.

I am seeking a position in an in-house legal department or boutique law firm. I bring a combination of highly developed interpersonal skills along with an expertise in finance. I also possess a sure grasp of current DRE requirements, essential for corporate paralegals involved in mergers and acquisitions. With market conditions driving a strong need for paralegals with this kind of background, I am sure some of your clients will be interested in my resume.

I have enclosed an updated resume that details my work history and education. If you would call me at (213) 555-1212 or e-mail at andy@sim??e.com, I would be happy to meet with you to further discuss job opportunities your firm presents. I am available to interview any time and look forward to your call.

Sincerely,

Andrew J. Johns

Enclosure

Cover Letter #3:
Prospecting

Date

Mr. Phillip Signey
Sr. Paralegal
Munger, Tolles and Olson
333 South Hope Street
Los Angeles, CA 90071

Re: Paralegal Positions

Dear Mr. Signey:

This June, I will receive my paralegal certificate from UWLA School of Paralegal Studies. I have already reinforced my paralegal training with an internship at Bet Tzedek Legal Services. My grades as well as my internship evaluation have been excellent, and I am ready to join a firm such as yours on a permanent basis.

My former career as a teacher has enhanced my ability to pay attention to detail, to work under a sometimes stressful environment, and to juggle multitask assignments. Of greatest value to you, however, is my commitment to the paralegal profession and willingness to do what it takes to get the job done.

If these are the qualities you may be seeking in paralegals at Munger, Tolles and Olson, I hope you will contact me. I will be happy to interview with you at any time and look forward to discussing my ability to work hard under any circumstances.

Sincerely,

Claire de Lune

Enclosure

**Cover Letter #4:
In Response to Article**

Date

Ms. Buni Valentine
American Legal Programs
1228 Capitol Blvd. Suite 100
Washington, D.C. 20001

Re: Paralegal positions within the corporation

Dear Ms. Valentine:

I read with great interest the article about your company in last week's *Legal Times.* I was delighted to see that firms such as yours are as interested in changing consumer laws as I am.

As you'll see on the enclosed resume, the depth of my experience as a financial advisor dovetails nicely with your needs for experienced professionals in consumer banking. As a recent graduate of the Georgetown University Paralegal Program, I have the background to research and analyze the multitude of documents ever present in banking. I am quite certain that my former career combined with my new paralegal career can be of value to your firm.

A personal interview would allow me to demonstrate my talents and show you how my combined background would fit nicely into your firm's practice specialty. Please feel free to give me a call at (202) 555-1212 so that we can schedule a meeting at your convenience to further discuss this opportunity.

Sincerely,

Joyce Brown

Enclosure (resume)

Cover Letter #5:
Networking

Date

Mr. Dallas Raines
Senior Vice President
Peoples National Bank
5454 South Expressway
Memphis, TN 12345

Dear Mr. Raines:

At the suggestion of a mutual friend, Jerri Hall, I am writing you to explore the possibility of working with your organization in the capacity of litigation paralegal.

As a recent graduate of the University of Tennessee Legal Assistant Program, I possess a solid understanding of the requirements an important corporation such as Peoples National Bank would have in order to hire a paralegal. My background as an account representative for a comparable banking institution combined with my paralegal training would be an asset to your company. I also possess a B.A. degree and more than 10 years' experience in the business world.

I would welcome the chance to talk with you to pursue any openings in the paralegal department for which you feel I may be qualified. Please feel free to call me at either number listed above. I look forward to your call.

Sincerely,

Joy Aquino

Enclosure (resume)

Cover Letter #6:
Response to Blind Ad

Date

Paralegal Position
c/o The Daily Journal
P.O. Box 12346
Atlanta, GA 00234

To whom it may concern:

I am writing in response to the ad for an experienced litigation paralegal placed in *The Daily Journal* yesterday. I am a graduate of St. George's University and a student in the Paralegal Institute Training Program in Dalton, Georgia.

With more than five years' experience in human resources and nearing completion of all requirements for a certificate from a very fine ABA-approved institution, I would welcome the opportunity to work for a firm such as the one described in *The Daily Journal's* advertisement. What my resume does not detail is my unique ability as a conceptual thinker and my strict attention to detail. I am also a self-starter and work well in a team.

I have enclosed my resume along with a description of the Paralegal Institute Training Program. I would welcome an interview at which time we can further discuss my capabilities and expertise. Please call me at (315) 555-1212 or e-mail at Linda@coldmail.com at any time. I look forward to hearing from you.

Sincerely,

Linda del Lavin

Enclosure

Cover Letter #7:
Response to Ad Requesting Salary History

Date

Ms. Carol Ann Chudler
Human Resources Manager
Brown, Goldman, White & Green
P.O. Box 1000
Falls Church, VA 78910

Re: Real Estate Paralegal Position

Dear Ms. Chudler:

Your ad in Sunday's *Washington Post* requests an individual who has a demonstrated track record as a transactional Real Estate Paralegal. I believe that my qualifications are precisely what Brown, Goldman, White & Green seeks from this individual.

As my attached resume indicates, I have a solid work history demonstrating increased responsibilities with each position I have tackled. My most recent position, that of Escrow Officer, has allowed me the opportunity to learn about real estate loans, documentation, and, of course, closings. While I would ordinarily be most willing to submit a salary history, please bear in mind that I am seeking an entry-level paralegal position. Therefore, I am eager to enter this field and be paid the market rate for a professional just entering the paralegal field.

Please review my enclosed resume. I would be happy to discuss my work history and how it relates to this significant job opportunity. I am available to interview at a time most convenient for your schedule. I look forward to hearing from you soon.

Sincerely,

Sue Ellen Greenberg

12

Where to Look: Resources, Techniques, and How to Use Them

"We all live under the sky—but we don't all have the same horizon."

—Konrad Adenauer

NETWORKING YOUR WAY TO A JOB—THE HIDDEN JOB MARKET

It's a well-known secret. Everyone talks about it: job seekers, job counselors, job placement directors, even those on the job. You'll hear it over and over: "One of the most effective tools you'll ever have is your network."

That's all very well and good if you've been in the field for a while, but what if you're just starting out? How do you get a network, and how do you use it?

Probably eight out of every ten good paralegal positions never make it to the newspapers. Those eight positions are filled by word of mouth, proving that time-honored saying, "It's not what you know, it's who you know." It's necessary, in this regard, to understand the workplace: Who will have knowledge before your supervisors that you are planning to leave your position? Your friends at the job, of course. When talking with other paralegals, remember: they have knowledge before the firm does that their friend or colleague may be leaving. They will know about openings long before the firm's hiring authorities get a glimmer that there's an upcoming vacancy.

Tapping into that hidden job market takes time, patience, and hard work. The first thing you have to do is meet working paralegals and attorneys. The next step is to earn those people's trust and respect. The final step is to let them know you're in the market for a job.

Probably the easiest way to meet working paralegals is to join and become involved in a paralegal association. Inquire at your paralegal school or local bar association to see if there is a local paralegal association, or a chapter of a state association in or near the city where you live. If none exists, how about starting one? What a great way to meet other colleagues!

137

Once you join the association, you will begin receiving its newsletter, which often contains a job bank or other such member service listing available positions in the immediate area. The newsletter will inform you of any membership meetings coming up. Begin attending the meetings and introducing yourself to people. Become a familiar face. Volunteer to work on committees. Paralegal associations are always looking for people to help plan meetings, prepare the newsletter, take care of membership enrollment tasks, or serve as a board member or officer. Another possibility is to offer to assist with pro bono projects. Pro bono publico is work done by those in the legal profession on a voluntary basis for members of the community who cannot afford to pay for it. Such work could include tasks like helping a women's shelter or domestic violence clinic prepare temporary restraining orders, or helping a senior citizen's home field elder law questions. The point of volunteering to work with the paralegals on these chores (other than, of course, the good feeling you get when you help those less fortunate) is to get to know them better and to let them see the caliber and quality of your work. Many associations also have a yearly "Paralegal Day" where there is some sort of community gathering. Here's another great way to meet the right people.

When a position opens up in the office next to them, these paralegals will think first about mentioning it to the person they have seen work so hard on one of their committees, not to a complete stranger. A side benefit of being involved in a paralegal association is the valuable skills you will learn running and being part of a professional organization.

If there is no paralegal association near you, contact your local bar association. Bar associations sometimes offer associate membership to paralegals and may allow them to attend meetings. It may be a little bit more difficult to get to know lawyers on this basis, so your best bet is to learn if the bar association has any pro bono activities that you could be invited to join. Many projects can be done by a paralegal-attorney team, such as visiting local high schools on career days. The important thing is to get teamed up with an attorney so that you can begin working with someone who may be a potential employer or who could recommend you to one of his or her friends.

And don't overlook the in-house corporate counsel. They have their own association called the American Corporate Counsel Association (ACCA). You can reach them in Washington, D.C. at (202) 293-4103, 1025 Connecticut Ave., N.W., Washington, D.C. 20036-5425 or online at www. acca.com, to find out the nearest local chapter to you. If they won't let you into the meetings, they probably won't protest too loudly to anyone attending their local or national seminars.

Reality Check

Go where lawyers and paralegals go. That's where you'll find lots of information about where the jobs are.

Another great networking resource revolves around your old classmates at paralegal school. If you are an experienced paralegal and lost touch with your classmates, contact your school to see how you might reach some of them.

For recent graduates, some of your classmates may have been hired by a firm they interned with. Some of them may have been legal secretaries who were promoted to paralegals upon graduation. Once those people are established, they may remember someone who was a good student and let you know about any new openings where they are working. Keep in touch with them.

Other key links in your networking chain are your instructors at the paralegal program where you graduated. Many instructors are adjunct faculty members who are actually practicing lawyers or paralegals. Approach any of the instructors who gave you a good grade about their advice on landing a position. If they are not in the market for a new employee, they may have a friend who is. Self-promotion does not come naturally to most people, but in this competitive job market, you have to make the most out of each contact.

Your paralegal school itself may have placement services for its graduates. If it doesn't, there is always an "informal" placement service existing. Many of the lawyers in the vicinity know the director of the program, and may call him or her to inquire after a promising student to fill a new position at their firms. Make sure your program director knows you are looking for a job and knows where to reach you after you graduate. More than one paralegal has gotten a job that way.

SEMINARS

Another great way to meet folks is at seminars—and not just ones geared toward paralegals. Try attending seminars for attorneys, administrators, litigation support staff, MIS staff, records managers, calendar and docket staff, and librarians—*any personnel that will have direct contact with paralegals or are actually the hiring authority.* Nothing is better than to meet someone in an informal setting and do a little "bonding." You can let them know right then and there that you are seeking a paralegal position. (Be sure to have business cards or even your resume with you.) Or you might give them a ring later and find out who the hiring authority is in their firm. Remember, you've already broken the ice.

Another trick is to send the seminar leaders a letter or to talk with them after the seminar (time permitting). They may come from a firm or in-house legal department or be vendors who are in amongst the hiring authorities. It's a safe assumption that they're pretty well connected, or they wouldn't have been asked to speak. They must know someone in law firms.

PRINT MEDIA

The next most common way to find a paralegal position is in one of the various newspapers, trade journals, trade papers, or other publications that contain job listings. The first thing that will come to mind, of course, is your local general circulation newspaper's classified ads. These will usually list openings under "legal assistant" or "paralegal" or perhaps "attorney assistant."

Many larger cities or regions have a legal or business newspaper that is specifically geared toward the legal profession. For example, there is *The Daily Journal* in San Francisco, Los Angeles, and the state of Washington. Washington, D.C., has the prestigious *Legal Times.* We enjoy publications such as *The Daily Journal* because of its interesting people-oriented articles in its weekly *California Law and Business* section.

These newspapers often list lawsuits that have been filed and bankruptcy filings. They will publish fictitious business name filings, default notices, and other legal notices. Along with these services, many of these newspapers contain classified sections that list openings for attorneys, paralegals, and legal secretaries. If you are not sure whether such a legal newspaper exists in your area, check the yellow pages in the telephone book or call a law office and ask someone there. Your local library may subscribe to the paper and keep recent copies there for your review.

Local and state bar associations typically publish newsletters or journals. Usually these are only put out once a month, so any job information in them may be somewhat stale. You may be able to find such publications at a law library in your area.

If you are not limiting your job hunt to your immediate area, another source of potential positions are some of the national trade publications. Following is a listing:

ABA Journal
750 N. Lake Shore
Chicago, IL 60611
(800) 285-2221
www.abanet.org/

This is a monthly journal published by the American Bar Association.

National Law Journal
345 Park Avenue South
New York, NY 10010
(212) 779-9200
www.nlj.com

This is a weekly newspaper. Its classified section, Law Journal Extra, contains on-line job listings at www.lawjob.com.

Lawyers Weekly
41 West Street
Boston, MA 02111
(617) 451-7300
www.lawyersweekly.com

A weekly newspaper.

The American Lawyer
600 Third Avenue, Second Floor
New York, NY 10016
(212) 973-2810
www.americanlawyer.com

A very slick monthly magazine focusing on hard journalism, people profiles, and big cases.

Trial
1050 31st Street, NW
Washington, D.C. 20007
(800) 424-2725
www.atlanet.org

This magazine is published by the Association of Trial Lawyers of America. It has its own job listings at www.atlanet.org/jobbank/openings.ht.

Corporate Legal Times
656 W. Randolph St. #500
Chicago, Ill. 60661
(312) 654-3500

A slick tabloid geared toward in-house counsel.

Law Technology Products News
It's FREE! http://www.ltpn.com
345 Park Avenue South
New York, NY 10010
Fax to (212) 696-1845 to receive a free subscription.

A tabloid with everything you need to know about information technology software and hardware. Mostly filled with press releases from software companies, this publication will give you the latest information on what's new with technology in the legal field.

Legal Assistant Today
James Publishing
3505 Cadillac Avenue, Suite H
Costa Mesa, CA 92626
(800) 394-2626

Just the very best in paralegal information. Of course, the fact that two of this book's authors are regular writers for the magazine helps.

Facts & Findings
National Association of Legal Assistants
1516 South Boston, Suite 2000
Tulsa, OK 74119
(918) 587-6828

Quarterly journal of National Association of Legal Assistants.

National Paralegal Reporter
National Federation of Paralegal
Associations
P.O. Box 33108
Kansas City, MO 64114
(816) 941-4000

Published five times per year by the
National Federation of Paralegal
Associations.

The Paralegal Educator
The Newsletter for
The American
Association for Paralegal
Education
2965 Flowers Road South,
Suite 105
Atlanta, GA 30341
(770) 452-9877

Published three times per year by the
American Association for Paralegal
Education.

The Health Lawyer
American Bar Association,
Publication Orders
P.O. Box 10892
Chicago, IL 60610
(800) 285-2221

A periodical published by the ABA
Health Law Section. $40 per year.

American Bar Association
750 N. Lake Shore Drive
Chicago, IL 60611
(312) 988-5522

Many of the special interest sections
publish periodic newsletters and
journals. Order the ABA Publications
Catalogue, which lists hundreds of
books, magazines, newsletters, and
pamphlets for $5.95, including
shipping.

*Association of Legal
Administrators*
175 East Hawthorn Parkway
Vernon Hills, IL 60061
(847) 816-1212

Publishes a journal, and newsletter
in alternating months, both include
classified employment opportunities.
Also publishes an annual directory
for members only and a very
comprehensive salary survey.
Membership is $200 annually.
Maintains a 24-hour job bank for
members.

Legal Assistant Management Association
2965 Flowers Rd. So. #105
Atlanta, GA 30341
(770) 457-7746
www./amanet.org

Publishes a quarterly newsletter containing employment opportunities, which is available to nonmembers for $45 annually.

Law Office Computing
James Publishing
3505 Cadillac Ave. Suite H
Costa Mesa, CA 92626
(800) 394-2626
www.lawofficecomputing.com

A wonderful magazine with all the latest technology for the legal field. A hands-on resource that legal professionals depend on!

Use your creativity when making use of these publications. *The American Lawyer* hosts a section called "Big Suits" and "Big Deals" by region. Fire off a cover letter along with your resume to the law firms involved, addressing how you read about the suit. Now's the time to inquire whether they can use a paralegal with your excellent blankblank skills to assist them in that suit or deal. Read these directories and trade publications creatively. They can give you a solid information base of who's who and what's what in the industry and keep you current in the field.

Look at the stories for hidden information on employment opportunities. For example, if you read about *Merrill v. Jones & Jones* and guess that this may be a huge case, you may contact either side to see if they can use a paralegal with your skills. Unlike the contents of more general business magazines such as *Business Week* or *Forbes,* trade publications can give you specific information.

Pay special attention to the "People on the Move" or "People in the News" columns. Drop a note congratulating the new promotee and see if there isn't something you can tie in about your background, perhaps the same college, hometown, or even associations. Briefly mention you are job searching.

Also look at the "Special Events" column. Are there seminars, events, or trade shows coming up that you might attend in order to network? Here is a perfect opportunity to work that room.

Don't forget a very important employer of paralegals seeking alternative careers: vendors. Being a vendor does not necessarily mean you wind up in sales (although sales can be a very lucrative position!). It may mean a position as corporate secretary, research and development, software training, deposition services, marketing and public relations, technical writer, trial support, data conversion, document processing, consulting, real estate services, information technology services, or recruiter, to name a few. And don't put down vendors, as is the case with many people in the law firm. Let's just name a few "vendors": IBM; Xerox; Prentice-Hall; LEXIS-NEXIS; West Publishing Group; Pitney Bowes; Hildebrant (consultants to law firms); PriceWaterhouse Coopers; Thompson & Thompson (trademark search); The Estrin Organization; Microsoft.

LEGAL AND OTHER DIRECTORIES

Legal directories list attorneys and law firms by city and state. These directories give a great deal of information about the firms, including the address and phone number of the firm, names and biographical data of the attorneys in the firm, a description of the types of law the firm practices, a list of the cities where the firm has offices, and a list of representative clients. Directories like these are useful. First of all, if you learn of an opening at a particular firm, you can do a little preliminary research to see if it is a place where you would be interested in working. Another use for legal directories is for blind mailings (see the following). Keep in mind that firms must pay a fee to be included in these books. Therefore, you will not find every attorney and firm listed. The local law library in your area should have one or more of the directories listed below.

Martindale-Hubbell Law Directory

This is the granddad of all legal directories, published since 1868. The volumes contain more than 900,000 lawyers, firms, and corporate law departments. The corporate section contains profiles of the companies listed, and a list of the attorneys and their titles. Many of the corporations have a "legal support personnel" listing that gives brief biographical information on the paralegals who work there, their education, and areas of responsibility. If you are interested in working as an in-house paralegal for a corporation, this would be a good place to check to see if the company employs paralegals. *Martindale-Hubbell's* Web site can be found at www.martindale.com.

Best's Directory of Recommended Insurance Attorneys and Adjusters

This directory, published since 1928 by A.M. Best Company, is targeted to insurance companies seeking counsel to represent their insureds. The law firms listed in this directory specialize in insurance defense litigation. Listings are similar to those found in *Martindale-Hubbell.*

Directory of Corporate Counsel

This legal directory is similar to *Martindale-Hubbell*'s corporate law department section. Published by Harcourt, Brace Jovanovich, it lists attorneys who are in-house counsel for various corporations.

Standard and Poor's Corporate Records

Boasting the top corporations in the country, this directory is chock full of valuable information, including tidbits on the legal department.

Million Dollar Directory

Published by Dun and Bradstreet, this publication lists substantial corporations throughout the United States.

Local Business Journals Book of Lists

The *Business Journal* in most cities publishes a yearly *Book of Lists,* which includes the top 50 or 100 law firms in the city or state, along with the Managing Partner or Executive Director. It will also list large corporations in various specialties, such as the largest banks, insurance companies, hospitals, real estate companies, investment bankers, health care companies, and more. Many of those companies have legal departments. Get on the phone and find out!

Parker's Directory

California has a directory that lists all the firms in the state by region, along with address, phone, and fax numbers. Most other states have similar directories.

Parker Directory
121 Chanlon Rd.
New Providence, NJ 07974
(800) 323-4958

Yellow Books

A series of fourteen directories of law firms, corporations, news media, associations, not-for-profit organizations, financial organizations, and federal, state, and other entities. These handy directories tell you who's who in the management of leading corporations, law firms, and other entities you'll need to research.

Leadership Directories
104 Fifth Avenue
New York, NY 10011
(212) 627-4140

Directory of Leading Private Companies

Reed Reference Publishing
121 Chanlon Road
New Providence, NJ 07974
(800) 323-6772

Moody's Industrial Manual

A listing of about 3,000 publicly traded companies.

Moody's Investor Service
99 Church Street
New York, NY 10007
(212) 533-0300

Thomas Register of American Manufacturers

A twelve-volume directory that lists almost all U.S. manufacturers—both privately held and publicly traded.

Thomas Publishing Co.
1 Pennsylvania Plaza
New York, NY 10119
(212) 695-0500

Directory of Legal Employers

A list of more than 1,000 private, government, and not-for-profit legal employers released annually by the National Association for Law Placement. Available in most law school career services offices or for $49.95 from the publisher.

Harcourt Brace
(800) 787-8717

Law and Legal Information Directory

Descriptions and contact information for more than 30,000 law-related institutions, services, and facilities, including bar associations, court systems, law schools, legal periodicals, public defender offices, and more.

Gale Research
835 Penobscot Bldg.
Detroit, MI 48226-4094
(800) 877-Gale

Dun's Directory of Service Companies

A comprehensive guide to service industries, including accounting, legal, research, motion picture, recreational, management consulting, engineering, and architecture services.

Dun's Marketing Services
3 Sylvan Way
Parsippany, NJ 07054
(800) 526-0651

American's Corporate Families
and International Affiliates

More than 1,700 U.S. companies and their 13,000 foreign subsidiaries as well as 6,000 U.S. subsidiaries of international companies.

Dun's Marketing Services
3 Sylvan Way
Parsippany, NJ 07054
(800) 526-0651

Directory of Corporate Affiliations

Divisions and subsidiaries of 4,000+ companies. You'll also get the names of officers at the divisions and subsidiaries.

Reed Reference Publishing
21 Chanlon Road
New Providence, NJ 07974
(800) 323-6772

Dun's Career Guide

Another of Dun's guides, here is a listing of employers by state. One problem with this guide, however, is that it is overly general and may not get you to the legal department.

Dun and Bradstreet Reference Book of Corporate Management

Covering executive bios, from the vice president level on up, this guide offers nice intelligence to be used in your cover letter or interview.

Dun's Marketing Services
3 Sylvan Way
Parsippany, NJ 07054
(800) 526-0651

Source Directory

A great listing of publications—technical, financial, business, and trade.

Predicasts
1101 Cedar Avenue
Cleveland, OH 44106
(216) 633-2938

Standard Periodical Directory

More than 85,000 publications in the United States and Canada

Oxbridge Communications
150 Fifth Avenue, Suite 302
New York, NY 10011
(212) 633-2938

Wall Street Journal

We've never really seen an ad for a paralegal here; however, we've seen plenty of ads for in-house counsel and attorneys for institutions. Chances are, if they need attorneys, they may need a paralegal. It also has great job-hunting articles and right-on-point articles about staffing trends.

Wall Street Journal
200 Liberty Street
New York, NY 10281
(212) 461-2000

Use local newspapers to help you with your job hunt. Find out from your paralegal network whether your region prefers to advertise in a legal trade newspaper or the local city newspaper or both. Remember to think creatively and review articles looking for hidden opportunities. If you are thinking about relocating, go to the nearest newsstand or get on the World Wide Web and research newspapers from the areas of the country you're thinking about.

To find the names of out-of-state newspaper and business publications, check

Gale Directory of Publications and Broadcast Media

Gale Research, Inc.
835 Penobscot Building
Detroit, MI 48226-4094
(800) 877-GALE

This directory is available at many libraries.

If you are seeking an alternative career outside the legal field, you may want to check a directory on trade associations and start there.

National Trade and Professional Associations

Columbia Books
1212 New York Avenue, NW
Suite 330
Washington, DC 20005
(202) 898-0662

National Association for Law Placement

An organization of legal employers and bar associations engaged in the recruitment and placement of lawyers. Where lawyers are hired, so shall paralegals follow.

1666 Connecticut Avenue, Suite 325
Washington, DC 20009
(202) 667-1666

Encyclopedia of Associations

More than 23,000 associations in the United States listed in seventeen categories, including trade, commercial and business, legal, government, public administration, military, and educational. Excellent resource for those paralegals seeking alternative careers.

Gale Research
835 Penobscot Bldg.
Detroit, MI 48226-4094
(800) 877-GALE

BLIND MAILINGS

Many paralegals have gotten jobs by simply mailing their resumes and cover letters to target firms. This is probably the only place in this book where you will find us allowing that a certain element of luck is involved (we place great emphasis on skill and perseverance). Your resume must hit the personnel manager's desk at exactly the right moment. That right moment is within a day or two of (1) a firm paralegal's giving notice; (2) a firm paralegal's having been fired; or (3) the firm's decision to create a new paralegal position.

Your best resource for doing such a blind mailing is one of the legal directories, such as *Martindale-Hubbell*. Peruse the listings in the city or cities where you are interested in working and find firms that practice the kind of law you would like to try. Send your resume and cover letter to those firms, addressed to the attention of the personnel manager. It is an extra nice touch if you call the firm first and obtain the name of the personnel manager or hiring attorney, so that the letter can be addressed specifically to that person. If nothing else, it shows that you are doing your homework!

Reality Check

If you're going to send a blind mailing, be sure you keep track of what resumes went where. Nothing is more embarrassing than not knowing who is calling. (Not to mention its impact on the firm's first impression of you!)

ARTICLES BY AND ABOUT THE FIRM OR CORPORATION

Read, read, read! By scanning the legal trade publications and your local newspaper, you will spot articles about firms, in-house legal departments, and individuals. Appeal to the ego. Let's say the *New York Times* wrote an article on John James, an attorney with White, Brown & Green regarding the fantastic settlement he obtained for the Voirdire Corporation regarding a copyright infringement matter. And, because you just happened to have a background in litigation, intellectual property, or publishing, you send Mr. James a letter congratulating him on his victory. Mention your background and include your resume. Be sure to sell the features and benefits as to why your background fits into his practice specialty. Point out why he needs you: in order to continue his wonderful success! Now is not the time to be shy.

THE OLD BOYS AND GIRLS NETWORK

Everyone is kind to his or her fellow alumni. While you are researching *Martindale-Hubbell* and other directories mentioned previously, be sure to look for schools attended by lawyers. Every time you see someone from your alma mater, mention it in your cover letter to that person. Usually, these resumes will get handled, some even get special attention. It's the oldest trick in the book, but boy, it sure does work!

AMERICAN SOCIETY OF CORPORATE SECRETARIES, INC.

For those experienced paralegals in corporate law, a bump up to corporate secretary in a corporation is a natural career path. The 1995 salary survey conducted by the ASCS showed salaries between $60,000 and $120,000 per year. While 60 percent of those surveyed were attorneys, the remaining 40 percent are nonlawyers such as yourself. Contact the association at 521 Fifth Avenue, New York, New York 10175, or call (212) 681-2000.

AMERICAN STAFFING ASSOCIATION

This granddaddy of staffing organizations can assist you in locating a full-time or temporary staffing organization that specializes in the legal field. Located in Alexandria, Virginia, they can be reached at (703) 549-6287. Call and ask for the membership directory services.

ALTERNATIVE CAREERS

Not all paralegal jobs have the paralegal title. Yet, by reading the job description or recruiting ad, you may discover that the position calls for paralegal skills. These jobs can be found through the normal channels of job searching. However, you'll need to have your investigator's hat on and be well versed with just what paralegals do in order to spot an opportunity. Alternative careers are great for experienced paralegals seeking something different from a traditional law firm or in-house legal department position. These positions are also very suitable for paralegals just completing their certificates.

One good way to find alternative careers is to just read the Sunday classified section of your newspaper. Read each and every ad. Look for jobs that require paralegal skills. Some will ask for contract administration background, real estate background, negotiating skills, research, fact-finding, or knowledge of legal terminology. Here are just a few of the careers found in alternative titles:

- Contracts Administrator
- Policy Managers
- Litigation Support Managers
- Documentation Specialists
- Legislative Analysts
- Financial Services Paralegals
- Regulatory Analysts
- Legal Analysts
- Compliance Officer
- Internet Research Specialist

Sounds like paralegal jobs to us.

Sample Advertisements

Trademark Administrator

We are looking for a take-charge individual who can work equally well independently and in a team environment, someone with strong interpersonal skills who can confidently interact with others at all levels. Responsibilities include planning, administering, coordinating, and implementing administrative processes and projects relating to trademark searches, registrations, renewals, agreements, investigations, and litigation activities. This includes adherence to company guidelines, protection of company interests, and identification of, and compliance with, common-law rights, and foreign, local, state, and federal regulations.

A college degree and at least 3 years' domestic and foreign trademark registration and prosecution experience required. Excellent writing and administrative/organizational skills with attention to detail are essential. Must be computer literate with strong database management skills.

Supervisor, Retail Contracts

XYZ Corporation, a Fortune 500 company, has an opportunity for a Supervisor, Retail Contracts. This position will be responsible for review and coordination of convenience store and retail gas station real estate contracts as well as assisting with branded concept agreements in retail marketing. Close coordination is involved with in-house and outside counsel as well as retail operations management. Candidates should have four or more years' experience in review of commercial real estate contracts, financing issues, and retail contract agreements. Some experience with mortgage and loan processing would be helpful as well as some supervisory experience. A Bachelor's degree is preferred in Business or a related discipline. We offer competitive salaries as well as comprehensive benefits, including a 401(k) savings plan.

Licensing Coordinator

ABC Books Worldwide, a leading computer and trade publisher known for best-selling book brands, seeks an experienced professional to assist our Manager of Legal Services with our growing licensing activities. You will be responsible for handling requests for permission to excerpt from our books, including researching all permissions issues, interfacing with the various departments involved in the process, and following up to assure compliance. The ideal candidate will have a minimum of 2 years' experience with granting permissions and good knowledge of copyright issues. Qualified candidates must possess computer database experience, excellent organization, writing, and interpersonal skills, with strong computer skills.

Paralegal/Research Specialist

San Francisco: Paralegal/Research Specialist at private company. Small, 20-year-old firm provides expert witness services to personal injury and employment law attorneys. Duties include assisting expert in working up cases, conducting on-line and phone research, reviewing/summarizing documents, writing reports. Requirements: Bachelor's degree and at least 1 year of experience. Excellent oral/written English skills, analytical/critical thinking skills. Proficient in WordPerfect 6.1 or higher, experience using database programs.

A very good book on alternative careers for paralegals is "Life Outside the Law Firm: Non-traditional Careers for Paralegals" by Karen Treffinger (Delmar 1995). In it, Ms. Treffinger interviews paralegals with very absorbing and rewarding careers. For those of you open to expanding the role of paralegals, we suggest you check it out.

ON-LINE JOB HUNTING

The newest way to search for a position is over the Internet. Many headhunters and legal staffing companies, attorney and paralegal associations, government agencies, and corporations advertise openings via the World

---

Reality Check

When it comes to alternative careers, we are reminded of the old adage "If it looks like a duck, talks like a duck, and walks like a duck, it must be a duck." Hmmmmmm.

Wide Web. Even large law firms post openings on their Web sites. The rewards for this for these employers is that they are getting job applicants who are already computer literate. Otherwise, they wouldn't be surfing the net!

Web-Based Job Databases¹

The top six job boards, according to the latest data from www.100hot.com (a group that measures the popularity of various Internet services), are the following:

1. Monster Board (www.monster.com)
2. Headhunter (www.headhunter.net)
3. Online Career Center (www.occ.com)
4. Career Path (www.careerpath.com)
5. hotjobs.com
6. jobbankusa.com

Legal Employment Sites (selected at random)
1. The Estrin Organization (www.estrin.com)
2. Law Mart (www.textlaw. com)
3. Attorneys@work legal jobs (www.attorneysatwork.com)
4. Cal Law Legal Classified Index (www.callaw.com)
5. Lawyer's Weekly Classifieds (www.lawweekly.com)
6. Law Journal Extra! Law Employment Center (www.lawjobs.com)
7. NationJob Network Legal Listings (www.nationjob.com/legal)
8. Paralegal Classifieds (www.paralegal-jobs.com)
9. The National Association of Legal Secretaries Job Bank (www.nals.org/bank)
10. NALA (National Association for Legal Assistants): www.nala.org. NALA has a career center. (See articles by the authors on this Web site.)
11. eattorney.com
12. legalstaff.com
13. Lamanet.org
14. lawinfo.com
15. TexLaw Career Resource Center: Paralegal jobs in Texas (www.texlaw.com)

---

¹Source: Law Office Management & Administration Report 1/99.

16. U.S. Justice Dept. Employment (www.usdoj.gov)
17. Legal Employment Search Site (www.legalemploy.com)
18. Commonwealth Employment Opportunities Jobs in Massachusetts (www.state.ma.us)
19. Federal Trade Commission Jobs (ftc.gov/ftc/personnel/jobs.htm)
20. Directory of Legal Recruiters, Legal Recruiters in California (www.callaw.com)
21. Employment opportunities with Kia (www.kia.com/employ)
22. Book of U.S. Government Jobs (www.federaljobs.net)
23. BestSFjobs, Jobs in San Francisco (www.bestsfjobs.com)
24. Findlaw.com

13

Wired for Work: A Guide for Finding a New Job On-Line

"Never before has the future so rapidly become the past."

—Arnold Glasow

We never thought we'd see the day when we welcomed a mouse into the house. Yet, mouse, modem, monitor—the three Ms—are the job search tools you need for the millennium. Gone are the days when you thought use of the Internet was for geeks only. The World Wide Web abounds with career-planning and job-placement sites. How many of them have abundant jobs for paralegals remains to be seen; nevertheless, passing up this resource would be foolish indeed.

The best of them save time and put career choices in your hands by offering easily searchable databases with job listings from around the country and even the globe. Looking for a paralegal job in Europe? Get on the World Wide Web. Search Yahoo (www.yahoo.com) under "employment" or "jobs" and you'll get hundreds of sites at this writing. Try The Riley Guide (www.dbm.com/jobguide) and find a comprehensive index of employment-related sites.

Research some of the legal periodicals and find job-searching areas on their Web sites. Many corporations and law firms post openings directly on their home pages. Some firms list their Web sites in the legal directories. Scan the firms listed in your target city(ies) and look for one that is the size and does legal work in the practice area in which you are interested. Make note of any Web site listed and then conduct a search to see if the firm has any openings for paralegals posted. To get you started, we've compiled a few established sites for both entry-level and experienced paralegals.

The Monster Board: www.monster.com

Well, it's not exactly the kind of name that is associated with staid, conservative law firms. But it is the most frequently visited job site on the Web. Easily searched (job category, location, key word), its listings come from top-notch companies. (In one search, we found offerings from MTV and a few of the Top 10 Law Firms in the country.) You can respond by clicking your mouse and E-mailing a resume to the employer. First, however, you have to register with the site and enter your work history in the "Resume City" database. Here's a handy feature: create a profile of your job needs, and a personal job

157

Reality Check

You can opt to keep your resume and other identifying information private. Not a bad idea, if your employer is also looking.

search agent named "Swoop" (we suppose in a law firm he would be Mr. or Ms. Swoop) will wire notification of a matching new listing directly to your "Profile In Box."

While the site averages 50,000 job listings, only a handful are for a paralegal position. However, it could be a very important handful. Learn to look past the job title "paralegal" and delve into the job description. It could be a paralegal job in disguise!

JOB-SEARCH TIPS

Here are a few tips for job hunting on the Internet. Remember: Keep it simple!

Reality Check

Be sure to read how employers want you to send your resume. Some do not want you to send your resume as an attachment because they are fearful of viruses. Your first test from an employer may be to see if you are following instructions.

- Take advantage of free search agents and E-mail bulletins that alert you to jobs matching your goals. With electronic notification, you won't have to keep logging on to check your favorite job-search sites. You'll automatically be notified. Make sure, though, that you receive notices through personal E-mail and not at your current employer's address.
- Build an on-line resume: There are many sites providing hand-holding and prompts. The builder will ask you to choose from various formats. Fill in the blanks and watch as your resume takes shape. When you're finished, you can copy and paste it into the resume builders of other job-search sites.
- Keep your resume in more than one format. Some employers will accept the on-line resume you've built, but others (mostly law firms) will want to get a hard copy by fax and/or mail. An ASCII format (plain text) is particularly useful. You can attach it to the body of an E-mail or translate it into any popular word-processing format and print.

CareerPath: www.careerpath.com

Here's a site that lets you customize your job search. After registering, you can create a personal home page to save the details of all searches. Sign up to receive E-mail notification of new job listings, and you'll be issued an on-site in-box to help track correspondence with employers. Check off the local and regional newspapers to augment the primary listings; check additional papers you want to search and from which you want to receive updates. Building a resume is relatively easy. All you need to do is copy and paste into blank fields. Privacy is guaranteed. The site reports 250,000 listings, "none more than two weeks old," and covers aerospace, banking, entertainment, law, real estate, and other areas.

CareerMosaic: www.careermosaic.com

There's a "CareerNetwork" section that allows you to pick a job description and canvass a range of industries. If that's too much to handle, view all available jobs within a single industry. If you still can't find what you want, use an index to search listings culled from Usenet Newsgroups (text-posting bulletin boards) across the Internet.

There are on-line job fairs on this site where large employers such as Citibank and Disney display company-wide openings and a career resource center with helpful advice on resume construction. Industries covered include accounting, health care, and insurance.

Headhunter.net: www.headhunter.net

This site promises that information won't be released without your specific permission. It is claiming more than 250,000 job listings; however, we found only around twenty-five paralegal ads. But don't let this deter you! Out of those twenty-five, you might just find the right one! Also, be aware of your alternatives: you may find a position that looks like, acts like, talks like a paralegal position without the title.

The CareerBuilder Network: www.careerbuilder.com

Here is a recent addition to the wired world of job searches. This site includes a "Personal Search Agent" that scans the site's job databases daily for new listings that match your search criteria. When it finds one, you receive an E-mail with a job description and instructions on how to apply. It has other interesting features: "Hot Companies" that are currently hiring, advice on marketing yourself, and "The Relocation Salary Calculator," which lets you select your current city and the city you're moving to, then enter your current salary, and view the salary you'll need to live in your new location. Read the monthly on-line 'zine, *Achieve,* for advice on finding your dream job. Listings cover a host of industries, including biotech, health care, and media, and top-notch companies from Andersen Consulting to *The Washington Post*—many prime targets for paralegal jobs.

Paralegals Classified: www.paralegalsclassified.com

Finally, a site dedicated strictly to paralegals nationwide. While many of the positions listed on the site are excellent, unfortunately, the site does not adequately cover some major cities. For example, Los Angeles, an active paralegal market, only listed two paralegal job listings at this writing.

Reality Check

Be aware that all employers can view your resume there, including your current employer!

However, it's definitely worth checking. There is a free period to view the site; thereafter, there is a small monthly fee.

Hieros Gamos Legal Employment Site: www.hg.org
Here is a site showing other legal employment sites.

WOMEN'S WEB SITES
Here are a few women's Web sites in the general job market (outside legal, specifically) that may be able to offer some solid advice:

Advancing Women: www.advancingwomen.com
Resources: Plan Your Career, Top Markets, Job Growth by Region, Industry Reports.

Electra Career: www.electra.com/caremain.html
Resources: Ask Our Career Advisors, Meet a Mentor, Right Resume, Solution Center, Back to School.

iVillage Career: www.ivillage.com/career/
Resources: A weekly E-mail career newsletter; forums and features such as Assess Yourself, Work Smarter, Work From Home, Dilemma of the Week, Ask the Experts.

Women's Wire Work: www.womenswire.com/work
Resources: Career Quiz, Ask Biz Shrink, Business Travel, Hot Careers, Management Tips, Where to Work, Work From Home, chat rooms, and message boards.

IF YOU GET STRESSED OUT OVER THE WHOLE DEAL
Mark Gorkin, a Washington, D.C., psychotherapist, offers a weekly chat room and biweekly newsletter on stress. He is a national seminar speaker on job-related stress and has lots of experience in the legal field. If you want to just let off some steam, find out about the Web site www.stressdoc.com. We think he's great.

Reality Check

Keep it confidential: If you're looking for a new job but don't want your current employer to know, here are a few pointers to consider when posting a resume:

- Make sure you can keep any identifying information private;
- Find out how to remove a posted resume.

Headhunter.net automatically "purges" resumes after 90 days. It and most other sites offer easy options for deleting your resume whenever you want.

- Get a secure E-mail address from an independent provider. Don't use your office network, which may not be secure. If the site you're using doesn't offer E-mail, sign on with a free Web-based service such as Hotmail (www.hotmail.com). Consider signing up for personal voice-mail as well.
- Know who can view a site's resume database. The Monster Board requires employers and recruiters to pay a fee to gain access, but job seekers can keep identifying information out of sight and get employers to respond to a private mailbox.
- Always ask enough questions through the feedback button or "FAQ" (frequently asked questions) section.

14

Getting a Staffing Organization to Work for You

"The trust that we put in ourselves makes us feel trust in others."

—Francois de La Rochefoucauld

STAFFING ORGANIZATIONS

Staffing organizations, formerly called employment agencies, are big business today, particularly in a thriving economy where the unemployment rate is low. A good economy generally means fewer available candidates. A bad economy, one where downsizing is rampant and the unemployment rate high, provides a wide range of available candidates. An overall healthy economy can force companies to turn to staffing organizations for a wider choice of qualified candidates.

Staffing companies today are more sophisticated than ever before. Offering a wide variety of services, the staffing industry is entering the new millennium ready and capable to tackle the staffing needs of the legal field. Many of them specialize in staffing legal professionals—a key indicator of their capabilities to assist in your job search. Those companies specializing in the legal field can offer opportunities for full-time, temporary, and temp-to-hire positions. Some may even offer additional services such as litigation support, court reporting services, deposition-summarizing services, and additional legal industry positions other than paralegal.

Because these organizations are often run by seasoned legal professionals, an entry-level paralegal can often get good advice and solid career coaching. Recruiters often know valuable insider information such as which firms consider entry-level candidates; who's hiring now; turnover rates (and why); firms and legal departments planning to expand. A good recruiter familiar with firm cultures can also assist you with tips for interviewing with specific firm employees.

If you live in a city offering several staffing companies, it's best to sign up with several. One agency in a large metropolitan area simply does not have all the job orders in town. Signing up with several good ones can speed up your job search process.

Before signing up, however, find out about the agency. Here are just a few questions you'll want to have answered:

- What is the agency's success rate for placing entry-level or experienced paralegals?
- Does the agency also offer temporary or temp-to-full-time opportunities?
- What is the agency's reputation within the legal community?
- What is the background of the recruiters? Are they from the legal field?
- What is the agency's policy toward temporary employees? Is there a personal touch? Or are you "just a number"?
- Does the temporary division pay competitive rates?
- What happens when you call? Does anyone know who you are? Is the call taken or ignored?
- Who are the agency's clients? Are these the firms or corporations on your target list?
- Is the agency employer retained? (This means all fees are paid by the employer.)

Employers utilize staffing organizations for several reasons:

- They do not want the general public to know there is a position open within the firm.
- It is easier, faster, and cheaper to use a staffing organization rather than to place an ad in the paper or to use other traditional recruiting techniques.
- They may want to try a candidate on a temporary to direct-hire basis and want to go through the staffing organization.
- The firm wants to take advantage of a guarantee period—if you don't work out as expected, the firm will get a refund or a replacement.
- Many of the more qualified candidates go through staffing organizations.

Treat the staffing organization as you would any other potential employer. In effect, these organizations are your "agent" and it is important to impress them with your skills, ability, and professionalism so they, in turn, can present a positive image of you to their clients. The more impressed they are with you, the better sales job they can do about you. Staffing organizations are impressed when you show up for their appointment

- on time, ready to fill out the paperwork
- complete with resume, references, and writing samples
- dressed professionally as though you were going to an interview
- with a positive and open mind, asking appropriate questions.

Ask your recruiter how their organization works. (Almost all staffing organization fees these days are paid by the employer. Be very careful if an agency asks you to pay a placement fee.) Some would like you to check with them weekly; some will tell you they will call you instead. Most should check your references prior to arranging an interview and particularly if you are also seeking employment as a temporary employee. The staffing organization handles the arrangements for setting up the interview and often will negotiate salary for you. Do not call the employer directly for anything. Employers choose to use staffing agencies so that they do not have to be on the firing line. They want the agency to handle all inquiries from candidates.

In most instances, if the firm decides to hire you, the staffing organization will also present the offer to you. When a recruiter does call with an appointment for an interview, ask them to give you as much information as they can about the firm:

- Have they placed paralegals in this firm before?
- What is the firm's specialty; how many attorneys/paralegals are in the firm?
- What are the minimum billable hours?
- How long has the firm been in existence?
- Why is this position open?
- What are the benefits?
- What are the responsibilities of this position?
- What software programs are you expected to know?
- What is the firm's culture?
- Exactly where is it located, and where do you park?
- What is the salary range for this position? Does the position pay overtime? Bonus?
- Who does this firm consider to be an ideal candidate?

Most recruiters want you to call them immediately after the interview before they talk with their client about you. They will want to know if there were any "red flags" and if you have any other questions. They will want to know if you discussed salary. They will ask if the firm indicated there was to be another interview. They should pick your brain for exactly what occurred in the interview so that they can successfully negotiate the deal. Be sure your recruiter is skilled, polished, and savvy in the ways of the legal field. Nothing is worse than to have a job opportunity crushed simply because the firm did not like the recruiter.

Establishing a long-term relationship with a staffing organization is good for your career. Once the staffing organization is familiar with you, they will call you from time to time even after you have found a position to present other opportunities to you. Although you may not be ready to make a move at that time, it is always good to know what the market is like. When you are ready to make a move, you already have an advocate in your corner. And, as your career develops and you become the hiring authority, you already have established a good working relationship with a staffing organization that you trust. In that vein, a good recruiter will already know to call you to present the very best and most qualified candidates to you before those candidates get out into the marketplace. A good solid bond with a staffing organization can be a very healthy relationship for all involved.

GUIDE TO LEGAL STAFFING ORGANIZATIONS*

Alabama

Amicus Legal Staffing, Inc.
Birmingham, AL
(205) 870-3330

Special Counsel
A Division of Modis
Birmingham, AL
(205) 870-3330

California

The Affiliates
A Division of Robert Half
International
Palo Alto, CA
(650) 812-9790

Bordwell & Associates
901 Dove Street, Suite 190
Newport Beach, CA 92660
(949) 724-1466

Cushing & Bickerton
595 Market Street, Suite 2500
San Francisco, CA 94105
(415) 495-1492

The Estrin Organization
1901 Avenue of the Stars,
Suite 350
Los Angeles, CA 90067
(310) 284-8585
fax: (310) 284-5733
E-mail: estrin@estrin.com

---

*This list is a partial listing chosen at random.

Landmark Legal Professionals
2055 Gateway, Place, Suite 400
San Jose, CA 95110
(408) 451-3911

Paralegals for Business and Law
Los Angeles, CA
(310) 474-1375

Special Counsel
A Division of Modis
Los Angeles, CA
(310) 649-6389

Special Counsel
A Division of Modis
Palo Alto, CA
(650) 833-5500

Special Counsel
A Division of Modis
San Francisco, CA
(415) 392-9246

Colorado

Special Counsel
A Division of Modis
Denver, CO
(303) 293-0344

Templeton & Associates
Denver, CO
(303) 571-0311

District of Columbia

The Affiliates
A Division of Robert Half
International
Washington, DC
(800) 870-8367

Kelly Law Registry
Fax: (202) 466-8985
E-Mail: McKinro@
kellylawregistry.com

Marsha Levey & Associates
(202) 659-0877 or (703) 519-0900

Paralegal Personnel, Inc.
Washington, DC
(202) 861-0100

Pat Taylor & Associates
Washington, DC
(202) 466-5622

Special Counsel
A Division of Modis
Washington, DC
(202) 737-3436

Spherion
(202) 347-0646

Stone Legal Resources Group
(202) 466-7560

Florida

The Affiliates
A Division of Robert Half
International
Miami, FL
(305) 447-4550

Special Counsel
A Division of Modis
Fort Lauderdale, FL
(954) 764-5474

Special Counsel
A Division of Modis
Jacksonville, FL
(904) 737-3436

Georgia
  The Affiliates
  A Division of Robert Half
  International
  Atlanta, GA
  (404) 264-0810

  Special Counsel
  A Division of Modis
  Atlanta, GA
  (404) 872-6672

Illinois
  The Affiliates
  A Division of Robert Half
  International
  Chicago, IL
  (312) 616-0220

  Paralegal Personnel, Inc.
  Chicago, IL
  (312) 782-8800

  Special Counsel
  A Division of Modis
  Chicago, IL
  (312) 814-0240

  Templeton & Associates
  Chicago, IL
  (312) 644-8400

Indiana
  ManPower
  Indianapolis, IN
  (317) 298-3230

Louisiana
  Amicus Legal Staffing, Inc.
  New Orleans, LA
  (504) 522-0133

  Special Counsel
  A Division of Modis
  New Orleans, LA
  (504) 522-0133

Maryland
  Paralegal Personnel, Inc.
  Baltimore, MD
  (410) 783-1234

  Special Counsel
  A Division of Modis
  Baltimore, MD
  (410) 385-5350

Massachusetts
  The Affiliates
  A Division of Robert Half
  International
  Boston, MA
  (617) 204-9100

  Bickerton & Gordon
  Legal Placement Consultants
  Boston, MA
  (617) 371-2929

  Paralegal Placement Consultants
  31 Milk Street
  Boston, MA 02109
  (617) 482-8515

  Special Counsel
  A Division of Modis
  Boston, MA
  (617) 338-7700

  Stone Legal Resources Group
  Boston, MA
  (617) 482-8515

Michigan
Special Counsel
A Division of Modis
Detroit, MI
(248) 593-6999

Minnesota
The Affiliates
A Division of Robert Half
International
Minneapolis, MN
(612) 349-2810

Esquire Search
Minneapolis, MN
(612) 340-9068

Templeton & Associates
10 South Fifth Street, Suite 990
Minneapolis, MN 55402
(612) 332-8079

Today's Legal Staffing
Minneapolis, MN
(612) 339-2772

Mississippi
Amicus Legal Staffing, Inc.
Jackson, MS
(601) 949-3000

Special Counsel
A Division of Modis
Jackson, MS
(601) 949-3000

Missouri
The Affiliates
A Division of Robert Half
International
St. Louis, MO
(314) 621-2223

The Esquire Group
8860 Ladue Road, Suite 120
St. Louis, MO 63124
(314) 862-1922

New Jersey
Special Counsel
A Division of Modis
Woodbridge, NJ
(732) 750-3331

Topaz International
West Orange, NJ 07052
(973) 669-7300

Update Legal Staffing
Newark, NJ
(201) 622-7575

New York
The Affiliates
A Division of Robert Half
International
New York, NY
(212) 557-7878

HireCounsel
575 Madison Avenue
New York, NY 10022
(212) 605-0570
fax (212) 605-0368
E-mail: hirecounsel
@earthlink.net

The Law Registry
A Division of Kelly Services
New York, NY
(800) 248-4LAW

Legal Assistant Corp.
New York, NY
(212) 557-7900

Legal Options
826 Broadway, 9th Floor
New York, NY 10003
(212) 505-8776

Robert Hadley & Associates
New York, NY
(212) 888-9090

Special Counsel
A Division of Modis
New York, NY
(212) 245-5599

Update Legal Staffing
New York, NY
(212) 921-2200

North Carolina
The Amicus Legal Staffing, Inc.
Charlotte, NC
(702) 529-5590

Legal Placement Specialists, Inc.
Raleigh, NC
(919) 829-2550

Special Counsel
A Division of Modis
Charlotte, NC
(704) 529-5590

Ohio
Major Legal Services
510 Park Plaza
11111 Chester Avenue
Cleveland, OH 44114
(216) 579-9782

Special Counsel
A Division of Modis
Cincinnati, OH
(513) 721-4400

Special Counsel
A Division of Modis
Cleveland, OH
(216) 622-2100

Pennsylvania
Special Counsel
A Division of Modis
Philadelphia, PA
(215) 569-0999

Templeton & Associates
Philadelphia, PA
(215) 772-0555

Tennessee
Amicus Legal Staffing, Inc.
Knoxville, TN
(423) 524-0008

Amicus Legal Staffing, Inc.
Memphis, TN
(901) 762-0111

Amicus Legal Staffing, Inc.
Nashville, TN
(615) 320-7700

Special Counsel
A Division of Modis
Memphis, TN
(901) 762-0111

Special Counsel
A Division of Modis
Nashville, TN
(615) 320-7700

Texas
Amicus Legal Staffing, Inc.
Austin, TX
(512) 494-9111

Amicus Legal Staffing, Inc.
Dallas, TX
(704) 529-5590

kforce
Houston, TX
(713) 439-1077

Special Counsel
A Division of Modis
Dallas, TX
(214) 698-0200

Update Legal Staffing, Inc.
Houston, TX
(713) 650-1000

Virginia

The Affiliates
A Division of Robert Half
International
Alexandria, VA
(800) 870-8367

Marsha Levey & Associates
(703) 519-0900

Washington

The Affiliates
A Division of Robert Half
International
Seattle, WA
(800) 870-8367

National

The Affiliates
A Division of Robert Half
International
(800) 870-8367
www.theaffiliates.com

Co-Counsel
A Division of Olsten
(415) 392-1414
www.olsten.com

kforce
425 California Street, Suite 1200
San Francisco, CA 94104
(415) 434-2410
www.romac.com

Law Corps
(888) 5LAWCORPS
www.lawcorps.com

The Law Registry
A Division of Kelly Services
(800) 248-4LAW
www.kelleyservices.com

Special Counsel
A Division of Modis
(800) 737-3436
www.specialcounsel.com

International

London, England
The Garfield Robbins Group
London, England
44 171 417 1400

Special Counsel
A Division of Modis
London, England
44 171 583 0073

Sydney, Australia
Dolman
Sydney, Australia
61 2 9231 3022

15

Let's Go Surfing!

"Warning! No Lifeguard on Duty"

—seen at every pool in California

*T*here are more Web sites today than, well, Web sites yesterday. Growing at a rate only known to kudzu,[1] the Web has furnished paralegals with an unbelievable wealth of information. Here are just a few Web sites[2] we have found that may assist you in your job search or even in your job. Use these Web sites to gather information about the legal field. Write and ask these vendors if they can use a paralegal with your skills. Remember that many of the vendors listed like to hire paralegals. Even though job listings may not appear on their Web site, you can also track down the hiring authority.

WARNING!!! Be forewarned that once you sign up for these services, you'll most likely experience an onslaught of advertisements, newsletters, listings, messages, and solicitations. Some have been known to generate up to thirty or forty per day! Also, things have a way of rapidly changing since the print date of books. Some services may now charge a fee or may have changed entirely. Of course, the Web sites were valid as of this writing, but like any other service, it's only as good as its volume of subscribers.

The following services and vendors were picked at random.

WEB SITES

There are over 40,000 job boards reported active at this writing. In the recent dot com shakeout, some have been merged, some purged and some downright obliterated. The sites come and go so quickly that from the time we wrote this book until its first edit, many of the sites disappeared. We offer only a few sites picked at random. The best thing to do for an on-line job search is to get on the search engines and type in "paralegal jobs," "paralegal education" or just "paralegal" and check out what comes up.

A.

American Association for Paralegal Education
www.aafpe.org
The American Association for Paralegal Education (AAfPE) is a not-for-profit organization for paralegal schools.

---

[1] An exotic plant seen in Georgia and North Carolina that has been known to grow more than a foot each day.

[2] Information provided by *Legal Assistant Today* magazine Nov./Dec. 1998 and May/June 1999 issues.

American Association of Law Libraries' Employment Resource
www.aallnet.org/services/hotline.asp

American Bar Association and the *American Bar Association Standing Committee on Legal Assistants*
www.abanet.org and *www.abanet.org*
Get information regarding lawyers, firms, seminars, chapter meetings, paralegals, unauthorized practice of law, books, and just about anything else you may need regarding the legal profession

America's Job Bank
www.ajb.dni.us
A nationwide selection of more than 100,000 jobs, primarily in the military and federal government, compiled from state employment offices. Provided by the U.S. Department of Labor.

B.
Bankruptcy
www.bernsteinlaw.com/publications/bankrupt.html
This Web site gives insight into all the legal jargon used in bankruptcy that can sometimes be confusing and frustrating. The terminology is simple and direct. The site contains twelve pages of the most commonly used language in the field. It is a terrific Web site for those who are entering the realm of bankruptcy law.

Barrister's New Javelan
www.barrister.com
Barrister Information Systems Corp. announced Javelan Practice Management System, which creates bills through Microsoft Word.

C.
California Association for Independent Paralegals
www.caip.org
Professional and educational organization for paralegals who work directly for the public without the supervision of an attorney.

California Law Information
www.parkerdir.com
The Parker Directory of California Attorneys has a Web site that lets you obtain information regarding legal services and law schools, expert witnesses, and court reporters in California.

Career Mosaic

www.careermosaic.com

Focuses on information about employers. Lists current openings and regularly hosts on-line job fairs. Many employers in high tech, financial, health care, retail, and telecommunications.

Career Path

www.careerpath.com

Listings from six of the country's largest newspapers.

CareerWEB

www.cweb.com

National job listings and information on developing on-line resumes.

Cornell University's Legal Information Institute

www.law.cornell.edu

LII's collection of recent and historic Supreme Court decisions, hypertext versions of the full U.S. *Code,* U.S. Constitution, *Code of Federal Regulation,* Federal Rules of Evidence and Civil Procedure, and much more.

CT Corporation

www.ctadvantage.com

Corporate and UCC services and corporate compliance solutions.

D.

DocLaw

washlaw.edu/doclawnew:html

DocLaw is a gateway to federal government Internet resources and other government-related material.

E.

Eclipse from LEXIS-NEXIS

www.lexis-nexis.com/xchange

Fee-based service, Eclipse searches are available in nearly all of the files on LEXIS-NEXIS. However, the E-mail delivery option is not available with any version of the LEXIS-NEXIS software. A one-time cost for creating an eclipse search runs between $8 and $105, depending on the library and file where the query is run. With the vast news sources available in the

LEXIS-NEXIS library, the potential for current awareness is overwhelming. If you are searching for articles about attorneys or corporations with which you would like to work, this time-consuming task can be automated to include many more sources than are available to you in print. It's pricey though!

Emplawyernet
www.emplawyernet.com
A nationwide on-line job listing service for lawyers. You can scan the list yourself or have selected listings automatically E-mailed to you. $9.95 per month for job-seekers. Call (800) 270-2688 for more information.

An on-line job search service requiring membership. To date, the service primarily provides job search services for lawyers. However, as we've taught you: where they need lawyers, they're sure to eventually need paralegals!

Employee Benefits Jobs
www.benefitslink.com
Employee Benefits jobs from BenefitsLink™ and its EmployeeBenefitsJobs.com division

The Estrin Organization
www.estrin.com
The Estrin Organization provides professional legal staffing services and corporate training to law firms and corporations. It's also a great way to get in touch with the authors of this book!

E-Span
www.espan.com
A national on-line employment resource that features more than 3,500 current openings.

F.
Federal Job Search Openings by Occupation
www.dsijobs.com/searchjobresults.asp
Federal job search openings by occupation by state

Federal Judiciary Home Page
www.uscourts.gov

Here is the federal judiciary's Internet Web site. The site has facts about federal judges, various types of federal courts and their jurisdictions, from the Supreme Court, Courts of Appeals, and District Courts to the more specialized courts, such as the Court of International Trade, Territorial Court, U.S. Tax Courts, U.S. Court of Appeals for the Armed Forces, U.S. Court of Veterans Appeals, and U.S. Court of Federal Claims. There are organizational charts showing the chain of command all the way from the Chief Justice of the U.S. Supreme Court to the court secretaries. *It also contains information on employment opportunities.* If you are considering a job in the federal court system, this site may be of value to you.

Federal Reports: Paralegal Careers by Federal Reports
www.attorneyjobs.com/paralegalcareers.html
Federal Reports Inc. provides valuable information concerning paralegal careers in both the public and the private sectors.

Federal Trade Commission
www.ftc.gov
The Federal Trade Commission hires attorneys. Check for paralegal openings.

Findlaw
www.findlaw.com
A wealth of linked resources, neatly categorized. Findlaw also provides job search links to many staffing organizations across the country. It's also a great starting point for legal research.

G.
GPO Access
www.access.gpo.gov
GPO Access, a service of the U.S. Government Printing Office, provides electronic access to important information produced by the federal government. The services are free.

H.
Headhunter.Net
www.Headhunter.net
An Internet resume bank for all walks of life, including attorneys and paralegals.

Hieros Gamos
www.hg.org
A searchable database of more than 50,000 law and government URLs, including vendor sites, Hieros Gamos is possibly the largest collection of law-related sites on the Internet.

Hot Jobs.com - Legal Channel
www.hotjobs.com

I.
InfoBeat
www.infobeat.com
For legal and nonlegal information, InfoBeat offers general news from Reuter, entertainment news, and stock updates. Stock updates can be a great tool for job seekers who are interested in checking out a potential employer's stability.

InMagic, Inc.
www.inmagic.com
A flexible litigation database and deposition management software using LiveNote.

Internal Revenue Service
www.irs.ustreas.gov
Don't run! The IRS has a user-friendly site for tax information, statistics, and help. The Forms and Publications sections are helpful.

Internet University
www.internetuniv.com/career
Web site with more tips on resumes, interviewing and researching potential employers.

J.
James Publishing, Inc.
www.jamespublishing.com
Meet the publisher of *Legal Assistant Today*—James Publishing, Inc. This amazing publishing company specializes in practical and affordable how-to-do-it books for attorneys and paralegals. Who knows! They frequently hire paralegals

as editors and in other interesting positions. They are always seeking excellent writers. Here is a great way to launch your paralegal writing career.

Job Board from Vault.com
www.vaultreport.com
A collection of reports from various industries including law. Each report has job listings.

L.
Law Employment Center
www.lawjobs.com
Site for the Law Employment Center, with legal job listings, classifieds, and nationwide ads for lawyers, paralegals, and law support staff.

Law Firms Online
www.ljx.com
Includes press releases. Look for interesting cases. Send your cover letter and resume with your qualifications and explanations as to how you fit.

Law Library Resource Xchange
www.llrx.com
Legal Assistant Today magazine calls this site a "terrific Webzine." It emphasizes research, management, and technology topics for the legal profession. Use it to find leads for law firms and corporations who may need paralegals!

Lawmatch
www.209.67.13.72
An Internet resume bank for attorneys, paralegals, law students, and other legal industry professionals.

Law Office Computing Magazine
www./lawofficecomputing.com
An interesting, cutting-edge magazine all about law office computing. Use it for up-to-date articles on law office technology. Vendors who advertise also like to hire paralegals. Use it as a great resource.

Legal Assistant Management Association (LAMA)
www.lamanet.org.
This national association for paralegal administrators offers a comprehensive salary survey of more than 3,100 legal assistants. The fee for members is $100; for nonmembers, $120.

Legal Employment network
www.legalemploy.com
Links to legal employment on the internet

Legal Profession Job Openings for Washington State
www.wsba.org
Legal professional jobs from the Washington State Bar Association

LegalTech
www.legaltechshow.com
One of the most informative trade shows and seminars dealing with technology in the legal field. This event is held several times a year around the country. Vendors, attorneys, seminar speakers, consultants, educators, paralegals, and law firms all about at LegalTech. Attending LegalTech is a great way to network for a new paralegal position!

LIVEDGAR®
www.livedgar.com
Research M&A, public offerings, employee benefit plans, contracts, and companies.

M.
Martindale-Hubbell
www.lawyers.com
Absolutely *the* definitive directory on lawyers, M-H has launched a new initiative to assist law firms in their use of the Internet to attract customers in need of legal assistance. The new Web site features a searchable database of lawyers and firms with detailed biographies, location information, and areas of practice. Use this fantastic resource to research potential employers. Walk into that interview with more information than you'll ever need!

Monster Board
www.monster.com/
Free to job seekers. Job openings and overview of employers. Mostly technical and sales positions.

N.

National and Federal Legal Employment Report
www.attorneyjobs.com
A monthly listing of available law-related professional positions organized by openings within the federal government in Washington, D.C. and across the country. A supplementary resource for those not focusing their search in selected legal markets. Subscription rate: $39 for three months.

National Association for Legal Professionals (NALS)
www.nals.org
Formerly the National Association for Legal Secretaries, this association provides the PLS (Certified Professional Legal Secretary) designation.

National Association of Legal Assistants
www.nala.org
The Web site for NALA, this interesting site provides news briefs and information on the industry as well as paralegal seminars on the Internet to help you stay current on industry trends.

National Federation of Paralegal Associations (NFPA)
www.paralegals.org
Pages and pages are devoted to career planning in this wonderful site. There is a calendar for seminars and events, legal resources, and a paralegal directory.

NetLizard
www.netlizard.com
Links to federal, state, and international sites providing court regulations and procedures, case law, federal and state government agencies, and international law sites. Check out what's new in the CIA or view the Office of Personnel Management.

NetSmart, Inc.
www.netsmartinc.com
The brainchild of a paralegal and Web consultant, this site provides links to software and technology sites, legal forms, news, financial information, and more. Created to serve the legal community.

Nolo Press
www.nolo.com
This publisher has a wide variety of books in their catalog designed to help you with all aspects of your job. Titles included are "Patent Searching Made Easy," "Paralegal Guide to UCC Filing," "Legal Writing," "Paralegal Discovery," and others.

O.
Oyez Oyez Oyez
www.oyez.nwu.edu
We don't know how this Web site can help you in your job search, but we thought we'd stick it in because it's so interesting. This is a multimedia database about the U.S. Supreme Court. It provides digital audio (RealAudio) of the oral arguments in many important cases. It's well worth a trip from time to time just to see what's there.

P.
Paralegal
PARALEGAL-L@lawlib.wuacc.edu
A paralegal and legal assistant discussion list. To subscribe, send the following message to listserv@lawlib.wuacc.edu: subscribe PARALEGAL-L your name.

Paralegal Classifieds Listing of Job Opportunities
www.paralegal-jobs.com

Paralegal Jobs
www.paralegalclassifieds.com/advertisedjobs.html
A listing of paralegal classifieds around the country

Paralegals
www.bls.gov
Occupational Outlook Handbook from the Bureau of Labor Statistics

ParaSource Inc.

www.parasource.com

A service providing continuing education via seminars and in-house training on a national basis, including Ethics, Skills Development, Substantive Law, and Computers and Technology.

Practicing Attorney's Home Page

www.legalethics.com/pa/index.html

Here is one of the older compendiums of Internet legal resources. It provides searchable links (and brief descriptions) to primary Internet legal resources.

Public Service JobNet

www.law.umich.edu/academic/opsp

Search public interest jobs by location, practice area, eligibility, and type of position.

R.

Recruiter Online Network

www.onramp.net/ron/

More than 1,000 executive recruiters, search firms, and employment professionals offer a resume posting service.

Researchers

www.researchersfyi.com.

A litigation support service providing services throughout the United States.

Shepard's

www.lexis.com

Shepard's Citations Service—citation research. A division of LEXIS-NEXIS.

The StressDoc

www.stressdoc.com

Because job hunting can be stressful, we wanted to point out this free newsletter available to you. Mark Gorkin, the StressDoc, has a specialty in law firm management. You may want to join his chat room on stress. He is also available for seminars through The Estrin Organization. Let him know you found him here!

T.

TechLaw, Inc.

www.techlawinc.com

A litigation support system and vendor featuring consulting, document processing, data conversion, training, and trial support. Approximately twenty offices throughout the country.

Technical Advisory Service for Attorneys (TASA)

www.tasanet.com

Expert witness services free of charge with more than 7,700 categories of expertise. Perhaps some of these experts need paralegals!

TechnoLawyer Listserver

www.technolawyer.com/

Another great way to network! This is a legal technology discussion for attorneys, paralegals, consultants, software developers, and other interested parties. To subscribe, send the following message to commands@technolawyer.com: subscribe listserver.

Telecommuting from Home

www.abanet.org/lpm/catalog

If you are thinking about telecommuting, check out *Telecommuting for Lawyers* by Nicole Belson Goluboff. This book encourages a telework arrangement due to increased productivity in the workplace statistically shown by increased efficiency, improved work product, and increased number of hours employees work.

U.

UnCover Reveal

uncweb.carl.org/reveal

A fee-based service, UnCover Reveal delivers up to twenty tables of contents or key word search strategies weekly to your E-mailbox for $25 per year. UnCover is a free database for searching through more than 14,000 periodicals, primarily nonlegal. Here is a great way to search for articles about potential employers. March into that interview armed with information!

W.
Westlaw

www.westgroup.com

The Westgroup comprises many publishers, such as Bancroft-Whitney; Clark Boardman Callaghan; Lawyers Cooperative Publishing; Westlaw and West Publishing.

WinServices Technologies

www.winservices.com

In conjunction with the National Federation of Paralegal Associations, WinServices Technologies has created the Virtual Law Library for attorneys and paralegals to locate case, statute, and administrative law, recent court decisions, bills, and advance sheets free on the Internet.

Y.
Yahoo!

www.yahoo.com/Government/Law

You cannot tell us you've never heard of Yahoo! We just won't buy it. The legal links area makes a good starting point for a broad search.

Z.
Z-Net

www.adnet.com

Z-net provides instant access to information about downloading sites, how-to tips on computing, freeware, shareware—the whole shebang.

16

Employment Verification, References, and Writing Samples

"The past, the present and the future are really one—they are today."

—Stowe

REFERENCES

You have created a cover letter describing a candidate any future employer would covet. You've put the finishing touches on a resume that bespeaks the highest qualified candidate possible. But, like the Emmy-award winning actress who showed up at the ceremonies in an Armani gown complete with shoes from Payless, you neglected to put the appropriate effort into your references. Whoa! Step back and revamp.

Just what is a reference? A reference is a person who either (1) knows you personally and can vouch for your honesty, background, and sparkling personality; or (2) knows you professionally and can confirm all of the above traits plus your work ethic, proficiency, and team spirit. Recent joiners of the career force and workforce may only be able to provide personal friends and teachers as references. Although teachers may make recommendations, particularly within the academic arena, employers are acutely aware that such recommendations are no indication how a candidate will do in the workplace. Back up academic references with actual experience. Experienced paralegals need to provide references from present and previous positions—and may have to go back as many as three positions. You'll need to draw references from several categories:

Professional References

After you have been in the profession for some time, you will have employers and coworkers to use as references. Consider the following factors when compiling your list of references:

- What is the position of the professional you've asked for a reference? The professional with the highest status and greatest responsibility usually makes the best impression on employers. Be sure, however, that they are familiar with your work. Name dropping can go "name thunking" if that person can't recall you.

187

- What is your relationship to the professional you've asked for a reference? Business relationships that transcend time are the best. Employers look for stability and your ability to deal with people. If time has severed the working relationship, choose someone else. Keep your list current and up-to-date.
- What is the gender and background of the professional you've asked for a reference? Today's buzzword is diversity. If your entire list is one gender or the other, you may be misunderstood. Demonstrate your sensitivity to issues of gender and diversity. Include references from a range of influential men and women.

Academic References

If you are just entering the field, your instructors in college or paralegal school may be of some assistance to you. They can verify what kind of student you were, your enthusiasm, your participation in class, your potential as a paralegal. They cannot, however, translate that experience into business experience.

Internal Endorsement

It gets pretty sticky when you want to make a change, don't want your present employer to know about it yet, but can't get the new job without references from the old. Employers insist upon the most recent references and want to hear about your current skill level and accomplishments. However, many people do not wish their present employers to know they are seeking a position elsewhere. This dilemma can be solved by confiding in a fellow employee, preferably someone high up enough in the company to have clout as a reference, but also someone who can be trusted to keep your secret. There is always some element of risk in doing this, and you may feel more comfortable going outside your current employer for references. If you can confide in someone above you without jeopardizing your position, you might want to ask this person to provide a reference. If there is absolutely no one you can trust with this very confidential information, you may provide your potential employers with references from the past. Upon acceptance of the job, you will be able to provide references from your current employer. This is a tricky negotiation, so make absolutely certain you'll get a great reference. Otherwise, the potential employer has every right to rescind the offer.

THE IMPORTANCE OF A GOOD REFERENCE

There's a lot riding on the employer to hire a perfect candidate. "Mishires" can misfire, causing the employer's reputation to deteriorate, workload to suffer, clients to be lost, and malpractice issues to rise. And there is the cost of turnover, which has been estimated at anywhere between $10,000 and $30,000 in costs to the firm. This cost includes advertising expenses, recruiting time, agency fees, downtime while the paralegal ramps up, and attorney time. By checking your references, employers are seeking reassurance they are making the right hire.

What are potential employers trying to learn when they call your references? Will the prospective employer even bother calling the references? How much will what the reference says weigh in the hiring decision? Who makes the best reference? These are all very valid questions, and ones that should be seriously considered when choosing the references to be placed on the resume.

REFERENCE LETTER MYTHS

Even though you may have a stellar letter of reference from a previous employer, people want to call your references anyway. First of all, they want to be able to ask questions that will pertain to their specific position. Second, and unfortunately, too many letters have been written by the candidate—even though they are signed by the previous employer. Reference letters, while great for the ego, just don't have the impact they used to. And because of the nature of litigation today, a previous employer can be sued by the new employer for giving a great reference for a disastrous candidate.

EMPLOYMENT AND ACADEMIC VERIFICATION

Most potential employers today will seek to verify your past employment. This is different from calling your references. Prospective employers may simply call the Human Resources Department and speak with anyone who can verify facts you have stated on the resume. Generally, they will ask

- Dates of employment
- Salary history
- Title and position
- Reason for leaving
- Whether you are eligible for rehire.

Because of today's litigious society, gaining access to information about your work history is often difficult. Most companies enforce policies that will only confirm the dates employed and salary history. Any other

Reality Check

Just don't lie. If you do, you'll probably get caught anyway. And if references, employment, and academic verifications are completed after your start-date and don't ring true, you may be dismissed from your new job.

Reality Check

Do not assume your references will gladly hand out raving reviews about you! Call all your references prior to listing them. Be sure that

1. You've asked permission from each person to list him or her as a reference;
2. They are not surprised when someone calls about you;
3. They are familiar with your work;
4. Both of you have the same recollection about your position;
5. They will give you a great reference.

information is strictly taboo and could potentially expose the former employer to a lawsuit by you (if they say something less than complimentary about you) or to a lawsuit by a prospective employer (if they give you a glowing report when you don't deserve one).

A reference, however, is a different matter. By listing a person as a reference, you are giving that person license to speak more candidly about you to the prospective employer. The personnel manager will learn much more about you by talking to your references than from employment verification.

Employers can also verify your academic history and degrees. Unfortunately, too many times people will lie on their resumes about receiving a four-year degree, paralegal certificate, and yes, even the J.D.

Case in Point

We recall one candidate whose resume stated she had a B.A. degree from a community college. Although we were puzzled as to how one could get a B.A. from a community college, we tried to verify the degree. Sure enough, this candidate not only did not have a B.A. but also did not hold an A.A. degree. When confronted with the "mistake" and asked to correct it, she told one of our recruiters she would never ever have anything to do with our staffing organization again. Why? Because she had claimed the degree for years and years, and we were the only ones who had the "nerve" to try to verify it. Furthermore, shame on us for not being more understanding of the fact that unless she says she has a degree, she might not get the job she wants.

But what if we asked the candidate how many jobs she has been disqualified for because no one told her they came up empty-handed when verifying her degree? Unfortunately for her, she'll never really know.

A potential employer calling references has several purposes in mind. First of all, she may be looking for third-party confirmation of some of the information in your resume. Primarily, employers are seeking an answer to: Did this candidate actually do what she says? What firms have you worked for previously? Were you actually president of the paralegal association? The employer will be curious about your work ethic. Were you punctual or always late? Did you pitch in and put in the extra hours when a trial was coming up, or did you leave daily at the stroke of 5:00? If asked to do unfamiliar work, did you balk or tackle it with enthusiasm? The employer will seek information on work product quality, your attitude, and your disposition.

Prospective employers know that you are going to paint a perfect picture of yourself in your resume. The only way to get a (supposedly) unbiased opinion of your work is to consult the references. Will they call? Count on it. One of this book's authors was offered a position based on the recommendations of her references. The hiring attorney said, "Your fan club says you walk on water!"

CHOOSING YOUR REFERENCES

If selecting a reference were an uncomplicated matter, most people would put their grandmothers on the top of the list. No one would give you a more glowing report than she. But it's not that easy. Different references have different strengths and weaknesses, and their testimonials must be carefully selected, depending on the intended audience. Your list of references may change, depending on the potential employer who will be reading your resume.

Here are a few examples:

Scenario # 1

You are a litigation paralegal with several years of experience with a few different employers. You are weary of this specialty and have decided to switch to something a little more people-oriented. Responding to an advertisement in the paper for a family law paralegal, you are keenly aware of your lack of experience in this area. The only references you have are former litigation employers. However, you have been volunteering for the last few years at the TRO clinic for the local women's shelter. A valuable reference on this particular resume would be the head of the women's shelter, who could vouch for your experience and skill in dealing with the upset individuals who come to the clinic.

Scenario #2

Applying for your first paralegal position, you are aware of your many different jobs in the past, which you terminated on good terms. Those employers could vouch for good work habits, but the work wasn't necessarily law related. Then you remember that during college you worked for four years in the reference department of the local university library. It was your job to assist students with their research projects in the various law books kept at the library. The head librarian would be an excellent reference.

Scenario #3

You have a lead on a great job with a plaintiff's environmental law firm. It is an area that has always interested you, but you have no working experience in this area. However, you used to put in a lot of volunteer time lobbying for the Sierra Club on a variety of environmental issues. A good reference from someone within that organization may be just what's needed to tip the scales in your favor.

These examples show the need to reach far back in time and into unexpected places for good sources of references. It is a good idea to keep the names, addresses, and phone numbers of the helpful people in your life, whether they are former teachers, employers, coworkers, co-volunteers, clients, or anybody else upon whom you have made a good impression. If you plan to include them on your resume as a reference, it is proper etiquette to call the person and ask permission. This serves a second purpose of warning the person that he or she may be receiving a call from a potential employer about you. This way, the person can be prepared for the call (the response "Now, refresh my memory about Jane. Just when did she say she worked here?" to a call out of the blue does not exactly create the good impression that you hoped for!).

Speaking of impressions, keep this in mind when choosing references: as noted earlier, the more prominent the person, the better reference he or she will be. The head of the paralegal program at your school will be a more impressive reference to a potential employer than one of the adjunct instructors. A senior partner's recommendation will have a much stronger impact than the same words coming from a junior associate at the same firm. Of course, don't list anyone who doesn't know you well enough to give a strong and convincing commendation, no matter how well the person is placed politically.

Following is a sample of a reference list, set up for use apart from the resume:

Professional References
for
Joyce Jones, C.L.A.
1428 SwissAlps Terrace
Boise, ID 00000
(w) (451) 555-1212 (h) (451) 555-1313 (e) Joyce@abc.com

Wendall Wilks, Esq.
Managing Partner
Wilks, Fredericks & Hart
12 Thurmond Lane
Chicago, IL 60606
(312) 555-1212

Anita L. Hill
Professor of Law
University of Illinois
College of Law
145 Summit Drive
Chicago, IL 60601
(312) 555-1414

Deanie Cohen
President
A Parent's Resource
1415 Midvale Avenue
Los Angeles, CA 90064
(213) 555-1616

Note that Joyce does not assume that potential employers automatically have their hands on her address or phone number. On this and on every application and document submitted, make certain your name, address, and phone number appears. Always make it easy for employers to contact you.

TESTIMONIAL LETTERS FROM CLIENTS, SUPERVISORS, AND COWORKERS

When you are doing your job well, testimonial or endorsement letters will cross your desk. These are letters, memos, and other forms of written communication praising you for a task done particularly well. They may come from clients or customers, from supervisors or from coworkers. Besides the immediate self-gratification these letters bestow, they also have another useful function. Store the originals or copies of such written communication away to use when applying for future positions. Nothing impresses a hiring partner more than spontaneous praises about you from completely disinterested third parties.

In the spirit of planning ahead for possible career moves, it is sometimes helpful to request a supervisor or a client who is pleased with your performance to write a testimonial letter or memo on your behalf. A little prompting from you is all they need to make the effort. Even if you never plan to leave your current employer, testimonial letters can come in handy for other purposes, especially at review time! (See Sample Testimonial Letters at end of chapter.)

WRITING SAMPLES

One of the most important requirements of a paralegal, no matter what area of the law you decide to specialize in, is being a good writer. Clear, concise writing will get your foot in the door of a firm even quicker than having knowledge of the firm's area of the law. It is many a manager's belief that anyone can be taught a particular legal specialty, but not everyone can learn to be a good writer. It is for this reason that many firms will request writing samples from prospective employees.

If you are already working in the paralegal profession, you may be asked to present carefully redacted pleadings, memos, letters, contracts, and other legal documents you have prepared for other employers. Make absolutely certain you have permission and are NOT violating attorney-client privilege in any manner, shape, or form. All dates, names, case numbers, places, things must be crossed out. Choose a case that has been closed for quite some time or a pleading that is of public record.

If you are applying for your first paralegal position and did not previously work in careers that required you to write, your best option is to submit materials that were done as part of your paralegal schooling. These could be motions prepared as homework for your legal research and writing class. They could be analysis memos written during a test in your litigation class. When submitting school work as your writing sample, it is beneficial to use papers that received a good grade, with the teacher's complimentary notes scrawled all over them praising your effort and thoroughness.

If you professionally wrote in your prior career and are trying to decide what type of work to submit as a sample, keep your target audience in mind. As a paralegal you will be asked to do such things as:

- Analyze legal research and show how it applies or doesn't apply to your situation.
- Review documents submitted by your client and give the attorney a synopsis of what has happened and what still needs to be done.
- Write a letter to a client explaining a case in clear and simple layperson's terms.

Attorneys and paralegal managers will be looking for writing samples that reflect how skills from your prior career will translate into these paralegal skills. Therefore, when choosing a writing sample, don't submit simple cover letters or inventory lists. Pick a sample showing you have the ability to analyze logically and communicate effectively. Some examples:

- A buyer for a department store writes a memo to her supervisor discussing fashion trends and giving recommendations on what styles the store should feature in its fall line.
- A customer relations supervisor for a building company is asked to investigate a customer's complaints about a new home and write a report to the manager regarding which items fall under warranty and should be fixed and which ones don't.
- A banking customer is unable to balance his checkbook. The account manager at the bank reviews the customer's records, determines what the problem is, and writes a letter explaining to the customer step by step how to correct his figures.

Each of the above-described documents would be an excellent choice to submit as a writing sample. One important rule—always protect the confidentiality of customers and other individuals mentioned in your writing samples by blocking out their names, account numbers, addresses, and other related information.

It is difficult to find decent writing samples in a hurry when you are applying for a new position. Therefore, it is a good practice to save documents of which you are particularly proud in a file, so they will be handy when you need them.

ARTICLES BY YOU OR ABOUT YOU

If a public relations agent specializing in job search existed, she would probably coach you to use any articles written by, written about, or quoting you. Newsletter articles, magazine pieces, house organs, even chapters of books are all good endorsements that you are a credible and worthwhile person. It's probably best to provide professional articles as opposed to a poem or romantic short story. A good time to bring these out is during the first interview, or send them along with your thank-you letter.

Reality Check

There is an awful lot of power in the written word. Attorneys went to school for years to learn how to dispute it.

SAMPLE TESTIMONIAL LETTERS

Elliot S. Smith
P.A.T.H.
918 Fiske Street
Ocean Grove, New Jersey 00000

Date
Susan Peters
1234 Mustard Street
Midtown, NY 00000

Dear Susan:

I just wanted to drop you a note to let you know that I was most impressed with your participation at the People for the Homeless (P.A.T.H.) workshop last Friday.

It's not always easy to set up workshops, let alone make certain that more than 100 people are fed lunch, given materials, and provided child care! It was indeed a miracle in the making to see how you managed to pull this off on limited resources!

Susan, please accept my most sincere appreciation for a job well done!

Best personal regards,

Elliot S. Smith

Managing Director

Richard M. Nixon
President
The White House
Washington, D.C.

June 23, 1972

Mr. Gordon Liddy
The Watergate Hotel
Washington, D.C. 20001

Re: Plumbing Duties

Dear Gordy:

I just wanted to take a moment to tell you how pleased I was with your unique and ubiquitous ability to fix the plumbing over at The Watergate Hotel. And I was most impressed that you had no problem working the graveyard shift. Little did I realize you had such extraordinary talents!

Hopefully, this will turn into something really big. Keep up the good work.

Best regards,

Richard M. Nixon
President

17

Resume Tracking

"Do today what should be done. Your tomorrow may never come."

—Harry F. Banks

The final envelope is licked, and the last stamp is put on. You hear a loud thud as the pile of resumes hits the bottom of the mailbox at the post office. Hold on! Now is not the time to sit back with your feet up and wait for the phone to ring. Follow-up calls need to be made, and resumes need to be tracked. You need to keep tabs on which firms you have sent resumes to so that you do not duplicate your efforts. As a working paralegal, one of your jobs is to keep the attorneys you work for highly organized. Now is the time to keep those skills in practice by organizing yourself.

Form 17-1 shows a resume-tracking table designed to help you with this task. You can create a similar chart using the "tables" feature of your word-processing program. As each resume is sent out, note the date it was sent and the name of the firm or corporation to whom it was sent.

A more up-to-date method of resume tracking is to utilize a good contact manager software program such as ACT! or Goldmine. These easy-to-use, reasonably priced programs allow you to track resumes along with all follow-up calls. You can set the "alarms" and program your computer to sound an alarm on the day, too. The program allows for one or multiple contacts at the firm, phone numbers, faxes, E-mail, action taken, results of last contact, and more. You can even send letters through the program.

When should you follow up on an outstanding resume? A few days? A few weeks? The trick is letting potential employers know you are very interested and enthusiastic without becoming a pest. Personnel managers quickly become exasperated with overeager job hunters who plague them every few days with phone calls or who drop in unexpectedly. That is one way to ensure that you will not get the job. A safe assumption is to allow three days to one week to follow up. This should give the firm ample time to collect and mull over a good selection of resumes. Any more time than that and the resume gets cold, too soon and you may appear to be too anxious.

Sometimes you can take your cue about when to start making follow-up calls from the advertisement for the job. Some positions will indicate a closing date, specifying when all resumes must be received. It is not appropriate to make a follow-up call before that closing date has passed. Most employers prefer to choose from as large a pool of applicants as possible. It is rare that they would begin setting interviews before the closing date has passed. If such a deadline is indicated in the advertisement, you should wait a day or two past that date for the firm to contact you. Then you can make your follow-up call.

If you are doing blind mailings (i.e., not responding to any particular ad in the paper, but just sending resumes out to a list of firms), the firm will not be having to sift through a stack of resumes, since yours will probably be the only one they receive at that moment in time. It is acceptable to follow up the resume with a call a little sooner, waiting five to seven days before calling. This will give the personnel manager time to have received and read your resume, but not so much time that he or she will forget who you are.

With any luck, you may not have to follow up. You may begin receiving calls from the firms to schedule you for an interview. If this happens, note this on the tracking chart or in your contact manager and jot down the date and time of the interview in the appropriate columns. You can use the final column, "Comments/Other," to note the name of the person you interviewed with, any information about when they would be contacting you next, your thoughts about the firm (too big, too small, nice office, etc.), and any follow-up information the firm requested of you.

If you do need to make follow-up calls, note the dates of the calls and the results in the appropriate columns. If the follow-up results in an interview's being scheduled, you can enter that information. If the firm tells you they have not completed the review of incoming resumes, make a note to follow up again in a week's time.

Of course, there is always the possibility that the human resources manager will tell you that the position has been filled or that there are no openings at this time. Although this may sound somewhat final, there is always the possibility that things could turn out differently. Suppose the person who accepted the position was given a huge raise by her old firm and decided not to make the change after all? What if three days after you are told there are no openings, one of the paralegals walks into the manager's office and gives two weeks' notice? These things happen. So if you receive a "negative" response, don't dismiss it too quickly. Very pleasantly express your disappointment by telling the personnel manager how much you would have enjoyed working at the firm. Ask whether the firm would be willing to keep your resume on file for a while in the event another opening comes up. Use the situation to make a good parting impression and sell yourself a little. You never know when these extra efforts will pay off.

CHECKLIST FOR GREAT FOLLOW-UPS

_____ Make sure you have a designated hiring authority's name to whom to direct your resume.

_____ Is your cover letter customized according to the job for which you are applying?

_____ Is your cover letter free of typos and personally signed?

_____ Does the cover letter contain a phone number where you can be reached during the day? Did you include a private voice-mail number? E-mail?

_____ Is the envelope appropriately addressed? (Do NOT send a hand-written envelope—ever.)

_____ Did you enter the data into your contact manager or on your resume-tracking form?

_____ Have you marked your calendar for follow-up?

Form 17-1

Date Resume Sent _____

Position _____

Firm or Company _____

Attention _____

Phone Number _____

Follow-up _____

Results _____

_____

_____

_____

Interview _____

Follow-up _____

Results _____

_____

_____

_____

18

Golden Rules about Appearances

"I base my fashion taste on what doesn't itch."

—Gilda Radner

APPEARANCE COUNTS

Certainly at some point in our lives, we have all picked up the most current magazines and imagined ourselves in the latest rage from *Vogue* or *GQ*. And to wear these delightful garments, we've sucked in our tummies, tightened our bat wings, and shored in our love handles. All the while, listening to our loved ones who have assured us how absolutely stunning we looked. God bless 'em.

Social psychologists studying the impact of image have determined that you have only 30 seconds after someone meets you to form a whole laundry list of impressions about your character and abilities. An informative book about dressing for success by Susan Bixler, *The New Professional Image* (Adams Media 1997), lists the impressions that are created during the first 30 seconds:

- Educational level
- Career competence and success
- Personality
- Level of sophistication
- Trustworthiness
- Sense of humor
- Social heritage.

People base their opinion in those short 30 seconds just on what they see. This includes your clothes, hair, smile, carriage, and nonverbal communications. Like it or not, appearances do count.

According to Bixler, appearances count in cold, hard cash. She cites a study conducted by Dr. Judith Walters of Fairleigh Dickinson University, who researched the impact of an effective business appearance on a starting salary. Dr. Walters sent a group of identical resumes to more than 1,000 companies. Some resumes were accompanied by a "before" photo of the candidate and others by an "after" photo. Each company was asked to determine a starting salary.

Reality Check

Statistics have shown that an individual will have the opportunity to see him- or herself in a mirror or reflection up to 55 times each and every day. That means 55 opportunities to feel positive or negative about yourself. We're opting for positive.

Amazingly, starting salaries ranged from 8 to 20 percent higher as the result of upgrading a mediocre business appearance to one that was polished and effective. Employers are willing to pay for people who look the part. And they are willing to pay handsomely for it.

CASE IN POINT

"Gretchen" was an experienced, high-level paralegal who, after more than 10 years at her job, decided it was time to seek other employment. She was sent to a small firm with a very upscale Beverly Hills clientele. The firm administrator who conducted her first interview fell in love with her. "She is," he said, "by far the most intelligent and knowledgeable paralegal I have ever met." Gretchen had the same reaction. "This is my dream job," she said. "Here is where I feel I could stay until I retire." There was one show-stopping problem the administrator had before he felt he could bring Gretchen back to meet with the partners. "She dressed as though she came right out of the sixties," he said. "There's simply no way our clients will go for this." When Gretchen was presented with the problem, she immediately thought that the firm had an issue because she was overweight. "Not so," said the administrator. "We have people here who are much larger than Gretchen. Believe me when I say it's all about her professional appearance."

So we sent Gretchen to an image consultant who in turn shopped with her, sent her to a hairstylist who cut and shaped her waist-length hair, and sent her to a makeup consultant who instructed her in a more professional look—a total makeover. And, frankly, when she was done, she looked like a million bucks. It was to her credit that she had the character to change what was necessary in order to get the job. And, after a full afternoon with four partners, we're delighted to say she got the job. So far, all parties are happy.

"What should I wear for the interview?" is answered with "always err on the side of traditionalism." There is a caveat to this answer, however, and that is that it also depends on where you live. A red, wool crepe suit could work well for a professional woman in Los Angeles, Atlanta, Dallas, and Chicago but might seem too flashy in the financial districts of New York or traditional businesses in Boston or Milwaukee.

An interview wardrobe is mostly built in solid colors, which offer a more elegant feeling. Both men and women are advised to dress conservatively for the first interview. If you can, find out from your network or your staffing organization what the appropriate dress is for the firm and just how they expect candidates to dress for the interview.

If you are interviewing on a Friday that is casual day, you may still be expected to suit up for the interview. The most important thing to remember is that law firms are generally conservative. However, we sent one candidate from a large city to interview in a much smaller city. The candidate arrived wearing her most conservative suit. Although the administrator was more than impressed with the candidate's ability, she wanted the candidate to understand that the firm did not always dress conservatively and wondered whether the candidate would be better off in a much larger firm. Mostly, however, feelings run just the other way—most firms want to see candidates dressed in traditional, conservative "Brooks Brothers" looks.

ATTENTION GETTING YESES AND NOS

Men's and Women's Attire

Wear professional, conservative attire. Let's define professional attire: Traditional, tailored look without flashy or extremely trendy flairs.

> Stick to conservative colors.
>
> Shine your shoes; make certain heels aren't run down.
>
> Check for missing buttons, hanging threads, correct lengths.

Briefcase

Bring a professional looking briefcase or portfolio. Make certain it is clean, in good shape, shined, and of quality leather.

Hair

Make sure your hair is washed, groomed, and recently cut. *Don't* use highly perfumed hair spray, gels, mousse, or shampoo. If you don't know the environment, stick with conservative haircuts for the interview. *Don't* wear clips or excessive hair decorations.

Tatoos

It's probably best to cover them for now.

Perfumes, Scents, and Aftershave: (Be honest with yourself—have you taken a holiday from hygiene?)

In this day of high sensitivity and allergy-free products, it's probably best not to use any perfume or scents whatsoever. Try to keep everything, including antiperspirants, unscented.

DRESSING TO GET THE JOB

Jewelry

Earrings

Men, unless you are absolutely certain it will be accepted, you may be better off leaving the earring at home. Women, don't wear dangling earrings. Keep earrings small and in good taste. Don't wear heavy necklaces, diamonds, or lots of gold.

Watches

Keep it simple.

Rings

Wear only one (two if wedding and engagement rings), and keep the look simple. Don't wear them on all your fingers.

Bracelets

Wear only one. Keep it simple.

Ankle Bracelets

Forget about them.

Glasses

Men and Women

How long has it been since you've gotten new frames? We know one fellow who wore heavy, silver, '70s-type frames and didn't understand why people perceived him to be, shall we say, somewhat less professional than he perceived himself to be? (He looked like a thug.) When he invested in up-to-date round, thinner, tortoise shell frames, suddenly he was perceived as a very nice looking and intelligent professional.

Women

Manicures and Nail Polish

Make sure your hands are well manicured. Keep nail polish to neutral and classic tones. Nails should be short and professional looking.

Stockings/Hose

Wear plain and neutral stockings/hose. Stay away from patterns, no matter what the trends are. Take an extra pair with you just in case of emergencies.

Makeup
Use neutral and professional tones. Have a makeover at a department store makeup counter. Find out what professional look works for you. Don't forget to touch up your lipstick before the interview. If you have a full or half-day interview with several people, try to touch up in between.

Shoes
Wear low-heeled, closed-toe pumps with heels no higher than two inches. No boots, sling-back pumps, or open toes. Stick to professional, conservative looks. *Don't* wear white shoes. Ever.

Handbags
Carry only what you need. Don't use your purse for extra copies of resumes or work product. That's what your portfolio is for. Make sure the handbag doesn't look as though you've used it every day for the past 10 years. It should be coordinated with your shoes. Polish and clean, if necessary. Keep it light and on the small side, preferably made with good leather. Don't wear white. Stay away from cloth, vinyl, burlap or canvas, rattan, cloth, or plastic. Use a small-to medium-sized bag that closes. Don't walk in with a purse that contains every important item from the last 10 years.

Suits, Dresses
It's always best to "suit up." Think "Brooks Brothers" look. A professional, conservative suit with jacket and skirt or a tailored dress with jacket is preferred even when you are interviewing on "casual Friday"—unless you are told differently. Stay away from short sleeves, even in summer. Keep to light wools or silks and stay away from linen (it always wrinkles). Keep skirt lengths fashionable. However, if the trend is short skirts, keep length just above the knee.

The most conservative look is a matched skirted suit that has the skirt and jacket in the same color. The fabric is traditional and the most formal choice. If you wear a business dress, it may be best to wear a jacket over it. Never, never interview in a sleeveless dress. The message is much too casual.

Large or busy prints are not acceptable. Good, neutral colors are taupe, beige, navy, grays, or pinstripes. Be careful when wearing black. You don't want to look too severe. Make sure there's plenty of lightening of the mood with a white or pastel blouse. Black outfits must be accompanied with black shoes.

Even if you are dressing for spring or summer, be sure to stick to neutral colors. Bright pinks, yellows, or whites are not always wise choices. Keep thinking professional "Brooks Brothers" look, neutral, neutral, neutral, and tailored, tailored, tailored.

There is a lot of controversy regarding whether a woman should wear a pantsuit to an interview. We say if you do, please, please pick carefully. There are now laws in California and other states that make it illegal for an employer to insist that a woman wear only skirts on the job. However, you must know that you may send a too casual message if you wear a pantsuit to the interview. If you do choose to wear the pantsuit, make sure that it is a very professional one, with an upscale, elegant look.

Colors

According to *OfficeSystems97* magazine, colors are often thought to be unimportant. However, studies suggest that colors affect our perception and behavior. Painting pegboard store displays pale yellow results in increased sales. People have a tendency to distrust anyone wearing green (consequently, it should be avoided by job applicants). The eye constricts less for blue light (which is why police cars have blue flashing lights).

Red is an interesting color. Some image consultants warn candidates not to wear red on interviews because it is considered too powerful. If you do wear red, make sure it looks absolutely great on you.

Blouses

Neutral colors win again. If you wear a print, make certain it is not a loud color or large print. Check the neckline. A neckline doesn't have to be plunging to be suggestive. A candidate was turned down for a position because she wore a Vneck that "v'd" just a little too much. The candidate was incensed. She refused to believe the suit was cut too low because, she claimed, it was made by Armani.

Stay Away From

Peter Pan collars; lace; scarves that get in your way; casual pantsuits; boots; flashy outfits; dressy sandals (or sandals of any kind); clothes that are a bit too snug or slightly too large; heels higher than two inches; big jewelry; more than one bracelet; perfumed powders; colognes and perfumes; highly perfumed iron spray starches used right before the interview; gum; brand-new silk sweaters that have a slight "fishy" smell; slips that are too long; no slips; see-through materials of any sort; skirts down to the ankle; torn pantyhose; patterned panty-hose; hair bows; sleeveless blouses or dresses; linen; diamond earrings; political jewelry; fake finger nails; heavy makeup; false eyelashes; worn and torn coats and hats; glitz of any kind; skirts with side splits.

Men and Women Who Smoke

Smokers Beware: Most business offices today do not allow smoking in the building. But bear in mind that the public today is highly sensitive to cigarette smoke. This means that they can smell it a mile away. Even though you think that no one knows, having a cigarette shortly before the interview can be detected. The smell gets into your clothes, hands, hair, breath, and skin. It is highly detectable and unpleasant to many. Try not to smoke anytime too close to the interview.

Men and Women Exiting the Service

While you've probably been advised to wear civilian clothes to interview in the private sector, interviewing in uniform is fine if you are still in the service at the time of the interview. We don't advise combat fatigues, however.

19

The Interview

" 'I can't do it' never yet accomplished anything; 'I will try' has performed wonders."

—George P. Burnham

Congratulations! You've passed the Gatekeeper! Now you're presented with the opportunity to get in and sell yourself. Here is where all your homework will pay off. By this time, you've studied the profession, decided on practice specialties, written a great resume, researched potential employers, and positioned yourself to land that job.

In the best-case scenario, you'll receive a call for an interview sometime between 2 and 10 days from the time you submitted your resume. In the worst-case scenario, you won't receive a call at all. Somewhere in between, you may be asked for a phone interview or you may receive a standard rejection letter. Be prepared to experience it all.

Some candidates view the interview as an exciting opportunity, while others face it with mixed emotions. Selling yourself is no easy task, particularly if you haven't been on many interviews and are unfamiliar with the process. If you haven't interviewed in quite some time and feel out of touch, there's good news. Not much has changed in the actual process. While stricter laws now protect candidates from discrimination and force employers to hire on the basis of skills and capabilities, little else has changed over the past years. Because interviews are so predictable, they're easy to *control*. A potential employer can ask hundreds of different questions, but essentially these questions all lead to the same thing—can this candidate do the job well, and is there a personality fit? Other than that, very little else is relevant.

Candidates who are well prepared by anticipating questions they may be asked will get through the entire process more easily. Nothing is worse than fumbling for answers—particularly while under pressure to demonstrate your capabilities. Rehearse the interview with a friend who acts as the interviewer. Practice answering tough questions. Be certain your friend acts as a critical interviewer and not your friend.

The interview-to-offer ratio improves for those candidates who have diligently prepared themselves for the unexpected. Employers perceive candidates who interview well as most likely to be a better employee. That's because those candidates demonstrate an ability to interact with others and give an excellent presentation of their ideas. Positive interaction gets people hired and recruited for better opportunities.

Reality Check

More impressions are based
upon a handshake than we
realize. Make sure yours is
firm—but not overbearing.

The interview affords you an opportunity to take a random selection process and control it. But don't try out-controlling the interviewer! Your goal is to knock an interviewer's socks off. Programming your mind with effective answers to the most generic questions will enable you to respond to any variations that arise. Rehearse, rehearse, rehearse. Don't fight the process. Work with it. It'll make all the difference in the world.

DOING YOUR HOMEWORK

Once the interview is scheduled, perform a little research on the firm. Using one of the legal directories available, such as *Martindale-Hubbell* (see Chapter 12), look up the firm and read the listing. You will be able to learn a lot. The address will tell you what part of town it's in—ritzy or more working class. A Web site noted in the listing will give you an idea of how on the ball the firm is technologically. The firm may include in its description a list of practice areas, which will give you an idea of the areas of law you may be expected to work. Next will come a list of each of the attorneys in the firm, in order of seniority, with a biographical paragraph or two. Finally will be a roster of the firm's more prestigious clients.

If you are interviewing for a position as a paralegal in the legal department of a corporation, you can do the same sort of homework using the *Directory of Corporate Counsel* or the corporate law department section of *Martindale-Hubbell.* Request a copy of the corporation's annual report, which will give you an overall picture of the entire company. Get on the Internet and research articles about the company and find out what it's up to. Always walk into that interview armed with information—even if you don't get an opportunity to use it. The worst answer to the question, "What do you know about us?" is "Nothing."

Besides giving you an idea of the size of the firm, its culture, and practice areas, such homework can be useful when you are tailoring questions you wish to ask during your interview. If you are able to ask intelligent questions about the firm or company and exhibit some knowledge of its background and structure, you will impress the interviewer as someone who has taken the extra step of doing some homework and preparing for the interview.

THE DAY BEFORE

You've completed your research on the firm or company, and you've figured out what you're going to wear (see Chapter 18). Now you need to start pulling together the things you are going to take to the interview.

_____ Resume
At least five extra copies of your resume. You never know who you're going to meet. If you know ahead of time that the interview extends to more than one person, bring a copy for each. Never assume that the interviewer will have a copy of your resume.

_____ Professional References
No less than three professional references on stationery matching the resume. Must have name, address, firm/company, and phone number (See Chapter 16).

_____ Briefcase or Portfolio
A quality leather case that is shined, polished, and clean. Fill it only with what you'll need for each interview.

_____ Quality Pen
Don't whip out your 39-cent special! Make sure you have a decent writing instrument.

_____ Money
Enough cash to park and make phone calls, if necessary. Don't automatically expect validated parking or free use of the phones.

_____ Extra At-Risk Clothing
Additional pantyhose or tie and shirt, if necessary.

_____ Legal Pad
If you are asked to write information down, you'll be prepared. You'll also want to write up details about the interview minutes after leaving.

_____ Writing Samples
An assignment (with grade and teacher's comments) or actual work product. Make certain all confidential information such as names, places, and dates are redacted (see Chapter 16).

_____ Samples of Articles You Have Written
Newsletters, articles, or papers by or about you.

_____ Emergency Contact Numbers
For the application.

_____ I-9 Documents
Passport or driver's license and social security card or birth certificate.

_____ College or Paralegal School Transcripts
If required.

_____ Logistical Information
Directions to the interview and parking structure, phone numbers of firm and agency, and names of people to meet.

_____ Personal Hygiene Lifesavers
Breath mints (smokers and coffee drinkers are mentioned among the worst offenders), makeup, Kleenex, brush/comb, small bottled water in case of dry mouth (leave the bottle in the car).

_____ Cell Phone
Just in case. (Make sure it is turned off during the interview!)

INTERVIEW DAY

The big day has arrived. Be sure to arrive at any interview 10 to 15 minutes early. Any more than that and you're too early. Any less and you may not have time to complete the necessary paperwork. What paperwork you may ask? Some firms, despite the fact they require a written resume, also want prospective employees to fill out an employment application.

It may have been a while since you have completed an application for employment. You may view this request as an indication the organization does not view paralegals as professionals. Not necessarily!

In today's litigious society, it is incumbent upon the organization to find out as much information about potential employees as is legally possible. In that vein, your signature is generally required for permission to check references and as a validation that you have told the truth. Few organizations are willing to put themselves at risk.

The Application

Because you have brought extra copies of your resume with you, you'll attach it to the application. If you are unclear whether the application must be filled in even though you have a resume, ask the receptionist. Don't worry about how it looks. Be assured, she hears it every day.

Have a black or blue pen with you and any pertinent information not addressed on the resume. Fill in your name, address, phone number, and the position for which you are applying. If you are not required to complete the application in addition to the resume, write "See Resume" across the questions relating to employment history and education. Leave salary history blank unless specifically instructed otherwise.

Complete areas that are not addressed on the resume such as social security number, whether you have applied with the organization previously, whether you have criminal convictions, how you heard about the job, availability dates, and whether you were referred. You may be required

---

Reality Check

Interviewers often make conclusive, sometimes irreversible decisions about you in the first five minutes. However open-minded they are, these first impressions are rarely changed.

to provide a reason for leaving each position. The application or paperwork for temporary work may also require a contact in the event of emergency. Be sure to have the right phone number and address with you. Sign the application in the appropriate areas. Attach the resume and return the paperwork.

Affirmative Action

Affirmative action information may be asked. These answers are optional. Your name is not required. For quite a few years, this form has been required by the EEOC (Equal Employment Opportunity Commission), and any organization may be audited. Changing political climates may eventually eliminate requests for information about the firm's affirmative action program. But if a firm puts the form in front of you, assume the organization still complies with the EEOC. These records are not allowed to be kept with your application. They must be kept in a separate file.

Temporary Employee Confidentiality Agreement

If you are applying for a temporary position, you may be asked to complete a Temporary Employee Confidentiality Agreement upon hiring. This agreement varies from firm to firm but basically ensures confidentiality of information regarding all clients to whom you may be assigned.

Conflict of Interest

A conflict of interest inquiry may also be required. This inquiry is designed to find out whether you may have a conflict with the firm, the matter, the case, or the firm's client. A conflict of interest may question whether you have dealings relating to

- Other firms or corporations involved in the matter
- Participation you may have with the opposing side, such as stocks in the company or past employment, including that of your family
- Specific products or services you may use
- Contact you may have had with the opposing side
- Cases you may have worked on
- And more.

I-9

The Department of Immigration also has a say in the hiring process. You must be able to legitimately work in the United States. This means you are a U.S. citizen, have a green card, or have a valid work permit. The form is called an I-9. This information should be asked after the interview, and most generally, on the first day of hire. Some staffing organizations will ask you to bring documentation to the interview confirming your right to work in the United States. They will also require I-9 information within three days of filling a full-time position. This information is not allowed to be kept in your personnel file. It must be kept separately. You must bring either a passport OR a driver's license AND a social security card OR a driver's license AND a birth certificate. Technically, these documents must be provided prior to the start date. There are serious fines for each I-9 that is incomplete. Don't be surprised when employers insist upon this information.

References
Checking references is standard operating procedure for the majority of employers. However, it's very difficult today to get employers to talk about past employees, no matter how great they were. Firms and corporations may require a signed release from you to check past employment history and academic records. In some states, employers may ask about credit history. This may occur if you are required to handle cash or securities.

Some staffing organizations and human resources departments may ask you to fill out reference-checking "mailers" to past employers. These forms require names of past supervisors, rate of pay, dates of hire and termination, social security number, position held, and reason for leaving. The form also asks for the address or phone numbers of past employers. Be sure to arrive at any interview with this information readily available. (See also Chapter 16.)

Bonding
You may also be asked about bonding eligibility. A fidelity bond covers employers in the event of theft of cash or negotiables. Banks, lending institutions, and firms dealing with financial transactions may require this information. As part of your job duties, you may be asked to become a notary public. Some states require notaries to be bonded.

W-4
If you are seeking a temporary position, you'll probably be handed a W-4 either now or on the first day. Be prepared to answer how many deductions to take. Do not expect the interviewer, receptionist, or new employer to tell you what you should do.

Driver's License

If the position requires driving, proof of a valid driver's license may be required. Be prepared. Paralegals who visit sites or scenes of accidents and those who interview witnesses, for example, may be asked to use their own vehicle.

Proof of Other Licensing

When applying for a paralegal position that also requires another vocation, such as R.N., you may be asked for license verification. Be prepared by bringing the appropriate information.

STRUCTURE OF THE INTERVIEW: THE UNSPOKEN RULES

Most interviews follow a typical pattern. It usually looks like this:

Lobby Etiquette

Greet the receptionist pleasantly. Actually, she's really a spy and reports all candidates with attitudes to the powers that be. If you've copped an attitude, you are now dead in the water. But don't try to engage her in conversation, particularly if she is busy answering phones or typing. If you are wearing an overcoat, hang it up in the outer closet as directed. (Californians and Floridians will have no idea what we're talking about.) Don't choose the cushiest chair to sit in as you may look clumsy getting out of it.

Fill out the required paperwork as quickly as possible. (Take no more than 10 minutes.) On some occasions, the firm may ask you to take a test. These tests revolve around grammar, spelling, writing skills, knowledge of legal terminology, even computer skills. Corporations more than law firms have been known to require an intelligence, aptitude, or personality profile. If you don't take the test, you won't be considered further. An increasingly common test now is the drug test despite public controversy over whether it is legal. If you pass the first interview, you may be asked to report to a medical clinic for a drug test. A recent Gallup poll reported that 28 percent of large corporations (5,000 or more employees) screen applicants for drugs. Don't be alarmed. Firms nowadays want to know exactly what kind of candidate they're getting.

Meanwhile, back in the lobby: Do NOT whip out a book you've brought to occupy yourself—particularly a Danielle Steele novel. (This actually happened.) Observe your surroundings. Is this an environment you might enjoy?

Reality Check

There are only two parts to an interview: The first five minutes and the rest of the interview.

Phase One: Hello! Introductions and Chitchat

Shake hands firmly. Look the interviewer in the eye and SMILE. This is your first physical test. Chitchat as you are led to the office only if encouraged. Sit down where you are shown. If you're not sure, then ask. Put your purse and/or briefcase down on the floor—not on the interviewer's desk. Sit back in the chair—not on its edge. Don't take your suit jacket off unless it's an abnormally warm day and the air conditioning is off. Chitchat will revolve around "nice offices, wonderful view, great art." Do NOT comment on family photos or personal objects in the office. Do NOT mention how hard it was to find the place or how bad the traffic was. Do NOT mention anything personal, such as "I just love your earrings" or "What nice red socks."

While it's true that the first five minutes are critical to your success, don't take that too literally. Focus on creating just the right impression. The most important thing may not be *what* you say so much as *how* you say it!

Typical questions revolve around politeness: Did you find the place OK? (Always yes—you did get there, didn't you?) What's the weather like out there? (Even in a torrential hail storm that just put fifteen dents the size of golf balls in your brand-new Toyota your husband just bought for your anniversary, you absolutely love it.) Do you want anything to drink? (Unless you just crossed the Sahara desert in a sandstorm and your camel died during the journey, don't even think about it.)

CASE IN POINT

One candidate (let's call her Sally) rushed off to an interview scheduled for 9:00 A.M. Not anticipating heavy traffic and failing to scout out an unfamiliar area prior to the interview, Sally wandered into a school, where she illegally parked as she rushed to a pay phone to call and let the interviewer know that she was going to be late. Upon returning to her car, she found she had just gotten a parking ticket for $50! When she arrived at the interview, she was so upset that she prattled on and on to the HR Director about the unfairness of the situation. Graciously, the HR Director offered to pay for the ticket, which Sally accepted. Thinking that she had aced the interview before it even started, Sally then proceeded to deliver what she thought was a great interview. Unfortunately, the staffing organization had bad news for Sally.

Phase Two: You're On—Input from Candidate

OK, here we go with everything we've rehearsed. If you've reviewed the "275 Killer Questions You Just Might Be Asked in the Interview" (see Chapter 20), you're ready. Relax. Smile. First question comin' at you. No,

No! Don't duck. Maintain a professional demeanor and keep the conversation on business. If you wander into personal topics, keep it light. While it's harder to reject someone who has a distinct personality beyond the resume, interviewers do not want to hear about your recent divorce, knee operation, death in the family, or breakup with your boyfriend. You're not there to make a new best friend. You are on the interview to sell yourself professionally and get a job.

Typical questions in this phase generally revolve around education, why you are leaving your present and past jobs, staying power, present and past responsibilities, type of position and environment you are seeking, what you know of this firm.

Phase Three: They're On—Information about the Job and Firm

Here's where your listening skills really come in. Most law firm interviewers do not seem to like candidates taking notes. You are having a conversation, not taking an assignment. Taking notes during an interview is too impersonal and smacks of a contract. Listen as you look for questions to ask later. Listen to what the interviewer is telling you about the firm. Listen to key phrases you can respond to with, "Here's how my skills fit with that."

Typical questions after who we are, what we do, what the position is, and how paralegals fit in this firm or corporation are more technical questions regarding whether your skills fit in and more specific questions to determine whether you can do the job outlined.

Phase Four: About Money—Are We Talking Apples to Apples Here?

Now that you've bonded, here come the salary questions. Usually in the first interview such questions will revolve around two things: (1) how much you are currently making and (2) how much you are seeking. It isn't until the second interview that salary negotiations get under way—unless you are working with a staffing organization, in which case they can negotiate for you.

Phase Five: Do You Have Any Questions?

Of course you do. You didn't do all that rehearsing for nothing. Besides, here's where you want to impress the interviewer that (1) you've been listening and (2) boy, have they got the right person for the job sitting right here! DON'T, however, whip out a list. Tacky, tacky, tacky.

If the interviewer asks whether you'd like to add anything, now is the time to summarize your qualifications and re-emphasize why you are right for this position. Summarize only the main points. A good technique is to number your accomplishments: "There are three primary reasons why I feel this job is right for me. One . . ." This is an old Henry Kissinger technique. Kissinger, of course, is known for his negotiating tactics.

Phase Six: Good-Bye

This next step may involve discussion, reinforcement of your interest, and good-byes to your new Best Friend (just kidding). It's best to wait for the interviewer to indicate he or she is ready to close the interview.

Find out what the next step is: another interview perhaps? Ask when the firm will be making a decision. Will you be meeting more players? Know when to leave. Take your cues from the interviewer. Trying to add "just one more thing" may work against you. Typical questions here include your availability for another interview and/or start-date, references, writing samples, and interest in the job. Shake the interviewer's hand, be sure to look him or her in the eye, SMILE, and say thank you when saying good-bye. Save any hugs for Aunt Millie.

Bye-bye to the Receptionist

Nicely say thank you to the receptionist. Don't forget your coat. Don't ask for a parking validation unless you've already been told to. Smile, smile, smile—and exit.

SELLING YOURSELF

We've all heard the phrase, "sell yourself." Sometimes easier said than done. It's the old "the cobbler's children have no shoes." We are great at selling someone or something else, but when it comes to selling ourselves, we are tongue-tied and at a loss for words.

Selling yourself is no different than selling anything else. Stick to features and benefits of why you are the right candidate for the position. Link what you're talking about with why you should be hired. Don't just state what you did; explain how it fits into the firm. If you are entry-level or changing specialties and your background isn't exactly a perfect fit, be creative. It isn't always the best-qualified candidate who gets the job. It's the candidate who can convince the employer that her skills are appropriate by exuding confidence.

But let's face it. Reciting your work history can get boring. A good sales pitch is one that gets the interviewer enthusiastic about the candidate. It isn't necessary to go into great detail about each and every one of your skills or all of the assignments you have ever tackled. In fact, if you are looking to upgrade your position, de-emphasize those assignments that you don't wish to continue and emphasize those that will move you forward. For example, a senior-level paralegal who emphasizes deposition summarizing and indexing documents shouldn't be surprised if that's the kind of offer she receives. If you are seeking an upgraded position, emphasize more substantive assignments.

The Second Interview

Law firms and legal departments usually follow a pattern of two, possibly three interviews. On the second interview, you will most likely interview with the decision-makers, attorneys higher up on the food chain, or you will meet with your potential colleagues. In either case, this is the most crucial of all interviews. Be at your all-time professional best. You will be scrutinized very, very carefully.

Be aware that many corporate employees have undergone rigorous interview training. At one large corporation, candidates were asked in the interview to name three qualities they possess that qualify them for the job. In the second interview with a different interviewer, they were asked if they recalled what those three qualifications were and to repeat them. Obviously, they were being tested for sanity.

Be prepared to interview with a number of attorneys, paralegals, supervisors, even legal secretaries and other support staff. When scheduling the interview, ask how long it is expected to last and how many people you will see. Be sure to bring plenty of extra resumes with you. You may have to repeat the same story many times. Always attack it with enthusiasm. Don't get annoyed if every interviewer hasn't passed along your information to the next.

Negotiations for salary will be more likely to happen in the second interview. Most offers are made via telephone after the interview; however, some firms and corporations may ask you to come in for a third interview to discuss salary. Rarely will you be asked to accept on the spot. If you are, it's best to go home and think it over to be absolutely sure this is the job for you.

STRESS INTERVIEWS

"Stress interviews" are given by organizations that want to test how tough you are. It may seem to you that the interviewer wants your hide. This person represents the firm or company. Ask yourself, "Do I want to work here?" If the interview becomes abusive, nowhere is it written that you have to sit through it. But if you choose to stay, maintain your sense of humor and don't lose your temper or argue with the interviewer. Stress interviewers honestly believe that they are testing you to see how well you handle stress. It is hoped that these kinds of interviews are things of the past.

How do you handle a stress interview? Let's say the interviewer comments that your schooling is marginal. You might respond by saying: "Some people think my practical experience counts heavily. If you'll review my resume, I'm quite certain you'll see that I learned very quickly on the job. In fact, I was promoted because . . ."

Acknowledge the objection, don't argue with the interviewer, but don't agree either.

THE BEHAVIORAL INTERVIEW

The behavioral interview is the current favorite of those who believe that they are conducting the "new" type of interview. The objective is to get you to avoid canned responses. You can spot a behavioral interview when the question, "Do you have any questions?" is asked at the beginning of the interview. They are trying to see whether you have initiative.

Ask questions that immediately pertain to the position itself and those that will highlight your qualifications. Sound informed and up-to-date on public information about the firm. (Stay away from rumors, of course.)

> I found the article in *The National Law Journal* about your involvement in the asbestos litigation very interesting. It reminded me of my experience with Acme & Jones, where I was the lead paralegal investigating witnesses. What were the key elements to your success in that matter?

If you are absolutely belly-up with regard to information about the firm, its clients, or lawyers, go for expansion plans, utilization of paralegals, or technology. The old 80/20 rule is always good—get the interviewer to do 80 percent of the talking, particularly with those professionals who are not used to doing a lot of interviewing and may be somewhat uncomfortable. This approach gives them the opportunity to discuss what they know best: their work and their firm.

Now is *not* the time to start out with questions regarding vacation, benefits, or salary. You are still in the "here's what I can do for you," *not* the "what's in it for me," mode.

DAY-LONG INTERVIEWS

When some law firms get excited about the ideal candidate, they're sure to bring them back to talk with just about anyone. Sometimes you'll be expected to interview with attorneys or paralegals with whom you may only end up having marginal interaction. But since law firms run on government by consensus, the hiring authority may want to seek as many opinions about you as possible.

The all-day interview is generally a formalized process usually for entry-level or mid-level paralegals. It usually takes the place of a second or even third interview. You may meet with as many as six or eight people in one day. This group of interviewers can range anywhere from senior partners to paralegals to office managers.

The day usually begins with a short meeting with the first person with whom you interviewed. He will generally explain whom you will be meeting. If you are lunching, it will most likely be with the people with whom you will be most closely working.

Part of this process is to see how well you'll hold up. We have seen candidates who actually lose it by the end of the day. The various interviews all run together in their minds, and they cannot get everyone's name straight, let alone their ranking within the firm. This is very dangerous. You are being tested for stamina, personality, memory, and even your ability to concentrate and work under pressure. Now is not the time to get giddy.

Vary your interviewing style somewhat so that you remain fresh and spontaneous. As the day progresses and you've told your story over and over, it's pretty hard to take it one more time from the top, particularly when you are asked (for the seventh time, "Why are you leaving your present position."

- Act as if it is the first time you've heard each question. If nothing else, you'll be in great shape to audition for *The Young and the Restless*.
- Bring at least ten extra resumes with you. Someone may be called to your interview unexpectedly. A paralegal is a little like the Boy Scouts—"always be prepared."
- Be ready for the unexpected interview. Some interviewers are sympathetic to your plight and may just want to concentrate on a frivolous matter or other non-resume-related topics.
- Always, always remember everyone's name with whom you've interviewed. Ask for a business card, if the situation is conducive. Don't make the mistake of saying, "The fellow in the last interview told me . . ."

- Don't hesitate to ask for a bathroom and freshen yourself up. We don't want you looking like Hurricane Hanna by the time you reach the managing partner.
- Use what you've discussed in earlier interviews during later ones. It shows you are paying attention. "When I spoke with Roxanne Jones, she mentioned that paralegals are part of the firm's marketing strategy. How has this worked in your department?"

GROUP INTERVIEWS: IF YOU ARE INTERVIEWED BY A GROUP

Group interviews are used in firms to save time and to test your ability to interact with others. They're tough and sometimes grueling as you have to field questions from three to five or even more interviewers. Here are a few tips on how to handle these groups:

- Stay calm and organized. Don't give long-winded answers.
- One person is most likely to dominate the questioning. However, when answering, be sure to look around the room at each interviewer—not only the one who has asked the question. Don't ignore anyone. Sometimes the one who is the most frail looking and the quietest has the most hiring authority.
- Don't hesitate to make the points you want to make. Too many people go through group interviews passively. They simply respond to questions but don't initiate. Be brief, but don't let the interview proceed as though it were an interrogation. Treat the interview as if it were a regular interview. Don't get intimidated because there are so many interviewers. Ask questions, make points, and sell your skills and wonderful personality.
- Part of the screening process is to see how well you react to the rigors of a group interview. Maintain your sense of humor. Don't get impatient or thrown by different styles and personalities.
- We cannot overemphasize the importance of remembering names. Sales seminars stress the fact that the greatest compliment you can pay someone is to say their name. People just love hearing their name. Be aware of the firm culture, however. Don't automatically revert to a first-name basis if the firm is very conservative and call each other by Mr. or Ms.

LET'S DO LUNCH

The purpose of a luncheon interview or "power-breakfast" is to see how you handle yourself socially. We can't think of anyone who actually likes mealtime interviews, but they are very popular particularly for second or third meetings. Keep the following in mind:

- Stick to innocuous conversation. Don't assume you are being psycho-analyzed. Don't get too personal, and don't get into political or religious topics.
- It's probably best to avoid alcohol, even if your interviewers drink. It's better to keep your mind fresh. Above all, don't order alcohol if your interviewers don't. If you do find yourself ordering a drink, make sure you only have *one*.
- Check out Miss Manners. Don't talk with your mouth full; be mindful of your silverware; put your napkin in your lap; don't reach for the cream; don't put salt on your food without tasting it first; and order middle-priced dishes. Stay away from difficult-to-eat food (spaghetti, crab, finger foods); don't order dessert unless everyone else does first.
- Let the interviewer take the lead in the conversation. A hard sell may not be appropriate. However, do sell yourself by bringing up outside interests that reflect your personality and good character.
- If you are asked an awkward question, turn the question back to the interviewer so you can find out their opinion before expressing your own. Be aware the interviewer may be testing you.

How to Say It

Emphasize Specific Accomplishments

Talking about what a hard worker you are doesn't sell anyone anything unless you can back up your claim with an example that demonstrates how you saved the client fees, found the "smoking gun," closed the deal on time. Be specific. One candidate gave a great example: "On one case, I worked until midnight one night because I was certain that the smoking gun was in one particular stack of documents. Sure enough, right at the stroke of midnight, I found it!"

Always Talk Positively about Your Coworkers, Supervisors, and Attorneys

Bad-mouthing your colleagues is not only in bad taste but will also work against you in an interview. Even the meanest boss can be described as, "He's very tough, but I think that goes along with being a top deal maker."

Be careful how you describe your current atmosphere. Interviewers are convinced that if you are bad-mouthing your current firm, there is nothing to prevent you from bad-mouthing them. Be especially careful not to reveal confidential information about your current employer. That too will work against you. Confidential information can also be construed as, "The firm is having severe financial problems, so I'm bailing."

Don't Apologize

So often, we are more sensitive than others are of what we perceive to be our weaknesses. And many times, our audience doesn't even consider weaknesses what we consider to be weaknesses. We see this over and over again with candidates who feel they may be too old, experienced, or senior. We also see it in those who feel they are underqualified for the position they're seeking. Generally, they start with an apology: "I know this is a position for kids right out of school but . . ." or "I probably stayed too long in my present position. . . ."

Stay away from "buts." If your interviewer has any objections at all, let her figure out on her own what those might be. Don't give her any more ammunition! Stick with the advantages of why you should be hired. For example, "My 14 years of experience as a senior real estate paralegal would be advantageous to this firm because I know how to close deals and how the loans should be processed."

We recently read about a man in his sixties who brought a magazine article to the interview that reported senior citizens have better attendance, more stability, infinite patience, and greater productivity than younger people. He was hired immediately.

Overcoming objections isn't easy. But it is better to turn around and face the tiger than to apologize for who you are and what you stand for. (Even though there are age discrimination laws, it's better to sell an employer on your worth.)

Don't Sound Tentative

"Maybe," "hopefully," "in a way," "might," and "if you will" are tentative words that get in the way of allowing you to come across as confident and positive. And by all means do not use your fingers like little rabbit ears to emphasize a "quote." This gesture turns many employers off. If asked how you like this career, the answer is, "It's terrific!" If asked if you plan to stay in this career, say "yes," not "I hope so," even if you're not quite sure. Technically, an argument can be made that while you're in this position, you are staying in the career. You can always change your mind later. In the meantime, you sound positive rather than powerless.

Don't Lie—Ever

Estimates are that up to one-third of job candidates lie during interviews. Don't make that mistake. If you lie and are found out, you won't get the job. And if you are found out after the interview even if you've already been hired, you could create grounds for termination. Admitting to failures doesn't always hurt your chances of getting the job as much as you may think. Getting laid off or failing at a business isn't necessarily a bad thing for potential employers. What does matter is how you've dealt with it and what you can bring to the table.

If You're Caught in an Inaccuracy

Simply thank the interviewer for pointing out the inaccuracy. "Thanks for pointing that out. What I meant to say was . . ."

CLOSING THE INTERVIEW

Closing the interview is very much like closing a sale. You have to ask for the order. There are two types of closes: a trial close and the actual close. A trial close probes the "buyer" to see if they are ready to buy. In closing an interview, it may sound like: "I'm very interested in this position and know I can make a significant contribution to this firm. Can you tell me what the next step is?" This trial close will probe to see whether the interviewer is prepared to ask you back or make an offer.

An actual close may be a little strong for law firm positions. Toward the end of the interview, a candidate may ask, "Is there any reason you wouldn't hire me?" This close is structured to bring up any objections the employer may have. At that point, the candidate has the opportunity to counter and close with a confirmation, such as an agreement to meet again. Another overly strong close is asking (before you have received an official offer), "When would you like me to start?" These are very hard sells and should be used very carefully, if at all.

As the interview draws to a close, be sure to thank the interviewer. Too often, people are either forgetful of their manners or too embarrassed. You can't lose by thanking someone for spending time with you. It reiterates the message that you are the person for the job. "Thanks Ms. Wilson. I certainly appreciate this opportunity to talk with you about this position. I'm looking forward to meeting you again next week. And I would like to throw my hat into the ring for this position. This sounds like a great firm, and I know I could make a difference here."

20

275 Tough Interview Questions

"For me, hard work represents the supreme luxury of life."

—Albert M. Greenfield

INTERVIEW QUESTIONS

The most nerve-wracking portion of the interview is, of course, answering the many questions that may be posed to you. You may be asked a variety of questions, depending on the skill level of the person interviewing you. Some interviewers are not trained in the art of obtaining as much useful information as possible from a prospective employee. These people may spend much of the interview time talking about themselves and their practice, or pontificating on the firm and its philosophy. You may come away from one of these interviews knowing more about the firm than they learned about you! However, professional personnel managers know just what they need to ask to find out about you, your skills, your background, your attitude, and everything else they will need to know to decide whether you would make a good addition to the firm.

The best way to relax at an interview is to rehearse. With that in mind, we have listed below samples of questions that may be in interviewer's bag of tricks. Pose each of these questions to yourself and think about how you would answer it. If you go through this exercise, you should be able to give a natural, relaxed, well thought-out answer during the interview.

275 Killer Questions You Just Might Be Asked in the Interview

Education
1. Tell me about your college experience.
2. Why did you choose this major?
3. What do you intend to do with your degree?
4. Are you changing your original goals?
5. What was your grade point average (GPA) in college? in paralegal school?
6. Were you an honors student?
7. What was your favorite subject?
8. What was your least favorite subject? Why?
9. Tell me the areas in which you excelled.

10. Tell me your weakest subject areas.
11. Were you employed while attending school?
12. Are you planning to complete college/paralegal school?
13. Why did it take so long to complete your degree?
14. Why did you decide to become a paralegal?
15. Why did you change careers?
16. Why did you choose the ABC Paralegal School?
17. How has your education prepared you for a paralegal job?
18. What professional seminars have you attended in the past year?
19. What are your future educational plans?
20. Does your grade point average reflect your work ability?
21. Name three subjects you learned that could be used in this position.
22. Are you planning to attend law school or grad school?
23. Tell me about your best/worst assignment.
24. Did you participate in a paralegal internship program?
25. What did you gain from the experience?
26. Do you have a paralegal mentor/role model?
27. Why did you choose this person?
28. Are you a CLA (Certified Legal Assistant) or a PACE-registered paralegal (Paralegal Advanced Competency Exam), or have you applied to take either test?
29. How has this certification or registration helped or hindered your job search?
30. How do you react to on-the-job-training?
31. Did you bring college/paralegal school transcripts with you? Can you provide them?

Characteristics and Traits

1. Tell me about yourself.
2. How well do you work under pressure? Please give me an example.
3. What would you do if, during a peak work period, someone dropped a document on your desk and said, "please have this done in an hour?"
4. Do you get bored doing routine and repetitious work?
5. Tell me about your ability to pay attention to details. Please give me an example.
6. What stresses you? What *really* stresses you on the job?
7. Tell me how you cope with deadlines. Please give me an example.
8. How would your past employers describe you?

9. What are your greatest strengths?
10. What are your weaknesses?
11. How would your friends/former coworkers describe you?
12. How do you cope with a changing work environment?
13. Who are your role models?
14. Describe a work situation where you were the "hero."
15. Describe a situation you could have handled better.
16. Describe a situation that demonstrates you are a "self-starter."
17. What are your feelings about a dress code? Casual day?
18. Why should we hire you?
19. Our paralegals are expected to bill 1,600 hours per year. Can you do that?
20. Describe how you would handle an irate client/attorney/colleague/supervisor.
21. Describe how you would handle an overworked, stressed-out, about-to-go-to-trial attorney/client/colleague.
22. What is your greatest attribute?
23. How do you get along with others?
24. Are you better in a team environment or as an independent player?
25. Are you a team leader? If so, please describe an instance that demonstrates your leadership.
26. What would you do if you were faced with an unethical dilemma?

Creativity and Initiative

1. Tell me how you handled the most boring assignment you've ever been given.
2. What would you do if you were handed an assignment you didn't know how to complete?
3. What makes a paralegal successful?
4. Describe an assignment where you took the initiative.
5. If you were in a situation where work was trickling in, what would you do?
6. If you were in a situation where the volume of work was overwhelming, what would you do?
7. How do you motivate a team?
8. How do you go about making important decisions?
9. Can you work without direct supervision?
10. What process do you use when faced with a job-related problem?

Past Employment

1. Tell me about your past position. What were your responsibilities?
2. Why are you leaving your present position?
3. Why did you leave your past positions?
4. Describe your current responsibilities.
5. How does your current/past position relate to the paralegal field?
6. To whom did you report?
7. What do you enjoy most about your current position?
8. Were you required to bill time in your past position? If so, what were the requirements?
9. Why were you downsized? Laid-off?
10. What would past employers say about you?
11. Are you accustomed to working overtime?
12. Tell me about your toughest project and how you handled it.
13. Describe a typical assignment from your last position.
14. Does your present employer know you are leaving?
15. Were you responsible for training/supervising anyone?
16. Why do you want to change professions?
17. Who can we contact for professional references?
18. How did you get along with your boss? Coworkers?
19. Tell me about your last performance review.
20. Why do you want to work here?
21. Why should we hire you over other candidates?
22. What do you know about our firm/company?
23. When can you start a position?
24. What would you like to be doing in five years?
25. Have you ever written any articles/taught courses?
26. Your resume reflects a two-year gap. Did you work during that period?

Skills

(Please note: You may be asked a few of these questions according to the job's practice specialty.)

1. Did you bring a sample of your work product?
2. Can you provide a writing sample?
3. Have you had a legal research assignment?
4. Do you know how to use LEXIS-NEXIS or Westlaw?
5. Are you familiar with federal and state laws?
6. What specialty are you seeking?

7. Do you speak any foreign languages?
8. How would you rate your cite-checking abilities?
9. Tell me about your computer skills.
10. Tell me about your analytical skills. Please give an example.
11. How extensive are your factual investigation skills?
12. Have you ever interviewed a witness?
13. Can you put together closing binders? Trial binders? Exhibits?
14. Have you ever summarized a deposition?
15. Have you ever drafted pleadings?
16. Have you ever attended trial?
17. What do you know about the SEC?
18. How would you prepare for a real estate closing?
19. Can you prepare subpoenas? Notices of depositions?
20. Tell me about the judicial system.
21. Have you ever coded documents?
22. Tell me about your organizational skills.
23. How much experience do you have interfacing with clients?
24. What are your crisis-management skills? Please give me an example.
25. Describe your worst assignment and how to prevent it, if you could, today.
26. Describe an assignment where you were the hero.
27. Do you know your way around the courthouse?
28. What do you know about imaging and scanning?
29. Have you ever formed a corporation?
30. Do you have any experience working with government agencies?
31. What do you know about CERCLA?
32. Have you ever worked on the case/matter? (Checking for conflict of interest.)
33. To what extent have you been exposed to mergers and acquisitions?
34. Have you ever worked with Blue Sky laws?
35. Have you ever Bates-stamped? No? Have we got a surprise for you.
36. How are punitive damages awarded?
37. How do you prepare jury instructions?
38. Have you ever prepared a lease summary?
39. Have you been to/studied Family Court?
40. Are you familiar with products liability litigation?
41. Describe how a trademark is registered.
42. Describe the patent registration process.
43. What is the procedure to file a copyright?
44. Give me an example of your organizational abilities.

45. Describe the differences between Chapters 7, 11, and 13.
46. What skills do you possess to be a great paralegal?
47. Why have you chosen corporate law over litigation?
48. Why are you seeking a position with an in-house legal department?
49. What is the difference between arbitration and mediation?
50. What practice area most interests you and why?
51. What are your strengths?
52. What are your weaknesses?
53. How do you handle last-minute projects?

Salary, Bonuses, Overtime, and Expectations

1. What is your current salary?
2. What is your base salary?
3. Are you compensated for overtime? How much do you receive in overtime pay?
4. Did you receive a bonus? If so, what was it based upon?
5. Do you hold an exempt (not paid overtime) or nonexempt (overtime is paid) position?
6. What salary are you seeking?
7. *Excuse me????*
8. Would you be interested in a temporary to permanent position? If so, what is the hourly rate you are seeking?
9. What was your total compensation?
10. We start all our entry-level paralegals at $_____ per year. (You are expected to respond.)
11. Can you work overtime? (Requires a yes or no answer only.)
12. We offer a bonus based on merit. (You may be expected to ask a few questions here.)
13. Are you open for negotiation regarding your salary requirements?
14. Can you work weekends?
15. Are you available for the night shift?
16. What would you like to be earning in 5 years?

Career Objectives

1. What position do you expect to hold in another 2/3/5 years?
2. What are your plans to achieve that goal?
3. What other positions within the firm are attractive to you?
4. Are you planning to attend law school or grad school?
5. What is your 5-year plan?
6. What thought have you given to your professional future?

7. Have you joined a paralegal association?
8. Tell me about your dream job.

Temporary Employees and Assignments

1. Are you seeking full-time (permanent) employment?
2. Can you commit to the end of the assignment?
3. Can you work overtime?
4. What are your computer skills?
5. Have you ever worked in a temporary position?
6. What skills do you have for this position?
7. Do you take direction well?
8. What hourly rate are you seeking?
9. When does your current assignment end?
10. What guarantees do we have that you'll finish the assignment?
11. Do you need an office?
12. Can you manage others?
13. Are you available on the weekends?
14. What agency do you work with?
15. Can you start tomorrow?
16. Describe an instance where you were required to make an important decision related to a temporary assignment. How did you handle it?
17. Have you ever had an assignment like this before?
18. Can you travel to the document production site?
19. Can you get here on time?
20. When is your time card due?
21. Who is supposed to sign your time card?
22. What would you do if you completed your assignment early?
23. What would you do if you didn't understand the assignment?

Availability

1. Are you available to work overtime?
2. Are you available to travel?
3. Can you complete this temporary assignment by the deadline?
4. How much notice will you give your present employer?
5. When are you available to start a position?
6. Can you start any sooner?
7. When do you graduate?
8. Are you available for work before graduation?
9. Can you relocate?

10. Are you available for training in our corporate office?
11. Are you available to meet with the rest of the staff on Tuesday?
12. Are you available next week for a second interview/lunch with colleagues?

Computer Skills

1. How would you rate your computer skills?
2. What are your computer skills?
3. Tell me the software in which you are proficient.
4. Do you know how to use spreadsheets? Which ones?
5. Can you use a MAC? a PC?
6. What do you know about networks?
7. How experienced are you on the Internet?
8. What do you know about videotaped depositions?
9. How extensive is your knowledge about imaging and scanning?
10. Can you design databases?
11. Have you ever coded documents?
12. What legal forms software packages do you know?
13. Do you know Windows 98? Windows 2000?
14. Do you know Office 99? Office 2000?
15. Are you familiar with SQL?
16. Are you familiar with graphics packages?
17. Tell me about your technology expertise.
18. Tell me about your litigation support expertise.
19. Are you a fast learner?
20. How many year's experience with computers do you have?
21. How did you use the computer on your last job?
22. Do you have good data entry skills?
23. Tell me about your legal research skills.
24. Are you familiar with WordPerfect or Word?
25. Do you have a computer at home? A modem? Fax? DSL?
26. Do you own a laptop computer?
27. Do you consider yourself computer literate?
28. How up-to-date are your computer skills?
29. How do you keep yourself informed about the latest technology changes?
30. Are you familiar with EDGAR?
31. What is HTML?
32. Have you ever used Lotus Live Notes?

33. What is Explorer?
34. What do you know about Java?
35. Yahoo is not a term used by cowboys. What would you say it is?
36. How have you used these services?
37. Are you comfortable asking for help when learning a new program? Or do you tend to "tough it out"?
38. What experience do you have with E-mail?
39. What is LAN/WAN?
40. What is your opinion regarding copyright, privacy, and First Amendment rights concerning the Internet?
41. Do you think the Internet is misused?
42. Where do you think technology in the legal field is headed?
43. What do you know about computers in the courtroom?
44. How has technology impacted billable hours?
45. What is a browser?
46. What technology periodicals do you read?
47. How did you first learn to use a computer?
48. Can you use the redlining features?
49. Do you know how to burn a CD?
50. Did you take any computer science courses in paralegal school?
51. Are you familiar with any of the latest litigation support software? Which ones?

Reality Check

A candidate was asked by an employer to submit two writing samples. She sent back two paragraphs. One she handwrote, the other she printed. We don't think she got the job.

Americans with Disabilities Act

1. Is there any reason why you cannot perform your duties?

This question should not be asked any other way. The question requires a yes or no answer. (See illegal questions.)

QUESTIONS CANDIDATES CAN ASK DURING THE INTERVIEW

No matter what, be sure to ask questions. After the interviewer explains the position, benefits, and history of the firm, he or she may ask if you have any questions. If the candidate says "no," the interviewer may think the candidate does not go beyond what is presented or shows little interest. Of course, if you have had an extensive dialogue and the question is really asking, "Do you have any *further* questions?," you may be better off not extending the interview.

However, if you have talked a little about yourself, then listened as the interviewer explained the position, it's probably better to ask at least one or two questions. Make certain the question is related to

- Job responsibilities
- Information about the firm that might affect your position, such as expansion plans, new specialty areas, new laws
- Other areas of the firm that may affect your position, such as MIS, litigation support, word processing.

In this phase of the interview, stay away from "what's in it for me" questions such as

- "When do I go on vacation?"
- "When are salary reviews?"
- "Do you pay for parking?"
- "Do I get an office?" "Does it have a window?"

While these are questions that eventually need answers, now is *not* the time. You must *first* sell the employer on your skills and abilities to do the job. You'll find out quickly enough what goodies the firm will bestow upon you. This information will be important to you in order to negotiate the total compensation package.

Stay focused on what has been said, no matter how nervous you might be. Come prepared, armed with background information on the firm as well as questions to ask the interviewer. Don't take out a list though! Many attorneys and law office staff find a list suspect. Interviewers prefer to participate in friendly conversation rather than an inquisition. Here are a number of appropriate questions. Two to four questions should be more than enough. The time to ask about benefits such as vacation, parking, or tuition reimbursement is during a second interview or toward the end of the first interview and before salary negotiations. Asking too soon about benefits risks a hidden message, "OK, enough about you, what about me?," which doesn't exactly help to get the job.

The Firm/Corporation
1. What is the structure of the firm or in-house legal department?
2. Who is the person paralegals report to?
3. How long has the firm/legal department used paralegals?
4. What is the history of the firm/company?

5. How many attorneys are in the practice specialty?
6. What is the ratio of paralegals to attorneys?
7. What are the practice specialties of the firm/legal department?
8. How many employees does the firm/corporation have?
9. Do paralegals work with senior partners?
10. How are paralegals assigned work?
11. Is the paralegal program a profit center?
12. What are the number of required billable hours?
13. Does the firm/corporation handle pro bono work?
14. If so, are paralegals involved?
15. Does the firm/corporation have branch offices? If so, where?
16. What is the firm's philosophy regarding technology?
17. Are paralegals responsible for administrative time? If so, what kinds of duties are involved?
18. Will I have an office?
19. Tell me about secretarial support for paralegals.

Paralegals in the Firm/Corporation

1. How many paralegals are in the firm/corporation?
2. Have paralegals been promoted into other positions within the firm/corporation?
3. How many attorneys or paralegals have been promoted to vice president in this company?
4. Do paralegals meet on a regular basis?
5. Are paralegals included in department meetings? Client meetings?
6. Who supervises the paralegal's work?
7. Where do I go if I have questions?
8. How do paralegals receive assignments?
9. Do paralegals use the Internet?
10. Do paralegals perform legal research?
11. Do paralegals draft documents in this firm/corporation?
12. Does the firm/corporation offer continuing education or in-house training?
13. Do paralegals attend trial?
14. Do paralegals attend depositions?
15. Do paralegals have access to secretaries or word-processing support?
16. Does the firm/corporation have a litigation support department?
17. Does the legal department work separately from other departments in this company?

18. Can you tell me how paralegals receive updated information regarding laws, technology and clients?
19. Does each paralegal have a computer?
20. Can you describe the culture of the firm?
21. What are the long-term plans of the firm/corporation?
22. Has the level of paralegal assignments progressed over the years?
23. What is the average tenure of the paralegals here?
24. Does the firm have a career path for its paralegals?

The Position

1. Can you describe a typical assignment?
2. Can you describe a typical day in the life of a paralegal in this position?
3. Does the position have a full pipeline of work?
4. How many attorneys and paralegals will I work with?
5. Why is this position open?
6. How many paralegals have held this position in the past 5 years?
7. What are the computer skills required for this position?
8. If the senior partners retire, does the firm continue on?
9. What do you expect this paralegal to accomplish?
10. Will I cross-train in other practice areas of the firm?
11. What access do paralegals have to word processing?
12. What access do paralegals have to the law library?
13. How long has this position been open?
14. What are the precise characteristics to be a successful candidate?
15. What is the skill level required for this position?
16. What software packages will I be expected to know?
17. Does the firm/corporation have a structured paralegal program?
18. What is the hiring process?
19. Would you like a writing sample?
20. Does the firm have a training program for entry-level paralegals?
21. Is the relationship between managing partners and paralegals favorable?
22. What are the most important duties in this position?
23. What causes a paralegal to fail in this position?
24. How is my performance evaluated?
25. What opportunities are there for advancement?
26. I have some interests outside work. Will I be able to pursue these after hours?

27. Do you have any other questions regarding my qualifications for this position?
28. Since I will be working with (five) attorneys, is there a formalized policy for prioritizing the work?
29. Will I have client contact?
30. What are the most important goals of this position?
31. When will you make a hiring decision?
32. Does the paralegal in this position have an office?

Benefits, Perks, Vacations, Time Off
(Be careful about when you ask these questions!)

1. Can you describe the benefits package? (Includes vacation and parking.)
2. Does the firm/corporation offer a 401(k) or other retirement packages?
3. Does the firm/corporation reimburse or pay for continuing education?
4. Does the paralegal in this position have an office or secretary?
5. What is the vacation policy? How is it accrued?
6. Does the firm/company endorse participation in paralegal associations?
7. Does the firm/company pay for association dues?
8. Are year-end or holiday bonuses offered?
9. Does the firm pay for parking or offer a transportation allowance?
10. Can you describe the health benefits?
11. Does the firm/corporation offer dependent coverage?
12. Do employees pay any part of the insurance premium?
13. Does the firm offer long-term disability or life insurance?
14. Does this corporation offer profit sharing?
15. Will I be able to attend paralegal association seminars? Does the firm/corporation reimburse or pay for these seminars?

Technical Savvy of the Firm
Just because the firm may ask you questions relating to your technology skills does not mean that you are prohibited from finding out just how technologically savvy they may be! If you are a new paralegal or a veteran exploring a job change, here are sixteen questions you can ask to help you

evaluate your potential new employer's orientation to technology utilization in the practice of law:

1. What programs are paralegals expected to know, and how are those programs used?
2. Do members of the firm use E-mail internally to communicate with each other? With their clients?
3. Are paralegals provided laptops? Are attorneys provided laptops? Do they use them?
4. Does the firm have a Web site? How often is it updated? Are paralegals included on the Web site?
5. Does the firm have a technology committee? Do any paralegals sit on that committee?
6. What ongoing training does the firm provide to maximize comfort level with new and existing technology?
7. What is the firm's attitude toward the virtual office? Do any paralegals in the firm work from home or a client's office?
8. Is the firm's computer technology compatible with clients'?
9. Does the firm have an MIS director, and if so, what is that person's relationship to the firm's management committee? How much interfacing is there between the MIS director and the paralegals?
10. What is the firm policy regarding the Internet and employee privacy issues?
11. If the firm has multiple offices, are they networked? Does the firm have an Intranet or Extranet?
12. What operating system does the firm utilize? (Is the firm still using DOS?) What are the plans for the future?
13. Does the firm have an in-house litigation support department? If outsourced, to whom?
14. How does the firm utilize imaging and scanning services?
15. How does the firm market its technology to clients?
16. Does the firm utilize computers in the courtroom?

Salary
(Timing is everything—don't ask about salary too soon!)

1. Is salary based on years of experience or performance levels?
2. When would I receive a performance review?
3. When would I receive a salary review?

4. Does the firm offer a bonus? What are eligibility requirements for the bonus?
5. Can you give me an approximate range of the bonus?
6. Does the firm/corporation offer compensatory time off in lieu of overtime?
7. Can you provide a salary range for this position?
8. How does the firm recognize and reward performance?
9. Does everyone in the firm/corporation receive salary reviews at the same time or on anniversary dates?
10. Since I would not have been with the firm for an entire year when reviews are given, will I be eligible anyway?
11. Since I would not have been with the firm for an entire year when bonuses are calculated, am I eligible for a bonus on a prorated basis?
12. Is this position exempt (does not pay overtime) or nonexempt (does pay overtime)?
13. About how much overtime can I expect?

ILLEGAL QUESTIONS

It's hard to believe, but illegal questions do get asked, even in law firms! You're probably aware potential employers cannot ask certain questions. But prejudices sneak in, whether knowingly or "accidentally." You can choose not to respond, tell the interviewer the question is illegal, or lecture to the interviewer about Title VII. While this might make you feel better, the end result is likely to be an apology, not a job offer. However, under no circumstances are you required to ever answer a question about:

• Age (unless you are under the age of 18)
• Race
• Nationality
• Origins
• Religion
• Marital status
• Family life
• Physical appearance
• Disabilities
• Sexual preferences.

If you are asked an illegal question, your internal red flag should go up. No one has to take a position with a firm/corporation that jeopardizes his or her well-being. In light of that, it is important to consider the following questions, finding answers where possible:

- Is this the person with whom I am expected to work? (Ask yourself: If so, why would I work alongside someone with this bias?)
- Is this person responsible for evaluating my performance? Assigning work? Part of my team? Overseeing my assignments? Involved in the day-to-day operations of work flow?
- Does this person represent the culture and/or philosophy of the firm/corporation?
- Will I ever even see this person again if I work here? (Some corporations are so large that the first interview is all about getting past the Gatekeeper.)
- How many employees in this firm/corporation carry the same attitude?
- Is senior management aware of what's going on?

Even if employment with this firm means you'll never cross paths with this interviewer, be very clear this person does represent the firm. Taking a job with a company that discriminates is not necessary. Under no circumstances are you required to answer an illegal question. If, after the initial shock has worn off, you do decide to answer, it doesn't have to be directly. One of the best answers was given by a litigation paralegal with more than 20 years' experience. The question asked was, "How would you feel about working for a firm where all the senior partners are younger than you?" The paralegal's reply was immediate. "If what you are asking is, 'Do I have the energy for the job, the answer is yes.' " The key phrase is, *"If what you are asking . . ."* Get to the heart of the question. **What is really being asked?**

Another great response to an illegal question is taught by Susan Miller, a Los Angeles-based career counselor. Illegal questions may arise regarding children, child care, spousal approval, and family relationships. A typical question may be, "Tell me about your home life." This question is usually geared toward a woman of child-bearing years. The correct response, according to Miller, is, "Everything in my home life is supportive of my career." **If you were sent to the interview through a staffing organization, be sure to report the illegal questioning to the agency. They need to know.**

Reality Check

Don't deny what may have occurred. And never assume you can change the attitude or mind-set of someone else. You can, however, make an intelligent and informed decision as to whether this is the right environment for you.

SAMPLE ILLEGAL QUESTIONS/COMMENTS

Home Life

Do you live with your parents?

What does your husband think about your job?

What does your spouse do for a living?

Does your spouse approve of your taking this position?

What line of work are/were your parents in?

Does your wife/mother work?

Who is the boss in your family?

Do you live in an apartment or house?

Religion

What church do you go to?

What is your religion?

Do you take the Jewish holidays off?

Children and Child Care

What are your day care arrangements?

How many children do you have?

What time do you pick your children up from day care?

Is anyone home with your children during the day?

Physical Challenges

Were you born blind, or did you get that way later?

Do you have any health problems, like diabetes, that we should consider?

Have you ever been tested for HIV?

Is that a temporary limp?

Race or Ethnicity

Would you like to play on our basketball team?

Do you know any good Chinese restaurants?

Your last name is Herrera? Do you speak Spanish?

When you were in school, did you join an African-American fraternity?

What part of town were your raised in?

What area of town do you live in? (The question should only be asked "Can you arrive to work on time?")

Is English your native language?

Is that a (Filipino, Spanish, etc.) accent?

Where do you come from?

More of your people should be just like you.

Looksism

We're looking for "front-office appearance."

Is it true blondes really have more fun?

Do you think you can lose a little weight before you start?

Could you get rid of that gray hair?

Age

What is your date of birth? (If asked prior to hiring.)

Have your children left home yet?

What's it feel like to be in a protected class?

My parents/children are your age.

"When I was *your* age . . ."

"When I get to be *your* age . . ."

Did you ever think that at your age you would be changing careers?

Sexism

"Young lady."

"The girl . . ."

"We're really looking for a man for this position."

"We think a woman would do better in this position."

"Why would a guy want to be a paralegal?"

Sexual Preference

"I see you live in _____. Does that explain why you aren't married?"

Origins and Nationality

"Is your last name Italian?"

"Were you born here?" (The only question that can be asked is, "Are you a U.S. citizen?")

"Are your parents immigrants?"

"Where were you born?"

"Where did you grow up?"

Pregnancy

"Are you pregnant now, or do you expect to be in the near future?"
"What are your plans for having children?"

Residence

"Do you own your home, or do you rent?"

Political, Fraternal, or Other Affiliations Not Related to Your Job

"Please list all organizations you have joined in the past 10 years, including political parties, fraternal organizations and religious groups."

"Are you a Republican or Democrat?"

21

The Buzz on Objections to the Sale

"Press on. Nothing in the world can take the place of persistence."

—Ray Kroc

Behind every question lurks a possible objection. Basically, the interviewer continues to ask herself, "Why should I hire you?" They really consider objections as part of their job. No one is entirely gullible, and objections serve as guideposts to making the right decision about the right candidate.

Most interviewers assume you've read the current books and articles, gone to job search workshops, and have rehearsed standard, neat, pat answers. So they try very hard to throw you a curveball. Many of them avoid the general and obvious questions. Instead, they develop new methods of interviewing.

No matter what questions interviewers ask or what objections they may raise to hiring you, they are all pretty much after the same information: what are your skills, are you qualified for this position, does your personality fit, will you stay?

HERE TODAY, GONE TOMORROW . . .

In some industries, you have to explain why you stayed at a place for many years. In the legal field, even though people seldom stay for 10 or 20 years, job-hopping is still suspect in many firms. If you're a little jumping bean, the key to packaging your job history is to articulate why you left. Here is a list of organic explanations:

"I can understand how you feel. However, **I followed the opportunities for advancement,** which caused me to move up quickly in this field." A promotion shows both that you're valued and that you're managing your career aggressively.

"I followed the money." Few will argue with a move that gave you a salary boost—as long as money isn't the only reason why you left.

249

"I followed the rainmakers." Firms want people who bring varied experience to the table. For that reason alone, job-hopping makes you more marketable.

"I followed my spouse." Employers are typically understanding of this type of move. But they also want to know that your career matters too.

Most people have some gaps or false starts and phases of unemployment in the background. To some employers, the more changes you've been through, the worse you look. Downsizing has accounted for many stops and starts in otherwise stellar career histories. But if you are downsized several times, you are also suspect—even though none of it was your doing.

There's no easy way to get around this problem, but there are good strategies. The best one is to demonstrate how all of the stops and starts have led to this career and, particularly, this interview. *Remember the key concern of the interviewer: Will you stay if you are hired?*

- Stress that it's not in your nature to job-hop. However, the one good thing about it is that job-hopping has given you a variety of expertise you can now bring to the firm.
- Emphasize that you now have the knowledge to be absolutely certain about what you want to do. Be as strong and as determined as possible without overselling. Talk about what you have learned. But don't dwell on the topic. Move the conversation toward this job and the future.

GAPS, HOLES, OR VOIDS NOW BECOME HIATUSES, RECESSES, OR INTERIM PERIODS

If you are questioned about periods of unemployment and an uncomfortable pause arises, show how productive you were during the time frame. There is really only one way an interviewer can ask about a gap in your resume, and that is, "Did you work from blank to blank?" And, technically, you are only required to answer yes or no. The question is designed to protect stay-at-home parents or homemakers. But if you feel an explanation is required, you might say:

"During the six months I was unemployed, I spent a good portion of the time searching for just the right position in a downturned market. Rather than just sit at home, I organized my job-search time so that I could work as a temporary employee and volunteer the rest of my time helping inner-city youths get jobs. That's why I know I could be very effective in this job. I'm capable of handling several different kinds of tasks at once."

LOW GRADES DO NOT EQUATE
WITH LOW PERFORMERS

Don't worry about low grades after you get your first job; worry even less if you have an advanced degree such as an M.B.A. or M.A./M.S. Employment surveys show that having good grades is among the least important factors in getting hired. Although associates are almost always asked for their transcripts, paralegals are rarely required to produce them.

Stress the reasons for having had low grades that explain how other vital activities took away study time. You could explain that you held a full-time position during the day while attending night school. Or you may have had a situation where you were busy supporting your children, holding a full-time position, and going to school at night. Instead of getting blasted, you should probably have won an award. Never sound upset, and above all, never apologize. This should not be a question of your intelligence. You just didn't have enough time to study. A good response might be

> "I had a 2.0 GPA. As you can see from my resume, I also held a full-time position. This taught me how to burn the midnight candle and still succeed at the task at hand. I learned how to juggle many responsibilities, which is what interests me about this job."

On the other hand, if you simply weren't interested in school and actually did flake out, you may want to reconsider your decision to enter or stay in the paralegal field!

COMING FROM A FOREIGN STATE

If you have recently moved from another state, chances are you'll run into another kind of objection: "Gee, your experience looks great, but you don't know this state's laws." This kind of limited viewpoint surely must make you want to scream. Before you wail too loudly, realize what is actually racing around in the interviewer's little mind: "Hmm, her experience is good but may not be right on point. Therefore, it will take some ramp-up time to get her properly trained."

Well, if that's the major objection, then you're not in a bad situation. This is not a situation where you are incapable of learning, is it? You need to point that out (in a nice way) to this conceptually-challenged interviewer. Here is a good way to counter:

> "If what you are concerned about is that I won't be able to learn quickly, let me put that fear to rest. I have already acquired a copy of the State and Local Rules and read it to acquaint myself with any differences in procedure. As you know, any new person coming into the firm will have to learn the firm's unique procedures. I also intend to study your form files and to ask lots of pertinent questions. I don't think you'll find that it will take me very long at all to ramp up to speed."

"We Really Hadn't Intended to Spend That Much Money on Salary"

"And, I hadn't planned on taking that little." No, no, no. That's precisely the wrong answer. Objections to salary are quite common. In the paralegal field, you must immediately tie in your salary to three things:

- The firm can generally ask for a higher hourly rate for someone of your experience and background.
- You require less ramp-up time than would an inexperienced person and can probably be more efficient than a lower-level person would be.
- You are the best qualified candidate for the job.

"What Are Your Weaknesses?"

This has and will always remain the silliest question ever invented for an interview. If employers expect candidates to answer with, "Well, every time I form a corporation, I forget to include some of the documents," they are living in another world. The game is and always has been to turn this question into a positive answer:

> "I am so fascinated with forming a corporation that at times I spend a little too much time making absolutely certain I have completed everything I can on the assignment."

Whatever the objection, stay positive. If confronted with a question you don't know how to answer, say so. If a weakness is pointed out, switch to one of your skills that is a strength. It's all in how you play the game.

22

Follow-Up and Thank-You Letters

"Say thank you to the nice lady."

—The authors' mothers

FOLLOW-UP LETTERS

Traditional job-search workshops will advise you to write a thank-you letter after each interview. We would like to offer an effective variation on the theme: the follow-up letter. The purpose of the follow-up letter is to continue promoting yourself. It is a reason to contact the interviewer once again and remind him or her of your superior candidacy for the position.

You can use the follow-up letter to

- Send requested writing samples
- Remind the interviewer of your availability for a second or third interview
- Provide additional references
- Clarify or strengthen comments made during the interview.

All follow-up and thank-you letters must be typewritten. Handwritten notes are not appropriate in the legal field. You are not thanking a hostess for a Sunday brunch. Remember you are establishing a professional relationship.

Here are several follow-up letters you might consider:

SAMPLE FOLLOW-UP LETTERS

September 7, xxxx

Chandler Ross, Esq.
Landers and Brothers
100 South University Avenue, Suite 203
Denver, CO 80300

Dear Mr. Ross:

I appreciate the opportunity to present myself as a candidate for the Banking and Finance legal assistant position; an opportunity, I might add, about which I am very excited. It was a pleasure to meet with you and members of the firm.

As per your request, I have enclosed two writing samples for your review. These examples of my writing should demonstrate my attention to detail and thorough investigative skills. Throughout my career, I have worked to consistently achieve a high level of work quality. I am hoping to apply these skills in a position within a firm precisely as you described during our interview last Thursday.

As the firm's Banking and Finance legal assistant, I can bring the insight and experience necessary to maintain the firm's sophisticated clients. I can also streamline costs and increase the profitability of the paralegal program.

I will contact you next week to see when we might meet again to expand upon how we can make this opportunity happen.

Sincerely,

Andrew Ramirez

SAMPLE FOLLOW-UP LETTER

December 12, xxxx

Ms. Andrea King
Vice President
National Pizza Corporation
367 East Brookline Avenue
Chicago, IL 60601

Dear Ms. King:

Thank you for your time last Thursday to discuss the immigration para-legal position within your organization and your plans to expand your paralegal department.

As we discussed, the position is an exciting one for which I feel I am suitably qualified. It would be quite an honor to join your prestigious team. The opportunity to work with international chefs is quite a departure from the typical paralegal position! I feel I can bring a diversified range of skills that would allow your Associate General Counsel to devote more time to in-house matters and ultimately save the company significant dollars in outside legal fees.

I am providing two more references, which are attached. I will call on Monday as you suggested to see whether Mr. Widsell has returned from vacation and is available to meet with me.

Thank you again for your time. I look forward to seeing you in the next few weeks.

Sincerely,

Stephen Elliot

SAMPLE FOLLOW-UP LETTER TO PHONE INTERVIEW

January 23, xxxx

Ms. Chere B. Estrin, President
The Estrin Organization
1901 Avenue of the Stars, Suite 350
Los Angeles, CA 90067

Dear Chere:

   It was a pleasure speaking with you on the phone last week with regard to future employment. I enjoyed discussing the current needs of *The Estrin Organization* and addressing the strengths of my professional background to fulfill those needs. I am enthusiastic about the contributions I can offer your company as well as the opportunity to work with you in a team effort with respect to staffing today's legal professionals.

   As we discussed, I am eagerly looking to secure a position that will allow me to exercise my talents in legal recruitment and staffing. I am interested in the training opportunities your organization provides with regard to its LegalTrack series. In addition, I would like to congratulate you on your successful efforts in starting a training division. I strongly support your mission and admire your dedication for promoting integrity and education in the legal profession.

   I am sending you a hard copy of my resume under separate cover. Should you have any questions or require additional information, please feel free to contact me.

   Thank you for your time and consideration.

Sincerely,

Myrna Myerson

Reality Check

Few of the people you will meet during an interview are professional recruiters. They are simply law firm or in-house legal department attorneys or staff with a position to fill. A strong follow-up letter can remind them of your qualifications, narrow the playing field, and re-emphasize why you are the best person for the job.

THE THANK-YOU LETTER

Thank-you letters are for the sole purpose of expressing gratitude. You may be writing to thank someone for their time, an introduction, some advice, a referral, or a reference. You may even be writing to thank someone for a job opportunity you have decided not to pursue.

Thank-you letters express more than good manners. People like to be appreciated. Reinforcing your appreciation for their time or favors gives a very positive impression. And some firms even wait to receive a thank-you letter as a further validation that your writing skills are indeed superb.

Written documents are tangible evidence that you can indeed do the job. (Of course, a poorly composed letter indicating you were not quite clear about the position could work against you.) These documents are testimonials not only to your writing skills but also to your intellect, sense of humor, desire for the job, and personality.

The letter will refresh the interviewer's memory about you. Regardless of your persuasive abilities and charming personality in the interview, your impact may soon fade because interviewers are faced with a number of candidates for each open position. Interviewers who have interviewed several candidates quite frankly may be confused as to which candidate you are. This is particularly true of those interviewers who are not used to interviewing. A slow moving firm with inexperienced interviewers presents problems to job seekers. Candidates may not stand out as individuals; instead, they may all run together in the interviewer's mind. The thank-you letter will remind them one more time why you are just the right candidate. And if the interviewer was sitting on the fence, a great letter may just push indecision into an offer.

Even if you are scheduling interviews with other organizations, follow each completed interview with a positive, straightforward, typewritten thank-you letter to each and every person with whom you interviewed. These letters should be brief and to the point. Stationery should match your resume and cover letter, and the letter must be professionally typed. You must always send a thank-you letter immediately—preferably no more than 24 hours after an interview or act of kindness. In some cases, faxing the letter is fine. However, if the firm offers a very formal environment, a letter that has been mailed may be more appropriate. E-mail is probably too informal for most situations. Do not handwrite a note. Above all, do NOT send a thank-you greeting card.

Reality Check

Thank-you letters are not an option during your job search. They are a necessity.

Reality Check

Just because an agency sent you on the interview is no reason why you should avoid sending a thank-you letter. Don't assume that the letter isn't necessary!

Open your letter by referring to the occasion. Stay brief, businesslike, and clear. Here are a few sample openers:

- Thank you for fitting me into your very busy calendar. I appreciate your willingness to meet with me regarding the intellectual property paralegal position within the firm.
- I appreciate your helpfulness in assisting me with my job search. Taking the time to call Mr. Castle regarding a paralegal position within his firm was invaluable.
- Thank you for introducing me to Gail Stevens. I appreciate your assistance and the referral to such an outstanding colleague.

If you are sending a thank-you letter for an interview, connect something that was said in the interview to your skills or qualifications for the position. State your feelings and desire for the position. You may even want to add an additional reason for hiring you—one that was not discussed perhaps.

If you were referred to someone or given a great lead, immediately write to thank the person who helped you. This gesture can also help to establish a good solid network—one that is sure to become invaluable.

If you are sending a thank-you letter for an interview, the body of the letter should

- Pinpoint a topic discussed during the interview. This shows the interviewer
  1. You were listening;
  2. You've given thought to what was said.
- Tie in your qualifications, demonstrating how you can fit into the organization.

You want to provide some detail in the body. No matter how you attack the thank-you letter or for what purpose it is written, remember to be brief and to the point. Always remain positive and offer no apologies for anything.

- Now that I have heard more about Wind & Jammer's objectives for the contracts administration paralegal, I am more excited than ever to be a contender for this position. Your comment regarding the absolute

necessity to pay attention to detail hit home. In my present position, I am frequently relied upon to furnish the most obscure bits and pieces of information. I can only do that if I am extremely detail oriented.
- Wind & Jammer's excellent reputation for quality legal services only serves to reinforce my desire to obtain employment with the firm. This is precisely the type of firm where I learned the majority of what I now know about litigation, and I would welcome the opportunity to continue my career at a firm that meets or exceeds the standards of my present employer.

Close the letter with your intent to follow up or your desire to hear from the reader. If you have only met this person a few times, now is not the time to get personal. Keep the letter business-like and professional.

- I have always succeeded by seeking challenges and creating opportunities where others felt none existed. That's how I managed to become and remain the top billing paralegal at Damascus and Israel, and it's what I'll do for you. Let's make it happen.
- I am most excited at the prospect of working with the legal department at Purcell Industries. Please let me know if there is anything else I can do to demonstrate my ability for this position. I look forward to hearing from you.

SAMPLE THANK-YOU LETTERS

August 21, xxxx

Mr. Michael Waters
A Family Affair
1234 Main Street
Los Angeles, CA 90064

Dear Mr. Waters:

I wanted to drop you a note to thank you for a most informative and exciting interview last Thursday. Upon reflection on our meeting, I am further convinced that my experience as a certificated paralegal matches the staffing needs you described.

Always state when the interview took place to remind the interviewer who you are.

The opportunity to participate in your firm's growing family law practice is extremely appealing. Of greatest benefit for those who seek lower legal fees is your firm's commitment toward better utilizing paralegals. As a paralegal with more than 10 years' experience, it is refreshing to hear your firm's positive attitude toward professional development of paralegals. My training background can benefit the firm's progressive outlook toward training clients about the benefits of paralegals.

Reaffirms that you understood the firm's mission. Redirects attention to your qualifications.

I appreciate your willingness to meet with me and would very much appreciate an invitation to join the firm. If I have not heard from you within a week or so, I will call to ask if I can provide further information to assist you in making your decision. I look forward to hearing from you soon.

Restates interest in the position. Paves the way for further communication between you and your interviewer.

Sincerely,

Katie Andersen

Sample Thank-You Letter

August 23, xxxx

Mr. Bruce Willus
Manager, Human Resources Department
Moore, Sheppard & Peters
1234 Century Park East, Suite 400
Los Angeles, CA 90067

Dear Bruce:

Thank you for meeting with me last week to discuss the firm's entry-level paralegal position. Our conversation left me excited about the endless possibilities this position offers.

I was particularly impressed with the firm's cutting-edge technology. It's a bold statement to be able to claim that electronic evidence discovery is the wave of the future, as the process is clearly here. Those firms not utilizing this technology are certain to be left behind. It is the prospect of combining my engineering background with the recent training I received from St. Joseph's Paralegal Training Program that is particularly motivating. I am certain that Moore, Sheppard & Peters could benefit significantly through my background.

I would like very much to throw my hat into the ring as a serious contender for this position. I look forward to hearing from you next week regarding a second interview. Thanks again, Bruce, for your time and consideration.

Sincerely,

Brenda Johnson

Sample Thank-You Letter

January 23, xxxx

Mr. James Peterson
Paralegal Coordinator
The Health NetWork
5684 North Second Street
Omaha, NE 08000

Re: Litigation Paralegal Position

Dear Jim:

I'm so pleased that you were able to break away from your busy schedule to meet with me yesterday afternoon regarding the litigation paralegal position within the company. Thank you for your time.

The Health NetWork's unique and interesting slant toward using paralegals is of particular interest to me. Using paralegals to audit law firm bills makes tremendous sense. I am certain that my accounting background, years of experience in the legal field, and drive toward finite detail would be an asset to the department.

Please let me know what additional information you might require of me regarding my background, skills, abilities, or references. I look forward to the possibility of working with you and your team. Thanks again for considering me for this exciting opportunity.

Sincerely,

Kevin Syndor

Sample Thank-You Letter
to the Staffing Organization

December 30, xxxx

Mr. Andrew Spathis
Executive Vice President
The Estrin Organization
1901 Avenue of the Stars, Suite 350
Los Angeles, CA 90067

Dear Andrew:

Thank you for your valuable assistance in landing the job of my dreams. Never did I think that it was possible to achieve four of the five goals we laid out at the beginning of my job search.

I am very excited about starting the paralegal position at Frasier, Niles and Krane. This position is precisely what I wanted in order to launch my new career. Of particular interest is the opportunity to expand my software expertise. As you know, I have always wanted to be paid for learning!

Please keep in touch. I'll remember your advice about being the "new guy on the totem" and hope to have the opportunity to pass it along as I develop in this position. Thanks again for all your help. I'll be sure to pass the word along about your terrific staffing expertise!

Best personal regards,

Benny Goodman
Paralegal

Sample Thank-You Letter for Referral

November 17, xxxx

Mr. James Johnson
Hill and Dale
5859 North Main Street
Salt Lake City, UT 55555

Dear Jim:

Just a note to thank you once again for referring me to Diane Adams. Because of your enthusiastic recommendation, I had a great meeting with her last Thursday.

I had heard that it was a sometimes difficult task to break into a brand-new career. However, because former colleagues like you are willing to take a chance on us "wanna-bes," an otherwise difficult task now becomes much easier and certainly much more pleasant.

Thanks again for the referral. If I can return a like favor, please don't hesitate to give me a call.

Best regards,

Karen Jones

Sample Thank-You Letter for Referral

February 18, xxxx

Ms. Gloria Martin
Careers Unlimited
1800 Main Street
Los Angeles, CA 90067

Dear Gloria:

Thank you for referring me to the Hancock Company. I thoroughly enjoyed my interview with Mr. Dudley.

I couldn't have been more pleased when he told me that he only uses your agency when the company has a need for a paralegal. My sincerest thanks for giving me this opportunity to land my first paralegal job. You have become an incredible resource during this exhaustive but exhilarating time. I am most appreciative of all you have done.

I will be most happy to send you as many of my paralegal friends as I can who are seeking employment. You are the best!

Sincerely,

Joy Rogers

Sample Thank-You Letter (General)

October 11, xxxx

Amy Rice, Esq.
Rice, Weiner, Capstone & Butler
5657 South Main Street, Suite 400
San Francisco, CA 94110

Dear Ms. Rice:

I was very pleased that we were able to continue our discussions regarding the real estate paralegal position with your firm. I remain very interested in this challenging and interesting position.

Now that I have learned even more about your firm's practice specialty and its need for a motivated, hard-working paralegal, I am yet more excited about the prospect of adding my escrow background to the team. Joining a firm such as yours that recognizes the importance of paralegals is an exciting prospect. Certainly, your firm and I both thrive on the art of the deal along with the creativity and energy it takes to put one of these packages together.

I would welcome the opportunity to work with you. I'm eager to prove my abilities and successes to you on a firsthand basis. I'll keep in touch to see when we might meet again and if there is any other information I can provide in the meantime. Thanks again for your time and consideration.

Sincerely,

Jaime Rodriguez

Sample No-Thanks Letter

October 5, xxxx

Christine Lloyd, Esq.
Richman, Crane and Kirkland, L.L.C.
428 Madison Avenue
New York, NY 10003

Dear Ms. Lloyd:

Thank you for your time and interest during our interview last week. Richman, Crane and Kirkland's planned expansion into medical malpractice sounds challenging and inviting.

While the opportunity to participate in this startup practice area is extremely appealing, I must withdraw my name as a candidate for the paralegal position. I have recently been offered another position closer to home that will also involve travel to Asia.

In any event, I want to thank you for taking the time to explore what promises to be an excellent career for the paralegal who is fortunate enough to be hired for this position.

Thank you again for your interest.

Sincerely,

Ann Whyte

CALL TO ACTION LETTER

There will be times during your job search that you think the work you have accomplished with some firms via resume, cover letter, and interview have fallen into a deep chasm. You're betwixt and between regarding what to do. Continuing to call the firm is not always a wise idea as being a pest won't bring you any closer to getting the job. Never following up and waiting for a call that may never come isn't good either.

Whatever the cause for the unending silence, consider yourself an active candidate until you hear otherwise. Don't get discouraged—take action instead! Send a call-to-action letter, which is meant to move things along. Your goal is to promote yourself once again and possibly push the hiring process along. It is important to determine, however, whether the person to whom you are writing will be receptive to a little push.

If you are convinced it's worth a shot, then a well-planned, well-written positive letter may be in order. Determine the style and tone of the letter: is the reader a very conservative, Brooks Brothers type, or casual and less judgmental? Tailor your writing style to the style of the reader. The most important thing, however, is to remind the reader who you are, provide additional information, or ask for the job.

Reality Check

If the firm is still uncertain that you are the one for the job, try offering your services on temporary basis. After all, to know you is to love you.

Sample Call-to-Action Letter

November 9, xxxx

Paul Meeks, Esq.
Managing Partner
Schneider, Becker & Meeks, LLC
100 Main Street
Boston, MA 02003

Dear Mr. Meeks:

When we met last month regarding the opening in the firm for an intellectual property paralegal, I had just completed my last quarter of the work for my certificate at the University.

Since that time, I have completed an internship at the Department of Corporations. It was there that I was able to work directly with attorneys and paralegals and handle actual assignments. It was a most rewarding experience. I have enthusiastically enclosed a copy of the review I received, which you may find valuable in making your final decision for the appropriate candidate for this position.

I look forward to hearing from you soon.

Sincerely,

Bobbie Charles

ACCEPTANCE LETTER

On rare occasions, you may be expected to write a letter of acceptance, or you may feel it is appropriate. The letter should be short and precise. You can include brief points of your negotiation efforts and the terms of your employment. Make sure you are accurate whenever you offer a written document.

Sample Acceptance Letter

August 23, xxxx

Ms. Alaina Alda
Paralegal Administrator
Morris, Roberts & Hoffman
12345 Wacker Drive
Chicago, IL 60601

Dear Ms. Alda:

It is with great pleasure that I accept your offer as Corporate Paralegal. I look forward to joining the firm on March 15 with a starting salary of $32,000 per year.

I am particularly interested in working with the Business and Finance team as it develops. I am also looking forward to enrolling in the title review course offered by the University of Chicago.

Thank you for your assistance and support. I look forward to a long and continuing business relationship.

Sincerely,

Christian Zimmerman

23

Evaluating the Job Offer

"It's not over 'til it's over."

—Yogi Berra

Now that you been interviewed, interrogated, examined, and polled about your skills, abilities, personality, and attitudes, it's time to analyze and evaluate your initial response to a potential job offer. Perhaps you have never formally assembled this kind of information before and things have just come together for you in a natural, easy fashion. However, the new way of doing things is to prepare yourself for a negotiation by breaking it into logical, digestible, and manageable pieces. Figuring out what is important allows for an easier negotiation. You'll stay grounded and clearer in your thinking.

USING THE ESTRIN JOB OPPORTUNITY INVENTORY CHECKLIST

Use the inventory checklist to see how the potential job stacks up against your personal priorities. Put a check mark (✔) in the Personal Priority column next to each item that is important to you. In the next column, indicate how much the item is worth by ranking it from 1 to 10, with 1 being the lowest and 10 the highest. In the Potential Offer column, weigh the offer you are considering by giving it a 1 to 10 rating based on how well you perceive it stacks up against your priorities.

Job Opportunity Inventory

Priorities Priority Y/N	Personal Priority Rating	Personal Offer Rating	Potential Offer
1. Quality of work	❑	_____	_____
2. Work environment	❑	_____	_____
3. Specialty practice	❑	_____	_____
4. Opportunity for more technology	❑	_____	_____
5. Title	❑	_____	_____
6. Growth potential	❑	_____	_____
7. Friendly supervisors/colleagues	❑	_____	_____

269

8. Family-friendly environment ❑ _____ _____
9. Manageable billable hours ❑ _____ _____
10. No billable hours ❑ _____ _____
11. Progressive atmosphere ❑ _____ _____
12. Private office ❑ _____ _____
13. Corporate environment ❑ _____ _____
14. Work in new industry ❑ _____ _____
15. Annual bonus ❑ _____ _____
16. Paid overtime ❑ _____ _____
17. Tuition reimbursement ❑ _____ _____
18. Great health benefits ❑ _____ _____
19. 401(k) Plan ❑ _____ _____
20. Open, friendly environment ❑ _____ _____
21. Lots of client contact ❑ _____ _____
22. Have fair amount of autonomy ❑ _____ _____
23. On-site day care ❑ _____ _____
24. Travel a reasonable amount ❑ _____ _____
25. Become a road warrior ❑ _____ _____
26. Work directly with partners ❑ _____ _____
27. Opportunity for advancement ❑ _____ _____
28. Length of commute ❑ _____ _____
29. Ability to use my skills ❑ _____ _____
30. Increase my present salary ❑ _____ _____
31. Job-share ❑ _____ _____
32. Work from home part-time ❑ _____ _____
33. Paralegal Association volunteer work ❑ _____ _____
 supported by firm
34. More fun than present job ❑ _____ _____
35. More challenging than present job ❑ _____ _____
36. More stability ❑ _____ _____
37. Casual dress ❑ _____ _____
38. On-the-job training ❑ _____ _____
39. Associate level work ❑ _____ _____

Don't shortchange yourself. Go after what you want, and know when and where you can make compromises. Clarifying what is important to you enters into every part of upcoming negotiations.

YOUR INITIAL REACTION

Let's face it. Job hunting can be stressful. By the time an offer does come in, you may be ready to say yes just to end the ordeal. But guard against a quick response no matter whether your reaction is positive or negative. It is imperative that you think the offer through.

Few employers expect you to accept on the spot. So whether the offer has been presented over the phone or in person, it's probably best to wait at least 24 hours before accepting. This way, you can sleep on it. If you wake up in the morning feeling the same way, there's probably very little that can change your mind.

Guard against waiting too long to accept an offer also. Waiting a few days may be acceptable for most employers. However, waiting a few weeks may put them off. Upon receiving the offer, you first need to ask the question, "How soon can I get back to you?" Try not to go beyond a week. Employers don't like to stop their recruiting process for very long. It takes too much to ramp up again.

Some employers are put off by candidates who want to wait until all offers are in to evaluate and choose. They want to know that you are enthusiastic about their firm. Others accept the fact that some candidates will have multiple offers and have no problem understanding that they are competing. Frankly, the more highbrow the firm, the less likely they are to understand that a candidate wants to evaluate all offers. Such an attitude stems from something akin to arrogance. After all, they say, we are the Blank & Blank firm. We're the best. Why wouldn't someone jump at the chance to work here?

CASE IN POINT

One paralegal administrator talked to us about an entry-level candidate who wanted to evaluate other offers. The firm, a top firm with 200+ attorneys, withdrew its offer. "Can you imagine," sniffed the administrator. "An entry-level paralegal who didn't realize just who he had an offer from." One never knows.

Should you ask for an offer letter? Today, many firms and corporations follow up a verbal offer with an offer letter. This letter is not an employment contract. It is merely a letter that outlines the terms of the offer. It will include salary, benefits, and start date.

CASE IN POINT

One paralegal got extremely upset and angry with her potential employer after receiving an offer letter. "Everything we talked about is not in the letter," she said. "You didn't state that I need to take my vacation in July; that I need to leave early on Thursdays; and that you would announce my arrival in the newsletter." Not knowing the difference between an employment contract and an offer letter, this candidate was turned off by the firm. The red flag went up, and her arrival was somewhat tainted. Even though she ultimately accepted the position, she got off on the wrong foot, and the position did not work out.

Now that you have analyzed your priorities against the offer, it's necessary to analyze your understanding of how the employer arrived at his or her offer. Do you have all the facts? Do you need more information? Review the Offer Analysis Chart for just a few questions you'll need answered before making your decision.

Offer Analysis Chart

How did the law firm/corporation arrive at its decision?

- Do you have a clear picture of where your skills, expertise, level of experience, and education fit within the firm?
- In what areas of expertise do you compare to the person you may be replacing?
- How do your background and expertise compare to the original job description?

How does the final total compensation figure stack up?

- Do you know whether you are being offered market rate for your skills?
- Has the employer articulated when you are eligible for a salary review?
- How long has this position been available?
- Has there been a hiring freeze? If so, what impact did the freeze play upon salary and the level of expertise required of a candidate?
- Do the benefits and perks make up for a less-than-desirable base salary?
- Is the base salary less than anticipated but the chance for paid overtime an opportunity to earn some nice dollars?

What do you have to do to maintain the expectations of the firm regarding salary?

- Is your future raise or bonus tied to billable hours?
- Do you know what average billable hours (as opposed to expected hours) are achieved by paralegals in this firm?
- What happened to the paralegal who was in this position prior to you? Was she promoted? Did she move on? Is this a high-turnover position, or is it newly created?

How were things left after the offer was extended?

- Is the firm expecting you to negotiate?

If you are clear about the terms and conditions of the offer, you are now ready to compare them to your core priorities. By being clear, you will be more centered and able to calibrate terms of the job offer against something valid and stable. If your approach to the offer is void of in-depth self-evaluation, you will probably find yourself swayed by aspects of the offer that might have short-lived meaning and value.

But sometimes there's an offer for a position that is totally the opposite of what you originally intended. If that happens, yet you are excited by this opportunity, ask yourself three basic questions:

1. What was my original intent?
2. What is acceptable about this offer?
3. How does that differ from my original intent?

Your next step is to compare this information to your core priorities. The next three important questions to ask yourself are

1. What do I know about the offer?
2. What *must* I have? (Criteria that are absolutely not flexible.)
3. On what can I compromise? (Would be nice to have but really can be flexible.)

And above all, before you accept any offer at all, you must ask yourself *the* most important critical questions:

What is the downside of this position?

and

Can I live with it?

If an offer letter is forthcoming, wait until it arrives to fully evaluate your offer. There may be items in it that you had either not understood or not been aware of. In any case, the offer letter will provide a clearer understanding of the offer.

Before you can negotiate your offer, you must understand the employer's point of view. Knowing the goals, needs, and perspectives of the employer will give you a leg up in your negotiations. Review the Offer Analysis Chart to make certain you have the information you need. Here is where it is useful to work with a staffing organization. If they are good, they will know the ins and outs of the firm. They will know weaknesses of the employer and how to get you the best offer.

If you are not working with a staffing organization, however, there are certain things you'll need to know in order to prepare yourself for the actual negotiation. Gathering more information from the employer in a timely fashion could be difficult given how busy everyone is. Furthermore, you need to hit the employer just right. Pestering for information could give a very bad impression and push the employer into reconsidering his or her offer. Not asking enough questions could land you a job that you really don't want.

Plan to use E-mail and faxes as the quickest, least offensive way to gather information. Any exchanges on the phone to get your questions answered should be kept very brief (no more than 10 minutes). If you have a face-to-face meeting, you may want to send your questions along ahead of time in order to prepare your firm's representative and make your time together as substantive as possible.

Reality Check

You just might be dealing with inexperienced representatives from the firm. Be patient! The best thing to do is to help them along.

SAMPLE OFFER LETTER

January 3, xxxx
Ms. Jan Doe
1415 Willow Tree Avenue
Pittsburgh, PA xxxx

   Re: Offer of Employment

Dear Jan:

   We are pleased to extend an offer of employment as Litigation Paralegal with Brown, Brown and Green. Your primary areas of responsibility will include working with the Healthcare Litigation Team.

   We are offering a salary of $38,000 per year. Overtime will be paid after you have worked 40 hours in any one week. You will be eligible for an annual bonus that is based upon performance, merit, and billable hours. You will be eligible for benefits (a cafeteria-style benefits plan is enclosed) after completing 60 days of employment with the firm. In addition, you will be eligible to participate in our 401(k) plan (also enclosed) after one year of employment with the firm. Parking in the building or in nearby lots is your responsibility. We pay a transportation allowance of $65 per month.

You will receive a written performance evaluation after one year of employment. At that time, you will be eligible for a salary review. Categories for the review will include performance, attitude, billable hours, and quality of work. Any raises you may earn are based upon industry standards.

Jan, we look forward to having you on our team starting January 15. We are very impressed with your expertise and look forward to a successful joining of talent. We would like to hear from you regarding this offer no later than January 8.

If you have any questions, please don't hesitate to call me.

Sincerely,

Brenda Starr
Human Resources Manager

MAKING THE DECISION TO NEGOTIATE

When an offer finally comes through, you may experience a range of emotions. Regardless of whether you are an entry-level paralegal or one who has battled the Bates-Stamping Wars, the offer will make you feel great. Even if it's not ideal, an offer is a symbolic validation of your professional value. Make certain you recognize the accomplishment an offer represents.

When the afterglow of receiving the offer subsides, the reality sets in that the moment to negotiate has finally arrived. You can choose to negotiate. Yessiree! You do have the choice not to negotiate!

However, if the offer is not quite right and you decide that you cannot compromise, you'll find yourself going back to the bargaining table. Rarely is there no room for some negotiation. It is almost impossible to have found yourself at the offer stage without some understanding between you and the employer that there are some commonalities. Negotiating for a better offer does not have to mean that you will blow the offer right out of the water.

24

Negotiating to Close

"All negotiation is to look, discover and take risks."

—Francis Bacon

Congratulations! Finally, an offer that you can seriously consider! Up to this point, you've focused on packaging, presenting, and proposing. Now, attention turns to getting precisely what you want—and the ante is raised.

No doubt you have bandied about salary, total compensation, and perks of the job. Most likely you and your prospective employer are not far apart, or you wouldn't have made it this far. By now, some discussion has taken place with regard to your expectations and theirs. Only one slight problem: rarely do offers come in that exceed the candidate's expectations. On occasion, it does happen. But for the most part, employers still try to see if they can land the best candidate for the least amount of money.

With that issue on the table, it is now time to refine the offer. If you are perfectly happy with the dollars and the package the employer has laid out, by all means, don't tamper with it. But if it isn't up to your expectations, it is perfectly OK to negotiate a better deal. *This is the risk-taking portion of the program—you get to ask for what you want.*

Employers come at job offers from this angle: if they bring the candidate on board at a lower salary, hundreds and possibly thousands of dollars will be saved over the time the candidate is employed with the organization. As for you, starting at a salary that is far lower than you need will cause incredible angst as you try to make up the difference over the next few years.

Here are a few ways to better equip yourself to avoid possible friction during the actual discussions:

1. If you are planning to negotiate over the phone, make certain you
   a. Are in a private area so you can talk freely—eliminate all distractions
   b. Are not on a cell phone or car phone, which can lose the signal or create interference
   c. Have your resume, offer letter, paper, pencil, calendar, and calculator ready.
2. Make certain you know the employer's issues or concerns, such as
   a. Employer is concerned you may not have enough education or experience.
   b. You are asking for more than the employer bargained for.
   c. Employer may lack the authority to change the terms of the offer, causing the employer to feel disempowered. (For example, if an administrator has to go back to the managing partner to get more dollars.)

277

3. Pinpoint the roadblocks in the flow of communication that might arise because of your concerns or hot buttons. Don't get angry. Get over it.
4. Develop an outline with the main points you want to cover in a logical sequence.
5. Have your counteroffers ready.

Rehearse key phrases and wording that will help neutralize the employer's tissues and the resulting roadblocks. Here are just a few key phrases that might help:

"I can appreciate the pressure you must be under. I would like to find a way for us to resolve one area of concern. I'm hoping that the firm has some flexibility."

"Thank you so much. I was hoping to get this job offer. I would like to make sure that we won't be cut short in this discussion. I have some time to talk now. Would that be convenient for you, or shall I call you back around 3:00?"

"Thank you for this insightful offer. I'm delighted at the possibility of working for Jones & Jones. However, there is one remaining issue that I hope we can resolve together."

"I have some concerns about the level of assignment in regards to what the corresponding pay is. Can you clarify a few things for me?"

HOW TO ASK THE QUESTION

Frequently, employers are thrilled they have found the right candidate and are excited when they present the offer. It becomes incumbent upon you not to deflate their egos. How you ask the question to attain more dollars is central to your successful negotiation. Asking close-ended questions will most likely cause you and your potential employer to be on opposite ends of a spectrum:

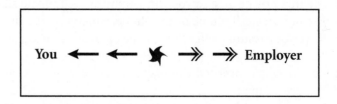

Closed-ended questions (which you do *not* want to ask) would be

"Can you change the base compensation?"	Asking questions that call for a yes or no answer do not allow for discussion. There's nowhere to go with it.
"I would like the base compensation part of the offer reevaluated."	Again, a closed-ended question. It's too easy for the employer to say "no."
"The base salary is lower than what I expected."	This is a statement of fact or an objection, not a question toward resolution.
"This offer is less than what I am currently earning."	Another statement of fact, which does not lead to resolution.

Your goal is to open up the discussion and create possibilities in an atmosphere that is comfortable. You can only do this by asking several questions and creating a common focus of resolving an issue together. You might try these open-ended questions:

"The base salary is lower than what I am currently making. Can you tell me what factors were revolved in arriving at this salary?"

"Are there ways in which we could include more in the base salary so that I do not have to take a 20 percent pay cut?"

Use salary survey information as a basis to point to for validation of your salary request. The Association for Legal Administrators offers a great salary survey. *Legal Assistant Today* magazine offers another excellent national survey. You may be able to obtain one from your local paralegal association. If not, you can always conduct an informal survey by calling local staffing organizations who may be willing to assist you. Your response to an employer's offer may be:

"According to recent salary survey information, this offer is slightly below market rate. How can we work together to bring it up?"

"Given your need for someone with my background and given my interest in this position, can you share with me how we might exercise some flexibility in this offer?"

"How can we reshape this compensation package?"

Reality Check

Many of these kinds of salary negotiations depend on what you bring to the table in the way of skills, expertise, education, and experience. More senior-level paralegals with highly sought-after skills or those in a low-candidate/high-demand practice specialty have much more negotiating power than do those who are just entering the field with generalized skills.

When putting together your negotiating tactic, take into consideration whether you bring something unique to the firm. Now is the time to be very honest with yourself about your present skill level and expertise. The strategy is to get the firm to acknowledge that you are bringing something to the firm that it does not already have. For example, a nurse entering the paralegal field may bring a value-added skill that the firm does not have but needs. It is therefore worth more dollars to the firm. An experienced paralegal seeking a higher salary may be replacing a more junior-level paralegal. In this instance, the candidate can use her experience level by saying:

> "I am very experienced in medical malpractice issues because of my four years at Smith and Jones. I will be able to complete assignments quicker than more junior-level paralegals could. You will be able to compensate for the additional increase in salary because you will be able to bill my services at a higher rate to the client."

WHAT TO DO IF YOU CAN'T GET MORE MONEY

Sometimes you won't be able to get the employer to up the base pay. You just can't. Either the firm has given you its maximum amount of dollars it feels it can for this position, or it just doesn't agree with you about additional dollars. In either case, you may still want the position. And it may still be a good one for you. The trick is to avoid the escalation of uncomfortable feelings that can often result in ineffective exchanges. The stakes remain high—this is your career, and a good portion of time and energy is about to be dedicated to this new firm or organization.

The following questions can be used as a pivotal turning of the negotiations from salary to benefits, perks, and action items:

> "In what ways can we redefine this offer?"

> "In what ways, other than compensation, can we think about changing the nature of this offer?"

Once you have turned the negotiations from salary to added compensation in other areas, you might ask for a replacement for actual base dollars. Consider asking for one of the following instead:

• An accelerated salary review in 3 to 6 months (make certain you ask for a *salary review,* not a performance review!).
• Tuition reimbursement for classes or seminars for the Certified Legal Assistant designation or specifically those aimed at your new position.

- Tuition reimbursement to finish your degree or certificate, provided you stay with the firm for a certain length of time after achieving the designation (usually one to two years or more).
- Stock options, if provided by the organization.
- Hiring bonus. (Entry-level paralegals, we're sorry, but generally firms do not give hiring bonuses to this level. They may make an exception, however, on very rare occasions, if they desperately need an entry-level with your particular unique skills and none is available anywhere.)
- Guaranteed year-end bonus.
- Four-day workweek.
- Laptop computer and telecommunications setup.
- Private or window office.
- Better or stronger title. (It will be useful for salary negotiations down the line. Or in the event you leave this position, a stronger title positions you to start negotiations at a higher level than here.)
- Salary in lieu of health benefits (if you can do it).
- Delayed start date.
- Additional vacation (not always negotiable).
- Car or generous allowance if one is required for traveling in the position (such as an investigative paralegal).

KNOWING HOW AND WHEN TO CONCEDE

Knowing how to handle objections to your requests is important. Navigating employers to close the deal is a learned skill. We weren't born knowing how to do it. Before addressing the employer's objections to your request, remember the employer is a buyer and you are the salesperson. A buyer, according to Garry Karrass in *Negotiate to Close* (Simon & Schuster), needs to feel satisfied. These "satisfiers" contribute to the buyer's satisfaction, which is imperative for smooth sailing once you have started with the firm. It does you no good to alienate the buyer. After discussions are completed, you'll have to work with this person, and you want that relationship to be comfortable and without ill feelings. Most potential employers want to

- Feel competent and confident they are making a "good hire."
- Avoid trouble.
- Look good within their own organization. A hiring authority's job may depend on whom he or she hires.
- Get relief from overburdening work.
- "Save face."

• Have the process over with.
• Be considered fair and nice.
• Be listened to and taken seriously.
• Feel as though they got someone that somebody else wanted.

In negotiations, according to Karrass, how you concede may be more important than what you concede. We try to make the "buyers" earn the concession. We hesitate, we ask for time to reconsider, we may even consider other job offers. Then the buyer feels better. She can go to her administrator or managing partner and say, "I couldn't get that candidate at the right salary. She wouldn't come down in dollars."

Another concession-making guideline: *Always give yourself room to negotiate.* What you ask for may not be what you are willing to settle for. For example, if you are negotiating salary points, you may ask for a salary slightly higher than what you might be willing to settle for. But don't pull the pin on the hand grenade, throw it over to the fence, and run for cover! If you cannot justify your request with solid aspects about your skill level, background, experience, or education, backed up by salary surveys, documentation, or market conditions, reconsider whether you should ask! And be careful not to give the employer the impression that your request is nonnegotiable when it is not. One good phrase to use is *"I would consider an offer at $40,000 per year"* rather than *"My bottomline is $40,000 per year."*

DEADLINES

Most good negotiators will issue a deadline. You must be able to determine whether the deadline is real. There is a tremendous amount of pressure to concede as the deadline nears. Stay calm. Most of the time, it's the employer who sets the deadline and the candidate who must adhere to it. However, if you have placed a counteroffer on the table, there's nothing wrong with asking, *"How soon can you get back to me?"* or *"While Jones & Jones is my first choice, I do have another offer to consider. Can you get back to me by Friday?"* Negotiations that continue on too long run into several dangers: confrontations, disinterest from both parties, or missed opportunities on both sides. It's better to set the expectation as to when the negotiations will conclude.

We want to make sure that not only you, the candidate, is satisfied with the offer, but also the employer is satisfied with what she is getting. You will probably be seeing this person quite a bit once you land in the firm. It's better to have made friends rather than enemies.

• Give in slowly and thoughtfully.
• Give yourself room to negotiate.
• Give in graciously.
• Don't mishandle a ridiculous offer.
• Don't ask for the moon if at least part of the moon isn't yours to have.
• Don't concede too much so that you are miserable after you start.

The overall concept of conceding is that we want to wring as much buyer satisfaction as we can out of each concession. We want the buyer to know that he earned the concession in some way. He'll feel better about the negotiation, and so will we.

Using a Staffing Organization to Negotiate for You

This is probably one of the few times in your professional life where a third party is at your disposal who can allay your fears, test the waters on your negotiating ideas, and inject some excitement and camaraderie into what is usually a lengthy and emotionally draining process. Good recruiters are highly trained in the negotiation process, and it is in their best interests to ensure that you get the job you want at the dollars you want.

An ethical recruiter will tell you about each stumbling block. Don't shoot the messenger! Employers will confide in the recruiter things that they cannot confide in you as a candidate. This gives you the distinct advantage of being able to correct the course as it develops. The recruiter serves as the conduit for feedback on both sides.

An employer will also give a recruiter an indication that you may be the firm's first choice, giving the go-ahead to discuss the parameters of an offer to get your initial read. Any objections can be headed off and a firm offer tweaked through this process. The recruiter can either negotiate between the two of you or pave the way for direct dialogue between you and the firm. But the process still belongs to you. You are at the helm, and you guide the process. Listen to what your recruiter has to say, but make up your own mind. Don't get pressured into taking something that you don't want. Ask your recruiter to amend your requests and carry your counteroffers. A good recruiter will facilitate the process but cannot and should not decide for you.

25

15 Ways to Leave Your Lawyer

". . . and set yourself free."

—Paul Simon

LAST IMPRESSIONS

Now that you have a job offer, you're going to have to give notice to your present employer. Don't get your knickers in a twist over how best to go about it! Just as you wanted to sway potential employers with your astounding skills and abilities, you want to leave your present employer with a good impression.

Last impressions are as important as first. This truism is doubly important in the legal field where "everyone knows your name." People talk, and when they're talking about you, it's important that the conversation remain positive. The time between the announcement of your resignation and your last day is a prime opportunity to ensure that today's coworkers become tomorrow's dependable references and contacts. Here are just a few suggestions as to how to go about it:[1]

Time to Get Ready, Freddie . . .

1. *Know when it's time to move on:* Working for someone is a dating relationship, not a marriage. At some point, unless you are a partner, it's probably time to move on to bigger and better things. It's just the reality of today's workplace.

Don't Cause a Storm, Norm . . .

2. *Never leave in a huff:* No matter how perturbed you may be or how much angst you have, it's never a good idea to walk off a job. Take a walk around the block instead. The legal field is a very small community. Trust us on this one. You're not going to want to burn any bridges.

Upgrade Those Skills, Jill . . .

3. *Take a look at your current skills:* Are your skills up-to-date? Have you been in one job so long that you have failed to familiarize yourself with the three Ts: technology, techniques, or tactics?

---

[1] Inspired by an article in *California Lawyer* magazine, "How to Leave the Law," by Susan E. Davis (1998). With apologies to the *California Lawyer*.

Before you quit, make certain that you have marketable skills. Do you know what practice areas are hot now? Are you in a dying practice arena and without cross-training into other specialties? Are you aware of how paralegals are utilized in other organizations? Is it time to finish your degree or certificate? Do your computer skills extend beyond word processing? Can you maneuver your way around, across, and through the Internet? Check with local headhunters to find out about current market conditions. Don't jump the gun on giving notice. It's best not to announce your departure until you've landed a new position for a couple of very good reasons:

a. You are more marketable if you are employed.

b. Some companies have an immediate termination policy, particularly if you are going to a competitor.

And, if your skills aren't marketable, you may have a long wait between jobs!

Don't Try to Look Back, Mack . . .

4. *Don't get fooled by counteroffers:* Remember why you decided to leave. If the issues go beyond the dollars, a counteroffer from your present firm does not always mitigate other issues. If all that was needed to make you really happy was a few more dollars, you may want to reconsider leaving. Other than that, ask yourself, "Once I get used to the salary increase, will other problems causing me to leave now cause me to leave again?" For example, "are they going to get rid of that old battle-ax down the hall or not?"

Create a Truce, Bruce . . .

5. *Mend broken fences:* Make peace with any adversary. Take her aside and mention a few things you enjoyed about working with her. Keep the conversation short and sweet—or write a personal note. Can you be accused of playing politics here? Sure! However, we'd rather see you leave your employer in a positive framework, complete with colleagues sorry to see you go. That's really so much better than that beastly dancing in the hallway the moment you are about to become a mere memory.

Extend Your Hand, Fran . . .

6. *Build lasting bridges:* Admire a particular colleague? Have a particularly close relationship with a coworker? Take her to lunch and let her know. Drop her a note mentioning what you learned from her. So

what if you kept getting passed over while she got all the goodies! Get over it. At least you'll leave on a positive note with a new best friend.

Write a Good Plan, Stan . . .

7. *Prepare a detailed status memo:* Nothing is worse than to leave colleagues confused about what you were doing. Take time to write a detailed memo that outlines the status of your current assignments, past cases, or matters that have a probability of surfacing. Don't leave thinking your successor will automatically get up to speed. Leave your job in an orderly and organized fashion.

Try to Leave Clean, Dean . . .

8. *Leave your desk in order:* Make certain to leave your desk neat, clean, and organized. Return all borrowed books, equipment, and the whatnots you borrowed from Susie in 1979. Perk up or—what the heck—throw out any dead plants. Answer all required letters and memos. Finish up every last assignment as time allows. Dust those window sills, and get those chocolate fingerprint stains off that computer. That last impression is as important as the first.

Respect the Firm, Herm . . .

9. *Take only what you are allowed to take:* Being an employee with the firm or company does not mean the tools you used, such as books, Rolodex, equipment, computers, post-its, or coat trees, belong to you. Do not take anything with you, including forms or client files. If you are not certain about an item, ask the appropriate authority.

Hire a Good Guy, Sy . . .

10. *Hire a great replacement:* If you are asked to hire your own replacement or to participate in the process, make certain that the person you hire is right for the job. You won't score any points by being remembered for approving the hire from hell.

Put on Your Tie, Clyde . . .

11. *Firm up outside contacts:* Use the news of your departure and successor's arrival to reconnect with former clients and suppliers. Vendors, in particular, can be very supportive and helpful. They have inside knowledge of the industry you never dreamed possible. You may want to let them know where you'll be landing. They can be critical to your future success.

Know When to Go, Flo . . .

12. *Give proper notice:* Two weeks' notice is standard. If you feel that more notice is warranted, try not to go longer than 30 days, no matter how long you've been with the firm. You're a "short-timer," and anything beyond a month is too long for you, your new employer, or colleagues to handle.

Pick up Your Files, Miles . . .

13. *Make certain you are aware of what is in your personnel file:* Many states have laws that protect employees' rights to access to their personnel files. Be sure that you know what is in your file before you leave. In most states, you are entitled to copies of your performance reviews. Take copies of "kudos" letters (correspondence in which clients, colleagues, or supervisors have acknowledged your good work). In this day and age of reference reluctance, it is very hard to get a firm or corporation to commit to anything more than name, rank, salary, and dates of employment. You may need these reviews and letters for future job searches.

Have a Good 'Tude, Dude . . .

14. *Maintain a positive and professional attitude:* Stay positive and professional while you are a short-timer. Continue to behave in a professional manner right through the time you leave. Don't start coming in late, leaving early, or using up your personal days because "it no longer matters." You'll only put pressure on your colleagues to pick up your slack and work overtime or harder to compensate for your attitude. This may account for the growling you now receive in lieu of "good morning." Your attitude could be the final impression your coworkers remember, and it's so much nicer if the memory of you is pleasant.

And Set Yourself Free.

15. *Ace the exit interview:* Anticipate questions about the firm and its staff. Be prepared to answer why you are leaving. Be sure to be diplomatic. Although the exit interview may seem like the time to spout off all those things you have been saving up for years, don't say anything you would not want repeated. And above all, think before you take aim. Offering suggestions to improve systems or operations is one thing, but harshly criticizing someone revengefully is quite another. Before decimating someone, be sure to ask yourself, "what purpose will this serve?" Leaving thoughtfully with an eye toward the future is the only way to go. Here's to outrageous success! Best of luck in your new endeavors!

26

Riding the Train from Temp to Full-Time

*"I believe the true road to preeminent success in any
line is to make yourself master of that line."*

—Andrew Carnegie

TEMPORARY STAFFING/AGENCIES

Some observers have expressed amazement at the skyrocketing growth of the temporary staffing industry. But given the fact that short-term staffing can be long on benefits for both employers and employees, experts believe the surge should really come as no surprise.

The soaring growth in temporary staffing has spurred dynamic changes in the temporary staffing industry. According to an article in *The Los Angeles Times,* temporary help services reached unprecedented levels in 1997. Receipts grew 15.4 percent to $50.3 billion; employment expressed as average daily employment rose 9.7 percent to 2,535,220 temporary employees. Growth in the temporary help and staffing services industry in 1997 was attributable to several factors:

Tight labor market: When business activity increases, there is greater demand for employees, both full-time and temporary, eventually leading to worker and skills shortages.

Changing worker attitudes: Rapid changes in the economy are changing the way workers view employment. They increasingly believe that traditional long-term job security with a single company is less certain and that employment security lies in having the right skills and knowing where to get those skills.

Expansion of staffing services beyond traditional temporary help: Staffing firms provide a far broader range of services than in the past.

In prior years, most legal staffing agencies were owned and operated by small business owners. In the past few years, increased consolidation and restructuring as well as enhanced sophistication have been among the changes. Big companies have grown much bigger, and several of the largest now post annual sales of more than $5 billion in clerical, medical, and light industrial arenas. The legal staffing component of these companies make up a very small part of revenues. These smaller divisions now place contract attorneys, paralegals, litigation support personnel, and administrative staff, including legal secretaries.

Meanwhile, "boutique" companies continue to enter the market. The barriers to entry are very low, so as one staffing company is gobbled up by a larger company, another one springs up to take its place. These businesses' basic assets are working capital.

With more temporary staffing companies vying to place workers, and unemployment at all-time lows (at this writing), competition among the companies has been ratcheted upward. Intense competition for dependable workers has meant even more good news for temps, some of whom now enjoy job benefits similar to those earned by full-time workers. Many staffing companies also offer referral bonuses paid to temps who refer other potential temporary workers to the company. The companies need to offer wages and benefits in line with those offered by other companies in order to remain competitive.

In these uncertain economic times, employers have taken the position that hiring temporary employees helps businesses get through peak demand periods without adding permanent staff and also permits them to try out prospective employees before awarding them permanent jobs. Temporary employees find much to like as well. Flexible staffing lets them tailor their jobs to their lifestyles and allows them to try jobs in different law firms and companies before committing to any one employer.

Like anything else, there's an upside and a downside to working as a temporary employee. The upside is that it gives you an opportunity to review several law firms in order to evaluate certain aspects of a firm or in-house legal department, such as size, culture, work environment, location, practice specialty, and philosophy to determine whether that firm or legal department is right for you. The downside, if you are seeking a full-time position, is that if you work as a temp, it is often difficult to land a permanent position. The theory (right or wrong) is that you might not be able to stay long-term with an employer. Unfortunately, there's no real definition of what constitutes too long.

Opportunities abound for everyone with any type of paralegal skill. For people who are just entering or reentering the workforce, a temporary position can be a bridge to permanent employment. Some statistics show that three-quarters of former temporary employees go on to permanent jobs. It's also an appealing option for those who don't want to move into

Reality Check

If you are seeking employment as a paralegal yet are constantly assigned document-coding positions, you may want to switch agencies. Having some document-coding positions on your resume may be acceptable to future employers. However, it is our experience that it is not always easy to attempt entry into the paralegal field with a long history of temporary document-coding positions. And, while this reaction may seem unfair, it is, nonetheless, an obstacle for some employers.

permanent jobs, at least not immediately, such as retirees and college students on summer breaks. An older person can get back into the workforce and take a position for shorter period. And younger people without a lot of skills can learn necessary skills to earn them a permanent position.

Temporary help agencies are not necessarily employment agencies. Some do not have permanent placement opportunities. Temporary workers are employees of a temporary help company and are recruited, sometimes trained, assigned, and paid by the temporary agency. This agency pays all payroll and social security taxes for its temporary employees, as well as any other benefits, such as medical coverage and, in some cases, vacation pay and 401(k) plans.

A Georgia State University study states that individuals who take transitional jobs "may be better off in the long run because a transitional job will relieve enough financial pressure to give them the bargaining power to hold out for higher wages and a better job." Bear in mind, however, that this report was prepared for the general workplace and not the legal arena.

The study further reported that taking a transitional job doesn't lessen a worker's chances for full-time employment and lengthens the search by just 5 weeks. Incidentally, according to an American Staffing Association (ASA) profile, of the temporary workers who were offered full-time positions as a result of temporary assignments, 38 percent turned down the offers because they enjoyed the benefits of temporary work.

In addition to those new or newly returned to the workforce, a number of others look favorably upon temporary work from a lifestyle perspective. This group is predominantly made up of people who seek optimum flexibility in their work lives. Actors, homemakers, students, teachers, writers, moms and dads needing flexible schedules make up this group. And there's a growing core of full-time temp workers who simply like to change their jobs from time to time.

Some legal assistants enjoy working temporarily and have no desire to seek any other kind of employment. In fact, you could say that there are actually permanent temporaries. Assignments are classified as short-term or long-term and can last anywhere from one day (usually, though, at least a week) to a year. If you are considering temporary work, be sure you have the right characteristics. You must be

- Able to hit the ground running, that is, take direction well the first time, assess the situation, and understand what must be done
- Available to work on short notice and be easy to contact

- Able to act independently yet unafraid to speak up and ask the right questions
- Flexible about location, times, acceptance of different personalities, and nature of assignments
- Adventurous
- Not too shy and enjoy being the "new kid on the block" all the time
- Respectful of different cultures
- Open to supervision
- Craving flexibility and variety
- Able to face some downtime between jobs, if necessary.

WHEN SHOULD YOU CONSIDER TEMPING?

You should consider a temporary position if you are

- Recently laid-off or downsized and need work immediately
- Interested in improving your skills before landing a full-time position
- Really looking to work project by project
- Unable to give a full commitment due to family matters, a personal project, travel plans, or school
- Looking to enter the field and need some experience behind you
- Retired from another career and don't need a full-time job
- Recently moved to a new location and want to get your bearings first
- Open to "let's get acquainted before either of us makes a commitment to each other" and looking to gain insight and exposure into a future employer
- One who just prefers it.

HOW AND WHERE TO BEGIN

Find a good agency that has a solid background in placing temporary paralegals. Tap into your network to find the "buzz" on the company. How long has the company been in business? What kind of clients do they have? What are typical assignments? What are the backgrounds of the recruiters? Is this an agency that places primarily secretaries or clerical help? Do they know what your needs are? What about benefits? Is there access to group health insurance? Are wages competitive?

Know the Temp Lingo

Contract: Generally a term for temp attorneys or IT professionals. They typically work on a project of several months' duration, such as taking a case through trial.

Temp-to-perm or direct hire: This is a position that starts out as temporary with the possibility of becoming a permanent or full-time position. The company for whom the temporary is working converts the temporary employee to a full-time employee through a conversion fee paid to the temp agency by the employer or with no fee, depending on the market or the length of time the temporary has been on the job. Steve Berchem, of ASA, says the term is applicable when an employer converts a temporary employee to a full-time employee, either through pre-arrangement (they want to try the candidate out first) or after the fact (they like the temp employee and want to hire the employee full-time). This is becoming a more widely used way of hiring paralegals and support staff professionals.

Temporary: Typically used to describe nontechnical employees who work for a period of short or indefinite duration in office-clerical, light industrial, or accounting positions.

Career Temporary: Those who find the flexibility of working with a staffing service to be a preferable means of working.

INTERVIEW TIPS FROM ASA

Interviewing with a temporary help service? This is a perfect time to explore your fringe benefits in detail, according to ASA.

The Association recommends that you ask the following questions:

1. Does the company offer paid vacations? If so, do hours accumulate from year to year?
2. Does the company fill both part- and full-time positions? If you are using temporary help as a bridge to full-time employment, ask about this. Some temporary help companies specialize in filling full-time openings, others do not. Also, ask about their policy regarding acceptance of a full-time position.
3. Is there a medical and hospitalization plan? What are the benefits?
4. Does the company have seniority bonuses?
5. Do you get a bonus for referring other workers?
6. How often are you paid? And are you paid locally, or are checks mailed from another city? (This may affect the ready cashing of paychecks.)
7. Is the temporary help/staffing service a member of ASA? Membership shows that the company has agreed to conform to the highest ethical standards in the industry and is up-to-date on all the latest developments and trends.

Don't forget to ask about your chances for being kept busy. If you feel that you won't be busy enough, register with other companies as backup. In fact, of those workers surveyed by ASA, 37 percent are currently registered with more than one company. In any case, make sure you are completely satisfied with the employment conditions of a temporary help company before registering.

Questions? You can log onto the ASA Web site at http://www.staffingtoday.net and search the membership directory for ASA-affiliated staffing firms in your area. Oftentimes, these firms will have links to their Web sites.

Because of liability issues, many firms refuse to hire temps directly onto their payroll and insist that you go through a temporary staffing organization. However, you might want to approach a few firms of your choice and ask whether they use temporaries. If the answer is yes, find out how they hire temporaries: directly onto their payroll or from an agency? If the firm uses agencies, find out which ones and sign up. Be sure to let your recruiter know you've done your homework and how you arrived at their agency. Most likely they will be pleased and should make an extra effort to place you at those firms as long as you meet the hiring requirements.

Don't expect to be an independent contractor, however. Few firms or agencies will take on independent contractors these days. Most will require an employee status. There is a list of twenty factors from the IRS that determine whether you will be considered an independent contractor.

Most paralegals do not qualify. These factors include working without supervision (questionable if you must work directly under the supervision of an attorney) and having a certificate of compliance that you have workers' compensation insurance—and very few do. Furthermore, you must pay estimated taxes quarterly, which can lead to some very costly problems if you fail even once.

WORKING WITH YOUR TEMPORARY AGENCY

Sign up with a couple of agencies in order to get maximum exposure to the temp market. Not all agencies have the same jobs. Establish a great rapport with your recruiter. Understand that a recruiting job is a high-pressure position that moves quickly. Consequently, your recruiter doesn't always get a chance to talk with you in depth. Be sure you are pleasant each and every time you call and that pleasantness extends to the receptionist, assistant, and other recruiters in the agencies who are trying to help you. They all talk to each other, and nothing is worse when recruiters stop taking your call because you're too difficult to deal with.

The most common assignment for temporary paralegals is in litigation. Frequently, law firms will need temporary paralegals for document productions, discovery, trial preparation, and large or complex litigation cases. Paralegals may also be called upon for due diligence projects, real estate closings, mergers and acquisitions, or data entry. On some occasions, you may even travel to other cities to work with the firm's lawyers and paralegals. You could be sent to a fancy office setting or out to a remote warehouse. The most important thing is to be prepared for just about anything!

Check in with your recruiter on a regular basis. Find out what's comfortable for your agency. Some want you to call in every day for availability, while others believe once a week is adequate. And even if you are desperate for a job, don't pressure your recruiter to death. Let them know you have an immediate need, be persistent, but don't expect your dire situation to become their dire situation. Most recruiters are empathetic and more than willing to help you, but as in any job, boundaries have to be set.

Be sure to let your agency know if you find a temporary job where you would like to settle in on a full-time basis. The agency may be able to negotiate a temp-to-perm position for you that would be a win-win for all parties.

Reality Check

Working as a temporary employee does not mean that you shouldn't have your own business cards, particularly if you are seeking a permanent position! Have business cards made up with your name, phone number, address, and E-mail address so that potential employers or your network can easily reach you.

27

Your First 100 Days
in Your New Job

"The secret of success in life is known only to those who have not succeeded."

—John Churton Collins

Your first 100 days as a new paralegal will be a whirlwind of activity and learning. Not only will you be getting used to a new office, new people, new procedures, and a new boss, but also you will be trying on your career "for real" for the first time. You may never have been a "boss" yourself before, so you may be unsure of how to treat the secretary who has been assigned to you. The best advice is to take a deep breath, keep calm, keep your ears open, roll up your sleeves, and get to work.

SAMPLE DIARY OF A FIRST DAY ON THE JOB AT A MID-SIZED FIRM

8:00   Arriving in the reception area, you are greeted by the office manager and shown to your office. You are introduced to your secretary.

8:10   You are taken on a tour of the firm and introduced to all available personnel. You are shown the various departments, including the file room, library, employee lounge, bookkeeping, word-processing department, and mail room.

8:30   The personnel manager takes you to his or her office, where you fill out all necessary legal and tax papers and are given a copy of the firm's employee manual.

8:45   You are turned over to your secretary, who helps you equip your desk with supplies and shows you how to log onto the firm's computer network.

9:15   Your supervising attorney pokes her head in the door and welcomes you. She sits down and gives you an idea of what she expects from you and asks you what your goals and interests are. She gives you your first assignment, a small research project.

10:00   You go to the library to start working on your research project. You are interrupted by the office manager, who wants to show you how to work the firm's telephone system.

10:30   You get back to work on your research project.

10:45   One of the firm's associates comes into the library to work on his research project. The two of you chat for a little while, and then he asks you to come down to his office so he can give you some depositions to summarize for him.

11:00   You get back to work on your research project.

12:00   You retire to the employee lounge with your brown-bag lunch.

12:45   You resume your research project in the library.

1:30   You complete your research project and go back to your office to prepare a memo. You realize that you don't know the proper format for the firm's memos or which directory you are supposed to save the document in. You call your secretary, who comes in and gives you a rundown of protocols on how information is stored in the firm's computers.

2:00   You are working on your memo when you are interrupted by the office bookkeeper, who wants to show you how you are supposed to keep your time sheets.

2:30   You are interrupted from working on your memo by yet another of the firm's attorneys, who comes in and introduces herself. She asks if you know how to use the firm's database program so that you can enter some documents for her on a case she is working on. You tell her you have used similar programs in school but not that particular one. She tells you to call the office manager and arrange to get some training on this database so you can help her with her case.

2:45   You finish your report and begin working on the deposition summaries. You realize that you don't have a sample of how this attorney likes his summaries done. You contact the word-processing department and have them print out some samples of previous summaries that have been done for this particular attorney.

3:15   The supervising attorney comes in and asks if you have finished your research memo yet. You tell her you have and that you have given it to your secretary for finalization and copying.

3:20   You call the office manager and ask her to get you trained on the firm's database program. She puts you down for Thursday at 10:00.

3:45   While working on the deposition summaries, you have a question on something that happened in the case. You realize you don't know the name of the client or where the file is kept. You contact your secretary, who shows you how to look up a client on the firm's computer printout and learn the file location.

4:30   One of the firm's other paralegals pokes his head in and invites you to a welcome lunch the next day so that you can meet all the paralegals. He has a large project due the next day and asks you if you'll have time to help him tomorrow.

5:00   Your secretary pops in to see if you need anything else for the day and tell you good-bye. She gives you a copy of the research memo that has been finalized.

5:15   You get a call from one of the attorneys in the firm asking if you have time to come down and see him first thing in the morning for a project.

5:30   You prepare your time sheet for the day's work. Realizing you are going to have a busy day tomorrow, you take one of the depositions home with you to summarize that evening.

SURVIVAL SKILLS FOR WORKING WITH ATTORNEYS

Attorneys, like any other people, are individuals, and it is impossible to generalize about them. Having said this, however, there are a few common characteristics that many attorneys seem to share. Knowing these characteristics in advance will give you an edge in working with them.

First of all, most attorneys, by the nature of their work, are pressed for time. It is important for you to understand that nowhere is the phrase "time is money" more important than in a law office. Attorneys (and paralegals too, for that matter) are judged, evaluated, and valued on how many hours they can bill each day to clients. Time spent sitting and chatting is time that must be made up elsewhere, probably over a lunch hour or in the evening when the attorney would rather be heading home. Keeping this in mind, when you are formulating questions to ask attorneys or preparing to go over with an attorney the information you have gathered for him or her, you must be organized and succinct. Ask your questions, note the answers, and then withdraw to continue your work. The attorney will appreciate it when you are not a time-waster.

Don't make the mistake, however, of being intimidated into not asking enough questions to properly perform your job. If after asking your questions and receiving some answers you are still unclear on what is wanted, you need to make a decision. If the attorney appears to be relaxed and willing to spend time with you, go ahead and ask for clarification. If, on the

Attorneys are usually creatures of habit. They will take their work to people they already know do a good job for them. It may take you a little while to earn their trust and get into the assignment "loop." Be patient and persistent. Keep knocking on doors and asking for work.

If no attorney has work for you, pester the paralegals. If no paralegals have work to hand out, ask the senior secretaries or even the office manager. If they don't have anything, study the firm's library books or a software manual for one of the firm's computer programs. The trick is to stay busy. You don't want the firm's senior partner to pop into your office and find you reading a *People* magazine!

other hand, the attorney has the phone in his or her hand and is giving you one of those "are you finished?" looks, you may want to retire and either try to figure out the answers yourself or seek clarification from another attorney or paralegal.

Checklist of Information to Get about an Assignment

- Who is the client? What is the file number? (You will need this information so that you can properly bill your time.)
- Legal and factual background of the case. (The more you know about the case, the better job you can do.)
- What task are you being given to do? (If the assignment seems vague, ask for more specifics.)
- How does that task fit into the big picture of the case? (If you know how your finished product will be used, it will help you focus your work.)
- Does the attorney want a written report of your work, or will an oral report suffice?
- How much time should this project take to complete? (This will help you budget your time for the day. Also, it will help you know if you are spending too much time on a particular task. See the section on billing, below.)
- What is your deadline for completing the project? (This will help you prioritize your many ongoing tasks.)

The second thing new paralegals need to know about attorneys is that they want things done *their way*. One of your jobs when you are assigned to work for a particular attorney is to learn all of his or her idiosyncracies when it comes to preparing forms, drafting documents, taking messages from clients, organizing files, keeping his or her calendar, or completing any of the myriad tasks you may be called upon to do. For example, some attorneys want you to put the client's file number on each phone message. Some want the correspondence to go on the left of the file, and some want it to go on the right. Each attorney has his or her own writing style that you will have to learn when you are drafting legal documents for his or her signature. This task is compounded when you are assigned to work for more than one attorney or when you are part of a "pool" where all attorneys in the firm have access to you. A paralegal who memorizes each attorney's preferences will be very valuable indeed.

One of the best things that a fledgling paralegal can do is locate an attorney mentor within the firm. A mentor can be an invaluable aid in a number of areas. If you are stuck on a legal question, a mentor can help you through the maze of the library or the on-line research. If you have a sticky ethical question or a political problem with a firm employee, a mentor can be a precious sounding board or source of insight. A mentor can stand up for you if someone registers a complaint against you or give you an idea of your chances for a promotion you have been wanting.

SURVIVAL SKILLS FOR WORKING WITH STAFF

Depending on the size of your office, there will be a number of different types of support staff available to assist you in your work. In most offices, there will be at least one secretary and a receptionist. In larger offices, there will be "gophers," whose job is to deliver packages to clients, file documents with the court, and run the other countless errands that a law firm generates. Your office may employ file clerks, whose job is to keep the stacks of letters, pleadings, and other documents filed away in their proper places. Some very large law firms have law librarians to manage the stacks of legal books and computer media, mail room clerks to sort and deliver mail, copy room personnel, who save you or the secretaries from having to stand at the copy machine, and case clerks, who perform some of the more mundane tasks that sometimes get delegated to paralegals, such as Bates stamping and data entry.

Although the firm may stress a teamwork concept, the larger the firm, the more likely that a social strata will develop, with attorneys at the top, paralegals and secretaries somewhere in the middle, and all other support staff at the bottom. Although this may very well be the reality of the firm, it is important that you not buy into such a notion. There are both humanistic and practical reasons for not doing so.

First of all, remember the Golden Rule: "Do unto others as you would have them do unto you." Would you appreciate being considered a less valuable employee? Then don't make others feel that way. Do you enjoy being left out of the lunch crowd because you are a paralegal and not an attorney? Then don't leave secretaries and runners out of your social circle.

On a more practical note, the law office does function on teamwork. If you are too proud to help out a secretary in the middle of a dire rush to get a bankruptcy petition on file before a deadline because it's not "paralegal" work, you can bet word of this will travel around the office. And may heaven help you when it's your turn to meet a deadline. If, on the other hand, you attain a reputation as a team player, the team will be there to back you up when you need it.

New paralegals sometimes complain that they are treated with contempt by the experienced secretaries in the office. This attitude stems back to a time before the paralegal profession had established a stronghold in the law office. Senior legal secretaries were actually performing paralegal work along with their secretarial duties. In fact, before there were many paralegal schools, most paralegals were secretaries who had moved up the ladder. Some secretaries who have the skills and experience, but not the title, are resentful over the perks and status that paralegals receive in the firm. Paralegals often have their own offices, don't usually have to punch time clocks, and are often on a higher pay scale than are secretaries. To add insult to injury, the secretary is assigned to work for this upstart paralegal. Paralegals must be aware that the seed of such resentment can be there and take care not to do anything to foster its growth into a full-fledged power struggle. Be compassionate and appreciative of your secretary. Don't lord your status over anyone in the firm. The self-importance may feel good at first, but the price you pay is much too high in the long run.

Another important thing to remember is to respect the firm's procedures and rules. They are usually there to make life easier for the staff that is in charge of that particular function. For instance, if you are expected to turn in time sheets daily or weekly, do it. If you turn in three weeks' worth of time on the last day of the month, it will not endear you to the bookkeeping department. If the firm wants you to forward your telephone calls when you are working in the library or another office, take the time to do so. Nothing frustrates a receptionist more than to search all over the office for you when a call comes in. Following these rules reinforces the fact that you are courteous and a team player. It shows your coworkers that you want to make it easier for them to get their jobs done.

WORKING WITH OTHER PARALEGALS

In a small office, you might be the only paralegal. In a large one, you may be one of dozens. Your relationship with the other paralegals in your office is vital. They will be your best source of information on a number of subjects. They will teach you many things that your attorney may not have time to. They will pinch-hit for you when you are ill or on vacation. In fact, it is a good idea to find a paralegal mentor as well as an attorney mentor. It is your fellow paralegal who will truly know what you are going through because he or she has been there too.

Sometimes it happens that competition may come up between paralegals for the "juiciest" case or to work for the "best" attorney. You should strive to keep these feelings from arising. Don't forget that you are on a team. After you have established yourself and your reputation for quality work is known, you will be rewarded with good cases of your own. You must be ready to pay your dues and work your way up. There are few shortcuts to that road.

THE LEARNING CURVE

You may have heard that employee turnover is expensive for employers because it costs thousands of dollars to retrain a new person. This expense is due to the learning curve, the amount of time it takes new employees to grasp enough information about their positions to be able to work with minimal supervision and begin to pull their weight. Until new employees are "up to speed" on what is expected of them, they are more of a liability to their companies than an asset. The company knows this and is willing to make the investment in the time, money, and energy it will take to train an efficient employee.

It is good to keep this in mind when you begin your new paralegal job. Your firm is investing its time and money in you in the hopes that you will become profitable and helpful to the firm down the road. Your job is to learn as much as possible as quickly as possible. If you can speed up the expected learning curve, you will rise in the esteem of your employers and coworkers. Have you ever heard the expressions, "She's fast on the uptake" or "He's a quick study"? This refers to someone who has zoomed through the training and left the learning curve in the dust. Do you have to have natural smarts to accomplish such a feat? Not necessarily. There are some tricks you can use to help you speed up your own learning curve.

1. *Take good notes.* Make a vow to yourself that no one will ever have to tell you something more than once. During your first 100 days in the law office, take a pen and pad of paper with you *everywhere you go.* Never get caught without them nearby. Every time someone explains how to use a particular computer program, how to use the phone system, what the procedure is for retrieving a file out of storage, how to keep track of the facsimile transmissions for billing purposes, anything at all, write it down. Don't think to yourself, "Oh this sounds easy. I won't have to write this down." It may be true, but when it's added onto the other two-dozen things you learned that day about office procedures, it will get lost in the shuffle. Plan to keep your

notes indefinitely. Some procedures you may only perform once in a blue moon, and you may need to refresh your memory occasionally.

2. *Keep samples of your work.* Whenever you draft a pleading or other document that is new and different, save a copy of it in a file that is kept at your desk. If you receive a well-written document from opposing counsel, save a copy of that too. Once you have built up a good "form bank" of your own, you will have a formidable library from which to draw for future projects.

3. *Don't try to reinvent the wheel.* New paralegals often think their tasks represent the first time such assignments have ever been given. What you should keep in mind is that whatever you have been asked to do has probably been done in that firm once before. Instead of trying to draft a set of interrogatories or prepare a grant deed from scratch, ask one of the other paralegals if he or she can point you to another case where this has already been done. It will give you a great starting place and save a lot of time. (Don't forget, time is money!) That does not mean you don't need to learn how to use the form books to prepare a document yourself if need be. It is merely a way to become more efficient. Once you are efficient, you have mastered the learning curve.

4. *Be willing to do a little homework on your own time.* Take home the employee manual and read it. Become familiar with the local rules of the courts nearest you. Spend a lunch hour browsing through the firm's library to see what resources are available. Have someone give you a tour through the office computer network. There may be all kinds of forms or legal research banks that have been loaded onto the computer. If your firm uses a type of software with which you are unfamiliar, take an evening course and learn how to use it. Any of these tools could help you move from "freshman" to seasoned paralegal in record time.

5. *Volunteer to help on firm committees or projects.* Firms often put together a group of volunteer employees to accomplish certain administrative tasks within the firm. Some such projects may be creating and maintaining a database of case law on a particular subject, organizing the firm's Christmas party or summer picnic, serving on an employee relations committee, or orchestrating a reorganization of the firm's storage warehouse. Employees from a wide area of the firm are sometimes grouped together to accomplish these tasks, and it will give you an opportunity to get to know and work with indi-

viduals whose paths you might never otherwise cross. This may help you later if you decide, perhaps, to transfer to a different department. It will also get you recognized by the firm higher-ups, who will appreciate that you are willing to go beyond the call of duty.

ACCEPTING RESPONSIBILITY WHILE NOT GETTING OVEREXTENDED

The first rush of beginning a new career is an exhilarating experience. You have finally realized a dream or accomplished a goal that you had set for yourself some time (possibly years) ago. You may be tempted to take on more projects than you can reasonably handle. This is done for a variety of reasons—for example, to speed up the recognition process, to be viewed as a hardworking, standout employee, or merely to immerse yourself in the sheer excitement of it all. While these are all worthwhile goals to accomplish, it is better to achieve them at less than breakneck speed. Too much too soon too fast will lead to burnout. Also, incomplete or hurried work or unmet deadlines will reflect poorly on you, no matter what your intentions were.

Sometimes, especially when you are working for multiple attorneys, you may be pulled in too many directions with multiple rush projects. Once you realize that you will not be able to get to everyone's assignments, let the attorneys know immediately. Of course, everyone will say that his or her project is *the* most important one on your desk. However, a determination can usually be made that some projects will take priority over others, perhaps because of a looming deadline. The most urgent ones will be taken care of first, and the truly less important ones will be assigned to someone else or placed on the "back burner" to wait their turns. Although you may be very capable of making this determination yourself, it is often wiser to let the attorneys fight it out amongst themselves. That way, you won't be accused of favoring one attorney over the other or exercising poor judgment.

THE "B" WORD: BILLING

There are fewer sources of anxiety for paralegals (or attorneys for that matter) than billing. As we have said before, time is money in the law firm, and the billable hour rules the office. Because it is so important to your life as a paralegal, it is something you should know about and be aware of during your first 100 days.

Although billable time is kept for a variety of management reasons, the two most important purposes of logging time are to create revenue for the firm and to track the productivity of firm employees.

Creating Revenue for the Firm

Your firm's managers have determined how much money clients can be billed for your time based on your years of experience, your specialty, and the going market rate in the area. Billing rates for paralegals range from $30 per hour in small towns for general practice paralegals to more than $150 per hour in big city firms for specialized work. Your billable rate says a lot about your experience and your status within your firm, and an increase in your rate is as high a compliment as any promotion.

Let's say the firm sets your starting rate at $35 per hour. That means if you spend four hours researching databases looking for a missing witness, your firm will charge that client $140. You have now created income for your firm. It is a wonderful feeling but also a great responsibility. You are now a profit center for your firm, and those employees of the firm who bill their time have a special status over the employees who don't bring in any revenue. Your compensation is usually tied to how much income you produce for your firm, so the more hours you can bill, the better. The money you bring in is used to pay your salary and your overhead (your office space, supplies, secretarial help, etc.), and the rest is considered profit for the firm's partners.

Now, for example, say that after you complete your first year with the firm, you are working very quickly and efficiently on projects. The firm ups your billable rate to $40 per hour. Now that same four-hour research project will cost the client $160 instead of $140. You are bringing in more money for the same effort. Your value to the firm has just gone up.

Tracking Productivity

Now, let's return to the first scenario, where you have a $35-per-hour billing rate. Suppose the attorney who is reviewing your time decides that it shouldn't have taken you four hours to do that research project, it should only have taken three. He will reduce your billed time to three hours, and the client will be billed $105. One hour of your time that day will have been thrown out the window. Suddenly it looks as though you worked only a seven-hour day instead of an eight-hour day. This process is known as being "written off" (e.g., the attorney just wrote off an hour of your time from the client's bill). There are many reasons why a firm may reduce your time on a client's bill:

- You may not have worked as efficiently as you could have.
- The attorney had made a deal with the client that the bill would not be more than a certain amount each month.
- New paralegals and attorneys are often written off to compensate the client for their learning curves.
- You may have spent longer on a project than the attorney had intended.
- Some attorneys have a reputation for writing off their paralegals' time so that the attorneys don't have to write off any of their own.

Being written off can be devastating because you feel as though you are not worth your salt. While write-offs can be a sign of trouble, sometimes they are done more for client relations or political reasons. If your firm shares its billing reports with you and you notice that your time is still regularly being written off after your first 100 days, you should make a point to talk to your supervising attorney or the office manager. It could be a sign that you are not working at an optimum level, and such write-offs will reflect poorly upon you during your next review.

When you were hired by your firm, you were probably told how many hours you were expected to bill per year. A common target figure for paralegals in mid-sized to large firms is 1,800 billable hours per year. Dividing this figure by 52 weeks gives us approximately 35 hours per week that you will need to bill to one of the firm's clients or another. At first, this does not sound particularly difficult, considering that you will be working at least 40-hour weeks. However, you will quickly come to learn that it is harder than it sounds. Here are some of the drains on the day's billable hours

- Stopping to chat with coworkers
- Forgetting to account for all of your time during the day
- Inefficiency, which leads to write-offs
- Volunteering to work on too many administrative projects
- Arriving late, leaving early, or taking long lunch hours.

Large write-offs and failing to meet billing quotas are common sources of reprimands for paralegals (and attorneys, too). Both indicate the employee is not productive enough and therefore does not bring in enough revenue to pay for his or her salary and overhead at the firm, let alone have enough left over to provide a profit for the partners.

You will learn about billing in paralegal school. There are also good books on the subject.[1]

AN EYE TOWARD THE FUTURE

Your first 100 days will be spent trying to survive. Your next 100 weeks will be spent honing your skills and really finding your stride. But what comes after that?

By the end of your first 2 years on the job, you will have a fairly good idea of whether you are happy in the specialty and the environment you have chosen. What if you're not? Or suppose you like what you are doing OK, but you are getting a little bored. If you are working in a mid- to large-sized firm, here are some things to explore:

- Approach an attorney in the firm for whom you have not yet worked and tell her you would like to learn more about her specialty.
- Strike up a friendship with a paralegal in a different department and offer to cross-train each other.
- Approach your supervising attorney and let him know you are ready to take on new responsibilities.
- Volunteer to work on a pro bono project at your firm in an area of the law that is unfamiliar to you.

By learning a new specialty area, you can either relieve your boredom or find a new niche within the firm. Some paralegals in large firms switch through several departments before finding a permanent "home."

Paralegals in small offices or working for sole practitioners don't have as much freedom of movement. If they are unhappy with what they are doing, their only option may be to look for another place of employment.

What about the future? What if you have other goals over and above your paralegal career? What if you have always wanted to try your hand at teaching? At writing? At going into management? Many paralegals have dreams of going on to law school. Others want to start their own freelance businesses. All these aspirations can be accomplished while continuing your paralegal career. Hone your writing skills by volunteering to author articles for your local or state paralegal association newsletters. Some legal newspapers also accept articles for publication. If teaching is your goal, stay in touch with the instructors from your paralegal program after you

---

Reality Check

Learning lots of interrelated skills at your firm serves many purposes, not the least of which is job security. Face it, when it comes to down-sizing, who is the firm going to keep? The paralegal who can prepare wills and trusts, or the paralegal who can prepare wills, trusts, and tax returns, file complaints, summarize depositions, and index documents?

---

[1] Dana Graves, *Counting the Minutes: The Essential Training Guide for Time and Billing Techniques* (Estrin Publishing 1992)

graduate. Offer to do some tutoring or volunteer to serve on an advisory committee for the program. Take some teaching courses at your local college. After you have enough years of education, some community colleges and business schools may desire your expertise.

If you are interested in becoming a manager, you should take some college management courses. You will also need to work in a city that has firms large enough to require paralegal managers. The Legal Assistant Management Association (LAMA) is a national organization made up of people who manage paralegals. For more information about the association, contact LAMA at 2965 Flowers Rd. So., Atlanta, GA 30341, call them at 770/457/7746 or visit their website at www.LAMAnet.org.

If you hope someday to become a freelance paralegal and contract your services to attorneys on an as-needed basis, you should begin to lay the groundwork as soon as you begin working for your first law firm. The key to being a successful freelancer is (1) to be very good at what you do, and (2) to have as many contacts as possible. Get to know all the attorneys in your office and keep in touch with them when they leave for other firms. Join your local paralegal association and mingle with as many of the members as you can. Each one may be a source of future work. Build an excellent name for efficient, thorough, and ethical work, and your reputation will precede and sell you.

Good luck and happy Paralegaling! We wish you outrageous success!

A

Legal Lingo

AAfPE   American Association for Paralegal Education, located in Atlanta, Georgia.

ABA   American Bar Association, located in Chicago.

ABA-approved certificate   A paralegal certificate awarded from a school which has met and passed criteria as set forth by the American Bar Association.

Accreditation   According to NFPA: A voluntary process by which an agency or organization evaluates and recognizes a program of study or an institution as meeting predetermined qualifications or standards. Accreditation shall apply to its institutions and programs of study or services.

Admin. Time   An abbreviated term for administrative time which covers nonbillable tasks such as filling out time sheets, management issues, and more.

ALA   Association of Legal Administrators. Holds a great yearly conference. Has local chapters. Located in Vernon Hills, Illinois.

All-nighter   You guessed it.

AO   The Administrative Office of the United States Courts.

Associate   An attorney within a law firm with anywhere from 0 to 10 years' experience who has not as yet reached partnership status. Is paid a salary from the firm rather than a draw against profits.

Baby associate   A first-year associate.

Bankers Boxes   Actually a brand name, but it has come to be used to refer to all types of flattened, premade cardboard forms that can quickly be folded into handled boxes with lids.

Bates stamping   A method of numbering documents or exhibits which may include hand-stamping. A Bates machine is a hand-held instrument that prints an identification number.

Billable costs   These are costs incurred by the firm that can be charged back to the client. Examples of billable costs are long-distance phone charges, copying expenses, travel expenses, and postage for large mailings. Costs that are not usually charged to the client include office supplies, library books purchased for a particular case, or other types of general overhead.

Billable hours   Hours that are billed to the client for your work. Billable hours have a fixed dollar amount, such as $75 per hour for your services. However, you do not share in the fee to the client.

Billing cutoff   The day on which the firm stops the monthly billing cycle so that a bill can be produced. Some firms use the last day of the month as the billing cutoff date. Some firms cut off the billing by the 20th or the 25th of the month so that bills can be prepared and mailed by the first day of the next month. Whatever day it is, it will be your last day to turn in time sheets for that month.

Boutique firm   A small firm that specializes in one practice area such as entertainment law, sports law, or securities law. Quite often a boutique law firm is a spin-off from a major firm.

Cafeteria-style plan   A type of health benefits plan in which the employee is given a choice of various benefits to make up the entire benefits package. An employee may choose between day care and dental care, for example.

Case clerk   A clerk position generally positioned below a paralegal. Responsible for clerical duties such as Bates stamping, putting files in chronological order, and indexing documents. Assignments are billable but more clerical in nature.

Case Management System (CMS)   A form of software that tracks cases and matters, including actions and events, financial information, parties and documents, calendars and dockets. Functionally, a CMS is a customizable database application capable of handling multiple case or matter types that manages information and activities. Centrally stores all key information related to cases.

CatLinks   A litigation support software package.

CEB   Continuing Education of the Bar.

CERCLA   The Comprehensive Response, Compensation and Liability Act of 1980 (also known as Superfund). Enacted by Congress to ensure that victims of hazardous substances releases are compensated for the injuries, that environmental damages are corrected, and that there are adequate emergency responses to halt and clean up unauthorized hazardous substances releases.

Certified   A voluntary process by which a nongovernmental agency or association grants recognition to an individual who has met certain predetermined qualifications specified by that agency or association. Such qualifications may include (1) graduation from an accredited program (2) acceptable performance on a qualifying examination or series of examinations and/or (3) completion of a given amount of work experience. Paralegals who earn their paralegal certificates are "certificated," not certified.

Chron file   A file of outgoing correspondence that is kept in chronological order. Most correspondence is kept in the file of the client on whose behalf the letter was written. Some firms like to keep an extra copy in a chron file so that there is a backup copy if a letter turns up missing.

CLA Certified Legal Assistant: a designation by NALA (National Association of Legal Assistants) that is awarded following successful completion of a two-day certification exam. It must be kept current through continuing education.

CLE Continuing Legal Education, generally for attorneys but also required for paralegals who have received the CLA designation from NALA or the Registered Paralegal (RP) designation from NFPA.

Coder The person who codes documents for entry into a database. (See coding.)

Coding A method of giving documents certain identification so that they may be entered into a database and searched by a software package. For example, a document may be coded onto a database via its date, recipient, author, and keywords.

Concordance A litigation support software package.

Confidential Information According to NFPA: denotes information relating to a client, whatever its source, that is not public knowledge or available to the public. ("non-confidential information" would generally include the name of the client and the identity of the matter for which the paralegal provided services.)

Contingency employment search firm Client pays after services completed.

Contingent workers People who are hired to perform a one-time task and are paid by the project. (Also referred to as contract or freelance workers.) Often, paralegals and attorneys are hired by a firm on a contract or contingent basis to help temporarily with a large case or with overflow work.

Corporate A practice area or department within a firm that specializes in assisting corporations with their day-to-day operations, such as preparing minutes, issuing stock, advising boards of directors, and related issues. Often corporations who do not have in-house legal departments will hire outside law firms to perform these functions.

Deposition summary A condensed version of a deposition usually prepared by a paralegal. For example, the paralegal may condense the deposition from 150 pages to 15. May also be referred to as an "abstract" or "deposum."

Deposums   Slang for deposition summary. Also, a vendor.

Direct deposit   A perk offered by some firms and corporations that allows your paycheck to be directly deposited into your checking account on payday.

Disclose   To communicate information that is reasonably sufficient to permit identification of the significance of the matter in question.

Discovery ZX   A litigation support software package.

DOA   Abbreviation for Director of Administration. You'll see it written but rarely spoken.

DOD   Department of Defense.

DOJ   Department of Justice.

Ethical Wall   According to NFPA: refers to the screening method implemented in order to protect a client from a conflict of interest. An Ethical Wall generally includes, but is not limited to, the following elements:

1. Prohibit the paralegal from having any connection with the matter;
2. Ban discussions with or the transfer of documents to or from the paralegal;
3. Restrict access to files; and
4. Educate all members of the firm, corporation or entity as to the separation of the paralegal (both organizationally and physically) from the pending matter.

For more information regarding the Ethical Wall, see the NFPA publication entitled, "The Ethical Wall—Its Application to Paralegals."

ETO   An abbreviated term used in some firms and corporations for employee time off.

Ex Parte   According to NFPA: denotes actions or communications conducted at the instance and for the benefit of one party only, and without notice to, or contestation by, any person adversely interested.

Family friendly   A firm or corporation that acknowledges employees do have a family life outside work.

File Room   The area in the firm dedicated to the storage of active client files. Files may be kept by client name in small firms or via a numbering system in larger firms. Small firms may allow employees to remove files from the file room at will to review at their desks. Larger firms employ a "checkout" system, so that the location of the file can be determined at any given time.

FOIA Request   Freedom of Information Act Request. A procedure by which an individual may request information from a federal agency that normally would not be considered a public record. Most states have a similar procedure for their agencies.

Form file   A file of sample forms, documents, and pleadings used by the firm. Individual paralegals can also keep their own "private" form files of their favorite documents.

Full-time   (1) A 40-hour-per-week position; (2) What used to be called a "permanent" position.

General Counsel   The term for top-level attorneys for in-house legal departments.

Halo effect   An employee that is often given a majority of the work even if that work is far below the employee's capability. This "halo effect" stems from the thought that this is the only person who can "get it right." The halo effect can sometimes backfire by burning out a competent, capable professional.

Home Page   A page on the internet that tells about an individual or company.

Hot doc   Refers to a "telling" document important to a case.

HR   Abbreviation for Human Resources department.

Hyperlink   A link in a computer document that brings the user to another document. These links are usually represented by highlighted words or images. (*Source: Business Words You Should Know,* by Brian Tarcy.)

Imaging   A process by which a document is scanned into a computer and converted by software into an image that can be viewed with a litigation support program. Most images are stored on CD-ROM disks.

Indexing   In litigation files, pleadings and other court documents are often indexed, which means they are number-tabbed into files in chronological order, with a sheet on top that indexes the number of each document, its title, and the date it was filed.

In-house   Generally a term referring to counsel or legal department within a corporation.

In-house legal department   The legal department within a corporation.

InMagic   A litigation support software package.

Insurance Defense   A practice area or department within a firm that is employed by insurance companies to defend their insureds against a lawsuit.

Intellectual Property A term used to mean, collectively, an individual's or company's patents, trademarks and copyrights. The firm's intellectual property department is composed of the attorneys, paralegals, and staff dedicated to filing and prosecuting patents, trademarks and copyrights with the U.S. Patent & Trademark Office in Washington, D.C. This department will, sometimes with the help of the litigation department, also handle any litigation arising out of intellectual property disputes.

Internet According to *The Los Angeles Times,* the Internet is a cooperatively run, globally distributed collection of computer networks that exchange information via a common set of rules for exchanging data.

KeyCite™ A citation research service integrating case law on Westlaw.

LAMA The Legal Assistant Management Association, an organization for paralegal managers.

LAN Local area network.

Legal Solutions A software package containing legal forms.

Legal Tech A popular yearly legal software and hardware convention, which usually is held in Los Angeles, New York, and Chicago.

Lexis/Nexis On-line legal research service.

Licensure A process established through an agency or branch of government that grants permission to qualified professionals meeting established criteria. The professional is then licensed to perform specified functions.

Litigation Support A term generally referring to the computerization of documents. Sometimes called "Lit Support."

M&A Mergers and acquisitions.

Major law firm Large influential law firm who may meet the Top 50 or Top 100 lists locally, nationally, or internationally. Usually hires only the "best of the best" attorneys from the top 10 to 20 percent of the top 10 to 20 law schools. Generally services large corporate clients.

Martindale-Hubbell A directory of law firms in the United States. Gives background information about the firm such as practice specialties, number of offices, clients, and biographies of partners and associates. Some paralegals are listed.

MCLE Mandatory continuing legal education required by state bar associations in order for attorneys to keep their licenses up-to-date.

Minimum billable hourly requirement The minimum number of hours you are required to meet in a law firm.

MIS   Manager of Information Systems (or Services).

MIS Director   Manager of Information Systems.

NALA   National Association of Legal Assistants. Incorporated in 1975 and composed of individual members and state and local affiliated associations. Located in Tulsa, Oklahoma.

NALS   The National Association for Legal Secretaries, based in Tulsa, Oklahoma.

NFPA   National Federation of Paralegal Associations. Formed in 1974 by eight paralegal associations in response to growing interest in the development of the paralegal profession. Located in Kansas City, Missouri.

Office Services   Sometimes referred to as General Services. This department generally handles photocopying, messengers, faxes, office supplies and purchasing, air couriers, mail delivery, office setups and repairs, and sometimes filing of court documents.

O.T.   Abbreviation for overtime.

Outsourcing   A term referring to the transfer of services to a company outside the firm. Facilities management (managing the photocopying, faxing, messengering, etc., services) is a popular outsourced function.

Overnight it   Slang referring to "send the package via overnight courier service such as Federal Express, Airborne, UPS, etc."

PACE   Paralegal Advanced Competency Exam: A new voluntary certification examination given through NFPA to test the competency level of experienced practicing paralegals. Those who pass the PACE exam and maintain the continuing education requirement may use the designation "PACE-Registered Paralegal" or "RP."

PACER   Public Access to Court Electronic Record service provided by the Administrative Office (AO) of the United States Courts. Includes the U.S. appellate, district, and bankruptcy courts.

Paralegal assistant   Generally the same as a case clerk. Assists the paralegal.

Partner   A seasoned attorney who has an equity share in the firm. Usually receives a draw against salary and splits profits at the end of the year.

Part-time   (1) A position that works fewer than 40 hours per week or (2) A confusing reference to temporary positions.

PC card   A device about the size of a credit card that is inserted into special slots on a notebook computer. They can be used to add a modem, network card, hard drive, or SCSI interface. Also known as PCMCIA cards.

PDO   An abbreviated term used in some corporations for paid days off.

Perks   Short for "perquisites," the benefits an employee receives from the firm.

P.I.   Private investigator. Also stands for personal injury, which denotes a practice area or department within a firm that represents plaintiffs who have been injured either physically or mentally or both and wish to bring a lawsuit.

PLS   The Certified Professional Legal Secretary designation provided by the National Association for Legal Secretaries.

Pool System   A system used in some firms in which paralegals and/or secretarial staff are not assigned to any one attorney but instead can be given work by all the attorneys in the office.

Pro Forma   A software package containing legal forms.

Public Records   Information maintained by certain governmental or quasi-governmental agencies that is made available to the general public for review. Such information includes recorded documents (such as deeds or birth and death certificates), filed information (such as lawsuits, criminal complaints, or bankruptcies), and licensing information (for example, for contractors, doctors, and attorneys).

Rainmaker   Attorney whose primary function is to bring new business to the firm.

RAM (Random Access Memory)   The main memory of a computer.

Redweld   A type of file folder that expands. Also called "cedar files" or "expandos" in some regions.

Registration   The process by which professionals or institutions list their names with an association or agency.

Regular hire   A new term for full-time position.

Retreat   A firm function held by a group of firm or department members for themselves away from the office. Annual retreats for partners are popular. Retreats can be held specifically for paralegals. Can be as simple as a one-day conference in a nearby facility or a week's working vacation in a first-rate resort.

RICO   Racketeer Influenced and Corrupt Organizations Act. Although enacted in 1970 as part of the Organized Crime Control Act, some provisions of RICO are also used in federal civil litigation claims, such as securities fraud, antitrust, and unfair competition actions.

Scanning   Typed documents can be scanned into and stored in a word-processing program through the use of a scanner. The main purpose of scanning is to save the time it would take to retype a long document from scratch.

SCSI   Small Computer System Interface. A type of port and device interface for connecting drives and other accessories to a personal computer. Rhymes with fuzzy.

Smoking gun   The document or exhibit that tips the case.

Storage   Off-site facilities where the firm stores its closed cases, dated internal records, extra furniture, and anything else taking up needless space in the office.

Suggested hours   Another term for billable hours.

Summation   A litigation support software package.

Summer associates   Law school students generally in their second to fourth year who are selected by the firm to work through the summer at the firm. These students are evaluated for potential offers of hire when they graduate.

Team concept   A structure within a firm whereby paralegals are assigned to work with either a single attorney or a small group of attorneys. Opposite of pool system.

Temp-to-hire   A staffing term referring to a position that starts out as temporary and could turn into a full-time (permanent) position.

Temp-to-perm   A staffing term referring to a position that starts out as temporary and could turn into a full-time (permanent) position.

Time sheets   A form created by the firm for tracking time that will be billed to the clients. Attorneys and paralegals are expected to fill out time sheets on a daily basis, which are turned in to the firm's bookkeeping department.

Transactional   An area of practice or department within a firm that deals with business transactions, such as leases, contracts, mergers and acquisitions, partnership agreements, limited liability companies, joint ventures, etc.

Transportation allowance   A benefit or stipend for parking, train, or bus fare.

WAN   Wide area network.

Westlaw   On-line legal research service.

White shoe firm   A term used more on the East Coast than on the West Coast. Refers to a "blue-chip," old-line conservative, well-respected firm.

Word Processing   Medium or large firms often have a word-processing department, consisting of typists dedicated to creating the larger, more complicated documents and pleadings.

Work product   Any work created by, between or for attorneys and their clients.

World Wide Web   The Web (World Wide Web) is a collection of millions of computers on the Internet that contain information that has been put in a single format agreed to by everyone–a format called HTML (hypertext markup language). By combining multimedia—sound, graphics, animation, and more—with incredible ease of use and connectivity among its many different parts, the Web has become the most powerful tool in cyberspace (*The Los Angeles Times*).

B

Choosing a Paralegal School

*I*n today's competitive world, choosing a suitable paralegal school is a necessity. As discussed in Chapter 19, two of the benchmarks for top programs are approval by the American Bar Association (ABA) and/or membership in the American Association for Paralegal Education (AAfPE).

The ABA has available for purchase a publication entitled *Guide for Legal Assistant Education Programs*, which lists ABA-approved schools. To obtain this publication, contact the ABA Service Center at (312) 988-5522.

AAfPE generously granted permission for us to reprint in this appendix the paralegal programs that were members in AAfPE at the time of publication of this book.

Alabama

Samford University
Division of Paralegal Studies
800 Lakeshore Drive, SU Box 2200
Birmingham, AL 35229
Fax: (205) 870-2783

Gadsden State Community College
Paralegal Program
P.O. Box 227, 231 Allen Hall
Gadsden, AL 35902-0227
Phone: (205) 549-8368
Fax: (205) 549-8444

Auburn University at Montgomery
Legal Assistant Education Program
209 Goodwyn Hall, 7300 University Drive
Montgomery, AL 36117-3596
Phone (334) 244-3697
Fax (334) 244-3826
E-mail: bailey@strudel.aum.edu

Alaska

Charter College
Paralegal Studies Program
1221 E. Northern Lights Boulevard, Suite 120
Anchorage, AK 99508-9990
Phone (907) 277-1000
Fax: (907) 274-3342

University of Alaska Anchorage
Paralegal Certificate Program
3211 Providence Drive–Justice Center
Anchorage, AK 99508
Phone: (907) 786-1810
Fax: (907) 786-7777
E-mail: ayjust@uaa.alaska.edu

University of Alaska Southeast
Paralegal Studies
11120 Glacier Highway
Juneau, AK 99801
Phone: (907) 465-6347
Fax: (907) 465-6383
E-mail: jfrch@acad1.alaska.edu

Arizona

Northland Pioneer College
Legal Assistant Program
P.O. Box 610
Holbrook, AZ 86025
Phone: (520) 536-7871
Fax: (520) 524-2313

Academy of Business College
Legal Assistant Program
3320 W. Cheryl Drive, Suite 115
Phoenix, AZ 85051-9576
Phone: (602) 942-4141
Fax: (602) 942-9082
E-mail: aob@netzone.com

American Institute of Paralegal Studies
3443 N. Central Avenue, #1800
Phoenix, AZ 85012
Phone: (602) 252-4986
Fax: (602) 274-1440

Arizona Paralegal Training Program
General Practice Paralegal Program
111 W. Monroe, Suite 800
Phoenix, AZ 85003
Phone: (602) 252-2171
Fax: (602) 252-1891

Phoenix College
Legal Assisting Program
1202 West Thomas Road
Phoenix, AZ 85013-4234
Phone: (602) 285-7568
Fax: (602) 285-7591

Yavapai College
1100 E. Sheldon St.
Prescott, AZ 86301-3297
Phone: (602) 445-7300
E-mail: mailto:pa_susan@yavapai.cc.az.us

Pima Community College
Legal Assistant Studies
1255 N. Stone Avenue

Tucson, AZ 85709-3030
Phone: (520) 884-6788
Fax: (520) 884-6201

Arkansas

Westark Community College
Legal Assistance/Paralegal
5210 Grand Avenue, P.O. Box 3649
Forth Smith, AR 72913-3649
Phone: (501) 788-7805
Fax: (501) 788-7816
E-mail: mlowe@systema.westark.edu

California

Southern California College
of Business & Law Paralegal Program
595 W. Lambert Road
Brea, CA 92621
Phone: (714) 256-8830
Fax: (714) 256-8858

West Los Angeles College
Paralegal Studies
4800 Freshman Drive
Culver City, CA 90230
Phone: (310) 287-4200
Fax: (310) 841-0396

De Anza College
Paralegal Studies
21250 Stevens Creek Boulevard
Cupertino, CA 95014
Phone: (408) 864-8563
Fax: (408) 864-5309

University of California Davis
Legal Assisting Certificate Program
University Extension
Davis, CA 95616
Phone: (916) 757-8895
Fax: (916) 754-5105
E-mail: mchaix@unexmail.ucdavis.edu

Coastline Community College
Legal Assistant Program
11460 Warner Avenue
Fountain Valley, CA 92708
Phone: (714) 960-7671
Fax: (714) 960-9581
E-mail: chet@cccd.edu

Fresno City College
Paralegal Studies
1101 E. University Avenue
Fresno, CA 93741
Phone: (209) 442-4600 ext. 8485
Fax: (209) 265-5719

San Joaquin College of Law
Paralegal Program
901 Fifth Street
Clovis, CA 93612-1312
Phone: (559) 323-2100
Fax: (559) 323-5566

California State University, Hayward
Paralegal Studies-Extended Education
25800 Carlos Bee Boulevard
Hayward, CA 94542-3012
Phone: (510) 885-3605 ext. 312
Fax: (510) 885-4817

University of West Los Angeles
School of Paralegal Studies
1155 West Arbor Vitae Street
Inglewood, CA 90301-2902
Phone: (310) 215-3339
Fax: (310) 342-5295

University of California-Irvine
Certificate Program in Legal Assistantship
P.O. Box 6050
Irvine, CA 92716-6050
Phone: (714) 824-3437
Fax: (714) 824-3651

University of California-San Diego
Legal Assistant Program
UCSD, 9500 Gilman Drive
La Jolla, CA 92093
Phone: (619) 534-3434, Ext. 0176
Fax: (619) 534-7385
E-mail: cboyl@ucsd.edu

University of La Verne
Paralegal Studies
1950 3rd Street
La Verne, CA 91750
Phone: (909) 596-1848
Fax: (909) 392-2707
E-mail: sanjuanv@ulvacs.ulaverne.edu

California State University, Los Angeles
Certificate Program in Paralegal Studies
5151 State University Drive
Los Angeles, CA 90032
Phone: (213) 343-2022
Fax: (213) 343-4954

University of California–Los Angeles Extension
Attorney Assistant Training Program
10995 Le Conte Avenue, Room 517
Los Angeles, CA 90024
Phone: (310) 825-0741
Fax: (310) 206-7249

Saddleback College
Legal Assisting Program
28000 Marguerite Parkway
Mission Viejo, CA 92692
Phone: (714) 582-4773
Fax: (714) 347-2431
E-mail: BOEN_P@sccd.cc.ca.us

Saint Mary's College
Paralegal Program
P.O. Box 3052
Moraga, CA 94575

Phone: (510) 631-4509 or (510) 273-8350
Fax: (510) 631-9869 or (510) 835-1451
E-mail: cmoscrip@stmarys-ca.edu

Cerritos Community College
Paralegal Program
11110 East Alondra Boulevard
Norwalk, CA 90650
Phone: (310) 860-2451 ext. 2710
Fax: (310) 467-5005

Sonoma State University
Attorney Assistant Certificate Program
1801 East Cotati Avenue ·
Rhonert Park, CA 94928
Phone: (707) 664-2394
Fax: (707) 664-2613

University of California–Riverside Extension
Legal Assistantship Certificate Program
1200 University Avenue, Extension Center
Riverside, CA 92507-4596
Phone: (909) 787-4111 ext. 1614
Fax: (909) 787-2456

MTI Western Business College
Department of Procedural Law
5221 Madison Avenue
Sacramento, CA 95841
Phone: (916) 339-1500
Fax: (916) 339-0305

Kelsey-Jenney College
Paralegal Studies
201 "A" Street
San Diego, CA 92101
Phone: (619) 525-1799
Fax: (619) 544-9610

San Diego State University
Legal Assistant Specialist Certificate
Program
5250 Campanile Drive
College of Extended Studies

San Diego, CA 92182-1924
Phone: (619) 594-7078
Fax: (619) 594-8566
E-mail: ngeiser@mail.sdsu.edu

University of San Diego
Paralegal Program
5998 Alcala Park, Serra Hall 316
San Diego, CA 92110
Phone: (619) 260-4579
Fax: (619) 260-2252

City College of San Francisco
Legal Assistant/Paralegal Program
50 Phelan Avenue, C106
San Francisco, CA 94112
Phone: (415) 239-3508
Fax: (415) 239-3919 (first)
E-mail: mvota@ccsf.cc.ca.us

San Francisco State University
Paralegal Studies Certificate Program
425 Market Street
Downtown Center, 2nd Floor
San Francisco, CA 94105
Phone: (415) 904-7770
Fax: (415) 904-7760
E-mail: leeg@sfsu.edu

Rancho Santiago College
Legal Assistant Program
17th at Bristol
Santa Ana, CA 92706
Phone: (714) 564-6813
Fax: (714) 564-6755
E-mail: deboerc@msn.com

Santa Clara University
Institute for Paralegal Education
M S B of A Building #507
Santa Clara, CA 95053
Phone: (408) 554-4535
Fax: (408) 554-5188

West Valley College
Paralegal Program
14000 Fruitvale Avenue
Saratoga, CA 95070-5640
Phone: (408) 741-2415
Fax: (408) 741-2145
E-mail: bobdiane@ix.netcom.com

El Camino College
Legal Assistant Program
16007 Crenshaw Boulevard
Torrance, CA 90506
Phone: (310) 660-3773
Fax: (310) 660-3774
E-mail: ohadley@admin.elcamino.cc.ca.us

Rio Hondo College
Paralegal Education Program
3600 Workman Mill Road
Whittier, CA 90608
Phone: (310) 692-0921 ext. 3941
Fax: (310) 699-7386

Colorado

Community College of Aurora
Paralegal/Legal Assistant Program
16000 E. Centretech Parkway, C208
Aurora, CO 80011-9036
Phone: (303) 361-7407
Fax: (303) 361-7374

Pikes Peak Community College
Legal Assistant Program
5675 South Academy Boulevard
Colorado Springs, CO 80906
Phone: (719) 540-7261
Fax: (719) 540-7254

Denver Paralegal Institute
General Practice Program
1401 19th Street
Denver, CO 80202-1213

Phone: (303) 295-0550
Fax: (303) 295-0102
E-mail: covingtonb@aol.com

Arapahoe Community College
Legal Assistant Program
2500 W. College Drive, P.O. Box 9002
Littleton, CO 80160
Phone: (303) 797-5878
Fax: (303) 797-5935

Connecticut

Sacred Heart University
Legal Assistant Program
5151 Park Avenue
Fairfield, CT 06432
Phone: (203) 371-7960
Fax: (203) 396-6543
E-mail: sdonohue@shy.sacred.heart.edu

Quinnipiac College
Legal Studies Department
Mt. Carmel Avenue
Hamden, CT 06518
Phone: (203) 281-8712
Fax: (203) 281-8709
E-mail: martin@quinnipiac.edu

University of Hartford
Legal Studies–Hartford College for Women
1265 Asylum Avenue
Hartford, CT 06105
Phone: (860) 768-5652
Fax: (860) 768-5693

Manchester Community–Technical College
Legal Assistant Program
P.O. Box 1046
60 Bidwell Avenue, Mail Stn. 8
Manchester, CF 06045-1046
Phone: (860) 647-6108
Fax: (860) 647-6238

Naugatuck Valley Community–
Technical College
Legal Assistant Program
750 Chase Parkway
Waterbury, CT 06708
Phone: (203) 596-8744

Delaware
Widener University Law Center
Legal Education Institute
4601 Concord Pike
Wilmington, DE 19803
Phone: (302) 477-2012
Fax: (302) 477-2054

District of Columbia
The George Washington University
Legal Assistant Program
2029 K Street, N.W., Suite 600
Washington, D.C. 20006
Phone: (202) 496-2274
Fax: (202) 973-1165
E-mail: parr@gwis2.circ.gwu.edu

Georgetown University
Legal Assistant Program
37th and O Street, N.W.—306 ICC
Washington, D.C. 20057
Phone: (202) 687-6245
Fax: (202) 687-8954
E-mail: silversg@guner.georgetown.edu

Florida
St. Petersburg Junior College
Legal Assistant Program
2465 Drew Street
Clearwater, FL 34625
Phone: (813) 791-2530
Fax: (813) 791-2601
E-mail: demerss@email.spjc.cc.fl.us

Santa Fe Community College
Legal Assistant Program
3000 NW 83rd Street, L17
Gainesville, FL 32606
Phone: (352) 395-5165
Fax: (352) 395-5895

Florida Community College at Jacksonville
Legal Assistants Program
3939 Roosevelt Boulevard
Kent Campus, C-205
Jacksonville, FL 32205-8999
Phone: (904) 381-3589
Fax: (904) 381-3462

Miami-Dade Community College
Legal Assistant Program
300 N.E. 2nd Avenue
Miami, FL 33132
Phone: (305) 237-3048 or (305) 237-3151
Fax: (305) 237-7429

Barry University
Legal Studies
11300 N.E. 2nd Avenue
Miami Shores, FL 33161-6695
Phone: (305) 899-3300
Fax: (305) 899-3346

University of Central Florida
Legal Studies Program
Phillips Hall 116/P.O. Box 161600
Orlando, FL 32816-1600
Phone: (407) 823-2603
Fax: (407) 823-5360

Valencia Community College
Legal Assisting
P.O. Box 3028
Orlando, FL 32802
Phone: (407) 299-5000 ext. 2551
Fax: (407) 299-5000 ext. 2552

Broward Community College
Legal Assisting Program
7200 Hollywood Pines Boulevard
Pembroke Pines, FL 33024
Phone: (954) 986-8011
Fax: (954) 963-8990

University of West Florida
Legal Administration
11000 University Parkway
Pensacola, FL 32514-5751
Phone: (904) 474-2336
Fax: (904) 474-3130
E-mail: sharrell@uwf.cc.uwf.edu

Edison Community College
Legal Assisting Program
2511 Vasco Street
Punta Gorda, FL 33950
Phone: (941) 639-8322
Fax: (941) 627-1661
E-mail: pseay@eworld.com

South College
Paralegal Studies
1760 N. Congress Avenue
West Palm Beach, FL 33409
Phone: (407) 697-9200
Fax: (407) 697-9944

Georgia

The National Center for Paralegal Training
Paralegal Studies Program
3414 Peachtree Road NE, Suite 528
Atlanta, GA 30326
Phone: (404) 266-1060
Fax: (404) 233-4891

Gainesville College
Legal Assistant Program
P.O. Box 1358
Gainesville, GA 30503
Phone: (770) 718-3760

Fax: (770) 718-3761
E-mail: jrnarler@hermes.gc.peachnet.edu

Athens Area Technical Institute
Paralegal Studies Program
800 U.S. Highway 29
North Athens, GA 30601-1500
Phone: (706) 355-5041 or (706) 355-5000
Fax: (706) 369-5753
E-mail: dacahill@admin1.athens.tec.ga.us

Hawaii

Kapiolani Community College
Legal Assistant Program
4303 Diamond Head Road
Honolulu, HI 96816
Phone: (808) 734-9100
Fax: (808) 734-9147

Idaho

Lewis-Clark State College
Paralegal Program
500 8th Avenue
Lewiston, ID 83501-2466
Phone: (208) 799-2466
Fax: (208) 799-2856
E-mail: bbowen@lcsc.edu

Illinois

Southern Illinois University
Paralegal Studies for Legal Assistants
c/o History Department
Carbondale, IL 62901
Phone: (618) 536-2162
Fax: (618) 453-5440

Loyola University Chicago
Institute for Paralegal Studies
820 N. Michigan Avenue, Room 307
Chicago, IL 60611
Phone: (312) 915-6820
Fax: (312) 915-6448

Roosevelt University
Lawyer's Assistant Program
430 S. Michigan Avenue, Room 462
Chicago, IL 60605
Phone: (312) 341-3882
Fax: (312) 341-6356
E-mail: sreardon@acfsysv.roosevelt.edu

Illinois Central College
Paralegal Program
One College Drive
East Peoria, IL 61635-0001
Phone: (309) 694-5386
Fax: (309) 694-5411
E-mail: thiggins@icc.cc.il.us

Elgin Community College
Paralegal Program
1700 Spartan Drive
Elgin, IL 60123
Phone: (847) 697-1000 ext. 7466
Fax: (847) 888-7995

Illinois State University
Legal Studies Program
Campus Box 4600
Normal, IL 61790-4600
Phone: (309) 438-8638
Fax: (309) 438-5310
E-mail: teeimer@ilstu.edu

William Rainey Harper College
Legal Technology Program
1200 W. Algonquin Road
Palatine, IL 60067
Phone: (847) 925-6407
Fax: (847) 925-6043
E-mail: pguymon@harper.cc.il.us

South Suburban College
Paralegal/Legal Assistant Program
15800 South State Street
South Holland, IL 60473
Phone: (708) 596-2000
Fax: (708) 210-5758

Indiana

University of Evansville
Legal Studies Program
1800 Lincoln Avenue–School
of Business
Evansville, IN 47722
Phone: (812) 479-2851
Fax: (812) 479-2872
E-mail: dh4@evansville.edu

Ball State University
Legal Assistance Studies
NW 240 Department of Political Science
Muncie, IN 47306
Phone: (317) 285-8780
Fax: (317) 285-8980

Saint Mary-of-the-Woods College
Paralegal Studies Program
Guerin Hall
Saint Mary-of-the-Woods, IN 47876
Phone: (812) 535-5235
Fax: (812) 535-4613

Vincennes University
Legal Assistant/Paralegal Program
Davis Hall #64
Vincennes, IN 47591
Phone: (812) 885-5764
Fax: (812) 882-2237
E-mail: lstearns@vunet.vinu.edu

Iowa

Kirkwood Community College
Legal Assistant/Paralegal Program
P.O. Box 2068
Cedar Rapids, IA 52214
Phone: (319) 398-5576
Fax: (319) 398-1021
E-mail: wgeertz@kirkwod.cc.ia.us

Des Moines Area Community College
Legal Assistant Program
1100 7th Street

Des Moines, IA 50314
Phone: (515) 248-7208
Fax: (515) 248-7253

Iowa Lakes Community College
Legal Assistant Program
300 S. 18th Street
Estherville, IA 51360
Phone: (712) 362-2604
Fax: (712) 362-7649

Kansas

Johnson County Community College
Paralegal Program
12345 College Boulevard
Overland Park, KS 66210-1299
Phone: (913) 469-8500 ext. 3184
Fax: (913) 469-2380
E-mail: atebbe@johnco.cc.ks.us

Kentucky

Sullivan College
Institute for Paralegal Studies
2659 Regency Road
Lexington, KY 40503
Phone: (606) 276-4357
Fax: (606) 276-1153

University of Louisville
Paralegal Studies Program
406 Ford Hall, Belknap Campus
Louisville, KY 40292
Phone: (502) 852-3249
Fax: (502) 852-7923

Midway College
Paralegal Studies Program
512 East Stephens Street
Midway, KY 40347-9731
Phone: (606) 846-4421 ext. 5331
Fax: (606) 846-5349

Morehead State University
Paralegal Studies Program
350 Radar Hall
Morehead, KY 40351
Phone: (606) 783-2655
Fax: (606) 783-2219
E-mail: s.herzog@morehead-st.edu

Eastern Kentucky University
Paralegal Programs
McCreary 113
Richmond, KY 40475
Phone: (606) 622-1025
Fax: (606) 622-4378
E-mail: govmccor@acs.eku.edu

Louisiana

Louisiana State University
Paralegal Studies Program
271 Pleasant Hall
Baton Rouge, LA 70803-1530
Phone: (504) 388-6760
Fax: (504) 388-6761
E-mail: amccror@lsuvm.sncc.lsu.edu

Tulane University
Paralegal Studies Program
Room 125, Gibson Hall
New Orleans, LA 70115
Phone: (504) 865-5555
Fax: (504) 865-5562

University of New Orleans
Paralegal Studies Program
226 Carondelet Street, Suite 310
New Orleans, LA 70130-2933
Phone: (504) 568-8585
Fax: (504) 568-8596
E-mail: klwpa@uno.edu

Nicholls State University
Legal Assistant Studies
Box 2089, Department of Government

Thibodaux, LA 70310
Phone: (504) 448-4610

Maine

University College of Bangor
Legal Technology, Paralegal Studies Program
210 Texas Avenue, Katahdin Hall
Bangor, ME 04401
Phone: (207) 581-6212
Fax: (207) 581-6069

Casco Bay College
Paralegal Certificate Program
477 Congress Street
Portland, ME 04101
Phone: (207) 772-0196
Fax: (207) 772-0636

Maryland

Anne Arundel Community College
Paralegal Studies Program
101 College Parkway (FLRS 202)
Arnold, MD 21012
Phone: (410) 315-7370
Fax: (410) 315-7099

Harford Community College
Paralegal Studies
401 Thomas Run Road
Bel Air, MD 21015-1698
Phone: (410) 836-4434
Fax: (410) 836-4198
E-mail: dsmith@smtpgate.harford.cc.md.us

University of Maryland
University College
Paralegal Studies Program
University Boulevard at Adelphi Road
College Park, MD 20742
Phone: (301) 985-7733
Fax: (301) 985-4615
E-mail: hkaufman@nova.umuc.edu

Dundalk Community College
Paralegal Studies Program
7200 Sollers Point Road
Dundalk, MD 21222
Phone: (410) 285-9794
Fax: (410) 285-9665

Villa Julie College
Paralegal Program
1525 Greenspring Valley Road
Stevenson, MD 21153
Phone: (410) 602-7423
Fax: (410) 486-3552
E-mail: dea-joyc@wpmsgsvr.vjc.edu

Massachusetts

Boston University, Metropolitan College
Paralegal Studies
755 Commonwealth Avenue, Room 205
Boston, MA 02215
Phone: (617) 353-2061
Fax: (617) 353-5532
E-mail: swidoff@bu.edu

Suffolk University
Paralegal Studies
41 Temple Street
Boston, MA 02144
Phone: (617) 573-8228
Fax: (617) 722-9440
E-mail: dahlborg@aol.com

Newbury College
Legal Studies
129 Fisher Avenue
Brookline, MA 02146
Phone: (617) 738-2407
Fax: (617) 730-7095

Elms College
Paralegal Institute
291 Springfield Street
Chicopee, MA 01013-2839

Phone: (413) 594-7787
Fax: (413) 594-8173
E-mail: currierk@elms.edu

North Shore Community College
Paralegal Program
1 Ferncroft Road
Danvers, MA 01923
Phone: (508) 762-4000

Bay Path College
Legal Studies
588 Longmeadow Street
Longmeadow, MA 01106
Phone: (413) 567-0621
Fax: (413) 567-9324
E-mail: jspadoni@baypath.edu

Anna Maria College
Paralegal Studies Department
Sunset Lane
Paxton, MA 01612
Phone: (508) 849-3380
Fax: (508) 849-3362

Bentley College
Institute of Paralegal Studies
175 Forest Street
Waltham, MA 02154-4705
Phone: (617) 891-2800
Fax: (617) 891-3449
E-mail: fsalimbene@bentley.edu

Michigan

Grand Valley State University
Legal Studies Program
237 Mackinac
Allendale, MI 49401
Phone: (616) 895-2910
Fax: (616) 895-2915

Kellogg Community College
Legal Assistant Program
450 North Avenue

Battle Creek, MI 49017
Phone: (616) 965-3931 ext. 2520
Fax: (616) 965-4133

Ferris State University
Legal Assistant Program
Bus 124E, 119 South Street
Big Rapids, MI 49307
Phone: (616) 592-2416
Fax: (616) 592-3548

Oakland Community College
Legal Assistant Program
27055 Orchard Lake Road
Farmington Hills, MI 48334
Phone: (810) 471-7643
Fax: (810) 471-7544

Davenport College
Paralegal Studies
415 E. Fulton
Grand Rapids, MI 49503
Phone: (616) 451-3511
Fax: (616) 732-1142
E-mail: rstevens@davenport.edu

Lansing Community College
Legal Assistant Program
P.O. Box 40010
Business Careers Department
Lansing, MI 48901-7210
Phone: (517) 483-1503
Fax: (517) 483-9740

Madonna University
Legal Assistant Program
36600 Schoolcraft
Livonia, MI 48150
Phone: (313) 432-5549
Fax: (313) 432-5393
E-mail: cote@smtp.munet.edu

Oakland University
Legal Assistant Diploma Program
265 South Foundation Hall

Rochester, MI 48309-4401
Phone: (810) 370-3120
Fax: (810) 370-3137
E-mail: gjboddy@oakland.edu

Delta College
Legal Assistant Studies
Office F-45
University Center, MI 48710
Fax: (517) 686-9144

Macomb Community College
Legal Assistant Technology Program
14500 Twelve Mile Road
Warren, MI 48093
Phone: (810) 445-7350
Fax: (810) 445-7014

Minnesota

Inver Hills Community College
Legal Assistant Program
2500 80 Street East
Inver Grove Heights, MN 55076-3224
Phone: (612) 450-8567
Fax: (612) 450-8679

Minnesota Paralegal Institute
12450 Wayzata Boulevard, Suite 318
Minnetonka, MN 55305
Phone: (612) 542-8417
Fax: (612) 545-1524

North Hennepin Community College
Legal Assistant Program
7411 - 85th Avenue
North Brooklyn Park, MN 55445
Phone: (612) 424-0915
Fax: (612) 424-0889

Hamline University
Paralegal (Legal Assistant) Program
1536 Hewitt Avenue
Saint Paul, MN 55104
Phone: (612) 641-2207

Fax: (612) 641-2956
E-mail: foreilly@piper.hamline.edu

Moorhead State University
Legal Assistant Program
1104 - 7th Avenue
South Moorhead, MN 56563
Phone: (218) 236-2862
Fax: (218) 236-2238
E-mail: nordick@mhdcb.moorhead.msus.edu

Winona State University
Paralegal Program
Minne Hall 212
Winona, MN 55987
Phone: (507) 457-5400
Fax: (507) 457-5086
E-mail: histdept@vax2.winona.msus.edu

Mississippi

Mississippi College
Paralegal Studies Program
P.O. Box 4092
Clinton, MS 39058
Phone: (601) 925-3812
Fax: (601) 925-3932

Mississippi University for Women
Paralegal Studies
Box W-1634
Columbus, MS 39701
Phone: (601) 329-7154

University of Southern Mississippi
Paralegal Studies
Box 5108, Southern Station
Hattiesburg, MS 39406
Phone: (601) 266-4310
Fax: (601) 266-5800

Missouri

William Woods University
Paralegal Studies Program
200 W. 12th Street

Fulton, MO 65251
Phone: (314) 592-4293
Fax: (314) 592-4574
E-mail: sstratto@iris.wmwoods.edu

Avila College
Legal Assistant Program
11901 Wornall
Kansas City, MO 64145
Phone: (816) 942-8400 ext. 2244
Fax: (816) 942-3362
E-mail: gibbsja@avila.edu

Missouri Western State College
Legal Studies
4525 Downs Drive, Room PS204
St. Joseph, MO 64507
Phone: (816) 271-5837
Fax: (816) 271-5849
E-mail: katz@griffon.mwsc.edu

St. Louis Community College, Florissant Valley
Legal Assistant Program
3400 Pershall Road
St. Louis, MO 63135
Phone: (314) 595-4568
Fax: (314) 595-4544

St. Louis Community College, Meramec
Legal Assistant Program
11333 Big Bend Boulevard
St. Louis, MO 63122
Phone: (314) 984-7376 or (314) 984-7575
Fax: (314) 984-7117

Webster University
Legal Studies
470 East Lockwood Avenue
St. Louis, MO 63119
Phone: (314) 961-2660 ext. 7747
Fax: (314) 968-7403
E-mail: hartch@websteruniv.edu

Montana

College of Great Falls
Paralegal Studies Program
1301 - 20th Street South
Great Falls, MT 59405
Phone: (406) 791-5339
Fax: (406) 791-5394

Nebraska

Lincoln School of Commerce
Paralegal Studies
1821 K Street
Lincoln, NE 68508
Phone: (402) 474-5315
Fax: (402) 474-5302

College of Saint Mary
Paralegal Program
1901 South 72nd Street
Omaha, NE 68124
Phone: (402) 399-2418
Fax: (402) 399-2686

Metropolitan Community College
Legal Assistant Program
P.O. Box 3777
Omaha, NE 68103
Phone: (402) 449-8559
Fax: (402) 449-8532
E-mail: vkorslmn@metro.mccneb.edu

New Hampshire

Rivier College
Paralegal Studies Program
420 South Main Street
Nashua, NH 03060-5086
Phone: (603) 888-1311 ext. 8266
Fax: (603) 888-6447
E-mail: repost@mighty.riv.edu

New Jersey

Middlesex County College
Legal Assistant Program
155 Mill Road, North Hall
Edison, NJ 08818-3050
Phone: (908) 906-2576
Fax: (908) 906-4194

Fairleigh Dickinson University
Paralegal Studies Program
285 Madison Avenue
Madison, NJ 07940
Phone: (201) 593-8990
Fax: (201) 593-8178

Atlantic Community College
Legal Assistant Program
5100 Blackhorse Pike
Mays Landing, NJ 08330-2699
Phone: (609) 343-4941
Fax: (609) 343-5122

Bergen Community College
Legal Assistant Program
400 Paramus Road
Paramus, NJ 07652
Phone: (201) 447-7191
Fax: (201) 447-0934

Mercer County Community College
Legal Assistant Program
P.O. Box B
Trenton, NJ 08690
Phone: (609) 586-4800 ext. 479
Fax: (609) 890-6338

Montclair State University
Paralegal Studies Program
Normal Avenue & Valley Road
Upper Montclair, NJ 07043
Phone: (201) 655-4152
Fax: (201) 655-7951
E-mail: tayler@saturn.montclair.edu

Cumberland County College
Legal Assistant Program
P.O. Box 517
College Drive & Orchard Road
Vineland, NJ 08360-0517
Phone: (609) 691-8600 ext. 290
Fax: (609) 478-0671

New Mexico

Albuquerque Technical Vocational Institute
Legal Assistant Studies
525 Buena Vista SE
Business Occupations Department
Albuquerque, NM 87106
Phone: (505) 224-3845
Fax: (505) 224-3850

New York

Lehman College
Paralegal Studies Program
250 Bedford Park Boulevard West
(Cont. Educ.)
Bronx, NY 10468
Phone: (718) 960-8512
Fax: (718) 733-3254

Long Island University
Paralegal Studies Program
1 University Plaza, Room LLC 302
Brooklyn, NY 11201
Phone: (718) 488-1066
Fax: (718) 488-1367
E-mail: ssobel@aurora.liunet.edu

New York City Technical College (CUNY)
Legal Assistant Studies Program
300 Jay Street, N622
Brooklyn, NY 11201
Phone: (718) 260-5124
Fax: (718) 260-5387
E-mail: msdny@cunyum.edu

Long Island University
C.W. Post Legal Studies Institute
Paralegal Program
720 Northern Boulevard
Brookville, NY 11548-1300
Phone: (516) 299-2238
Fax: (516) 299-2066

Corning Community College
Paralegal Studies
One Academic Drive
Corning, NY 14830-3297
Phone: (607) 962-9424
Fax: (607) 962-9287

Mercy College
Paralegal Studies Major
555 Broadway
Dobbs Ferry, NY 10522
Phone: (914) 674-7320
Fax: (914) 693-9455

Queens College
Paralegal Studies Program/CEP
65-30 Kissena Boulevard
Flushing, NY 11367
Phone: (718) 997-5709
Fax: (718) 997-5723

Nassau Community College
Paralegal Program
Garden City, NY 11530
Phone: (516) 572-7774
Fax: (516) 572-7750
E-mail: birdofj@sunynassau.edu

Hilbert College
Legal Assistant Program
5200 South Park Avenue
Hamburg, NY 14075
Phone: (716) 649-7900
Fax: (716) 649-0702

St. John's University
Paralegal Studies Program
8000 Utopia Parkway
Jamaica, NY 11439
Phone: (718) 990-6161 ext. 7417
Fax: (718) 990-1882
E-mail: ylbhssc@st.johns.edu

Sullivan County Community College
Paralegal Program
P.O. Box 4002
Loch Sheldrake, NY 12759
Phone: (914) 434-5750 ext. 338
Fax: (914) 434-4806

Interboro Institute
Lawyer's Asst. (Paralegal Studies) Program
450 West 56th Street
New York, NY 10019
Phone: (212) 399-0091
Fax: (212) 765-5772

New York University
Diploma Program in Paralegal Studies
11 W. 42nd Street, Room 429
New York, NY 10036
Phone: (212) 790-1320
Fax: (212) 790-1366

Syracuse University
Legal Assistant Program
610 E. Fayette Street
Syracuse, NY 13244-6020
Phone: (315) 443-2894
Fax: (315) 443-1928
E-mail: dhking@syr.edu

Mercy College
Paralegal Studies Program
277 Martine Avenue
White Plains, NY 10601
Phone: (914) 948-3666
Fax: (914) 948-6732

Ohio

College of Mount St. Joseph
Paralegal Studies Program
5701 Delhi Road
Cincinnati, OH 45233-1670
Phone: (513) 244-4952
Fax: (513) 244-4222
E-mail: georgana_taggart@mail.msj.edu

University College
Legal Assisting (Paralegal) Technology
P.O. Box 210207
Cincinnati, OH 45221-0207
Phone: (513) 556-1731
Fax: (513) 556-3007

David N. Myers College
Paralegal Education Program
112 Prospect Avenue
Cleveland, OH 44115-1096
Phone: (216) 696-9000 ext. 691
Fax: (216) 696-6430
E-mail: apiazza@dnmyers.edu

Capital University Law Center
Certified Legal Assistant Program
665 South High Street
Columbus, OH 43215
Phone: (614) 445-8836
Fax: (614) 445-7125

Sinclair Community College
Legal Assisting Program
444 W. Third Street
Dayton, OH 45402-1462
Phone: (513) 226-2932
Fax: (513) 449-5192
E-mail: gmcdonou@sinclair.edu

Notre Dame College of Ohio
Paralegal Studies Program
4545 College Road South
Euclid, OH 44121-4293

Phone: (216) 381-1680 ext. 229
Fax: (216) 381-3802

Lakeland Community College
Paralegal Studies Program
7700 Clocktower Drive
Kirkland, OH 44094
Phone: (216) 953-7352
Fax: (216) 975-4333

Lake Erie College
Legal Studies Program
391 W. Washington
Painesville, OH 44077
Phone: (216) 352-3361
Fax: (216) 352-3533

Cuyahoga Community College
Paralegal Studies Program
11000 Pleasant Valley Road–C247
Parma, OH 44130
Phone: (216) 987-5112
Fax: (216) 987-5050
E-mail: ellen.erzen@tri-c.cc.oh.us

Edison Community College
Legal Assisting
1973 Edison Drive
Piqua, OH 45356
Phone: (513) 778-8600
Fax: (513) 778-1920
E-mail: cooper@edison.cc.oh.us

University of Toledo, Community
& Technical College
Legal Assisting Program
2801 West Bancroft
Toledo, OH 43606-3390
Phone: (419) 530-3363
Fax: (419) 530-3047

Muskingum Area Technical College
Paralegal Program
1555 Newark Road

Zanesville, OH 43701
Phone: (614) 454-2501 ext. 439

Oklahoma

Rose State College
Legal Assistant Program
6420 SE 15th Street
Midwest City, OK 73110
Phone: (405) 733-7460
Fax: (405) 733-7447

University of Oklahoma College of Law
Department of Legal Assistant Education
300 Timberdell Road, Room 314
Norman, OK 73019
Phone: (405) 325-1726
Fax: (405) 325-7158
E-mail: rscott@hamilton.law.uoknor.edu

Oklahoma City University
Legal Assistant Program
2501 N. Blackwelder
Sarkeys Law Center 209
Oklahoma City, OK 73106
Phone: (405) 521-5189
Fax: (405) 521-5185

Tulsa Junior College
Legal Assistant Program
909 S. Boston, Room 416
Tulsa, OK 74119
Phone: (918) 595-7317
Fax: (918) 595-7343

Oregon

College of Legal Arts
Paralegal Studies
University Center Building
527 SW Hall, No. 308
Portland, OR 97201
Phone: (503) 223-5100
Fax: (503) 273-8093

Pennsylvania

Cedar Crest College
Paralegal Studies
100 College Drive
Allentown, PA 18104-6196
Phone: (610) 740-3792 ext. 3412
Fax: (610) 606-4614
E-mail: gmglasco@cedarcrest.edu

Mount Aloysius College
Legal Assistant Studies
7373 Admiral Peary Highway
Cresson, PA 16330
Phone: (814) 886-6304

Gannon University
Paralegal Program
Box 1027, University Square
Erie, PA 16541
Phone: (814) 871-5897
Fax: (814) 864-1311

Harrisburg Area Community College
Paralegal Studies
One HACC Drive
Harrisburg, PA 17110-2999
Phone: (717) 780-2515
Fax: (717) 236-0709

Manor Junior College
Paralegal Studies
700 Fox Chase Road
Jenkintown, PA 19046-3399
Phone: (215) 885-2360
Fax: (215) 576-6564

Community College of Philadelphia
Paralegal Studies Curriculum
1700 Spring Garden Street
Philadelphia, PA 19130-3991
Phone: (215) 751-8961
Fax: (215) 972-6388
E-mail: markphila@aol.com

Peirce College
Paralegal Studies
1420 Pine Street
Philadelphia, PA 19102
Phone: (215) 545-6400
Fax: (215) 546-5996

Duquesne University
Paralegal Institute
201 Rockwell Hall
Pittsburgh, PA 15282-0102
Phone: (412) 396-5128
Fax: (412) 396-5072
E-mail: klein@duq2.cc.duq.edu

Robert Morris College
Legal Assistant Certificate Program
600 Fifth Avenue
Pittsburgh, PA 15219
Phone: (412) 227-6478
Fax: (412) 281-5539

Marywood College
Legal Studies/Legal Assistant Program
2300 Adams Avenue
Scranton, PA 18509
Phone: (717) 348-6288
Fax: (717) 961-4742

Central Pennsylvania Business School
Legal Assistant Program
College Hill Road
Summerdale, PA 17093
Phone: (717) 728-2230
Fax: (717) 732-5254

Villanova University
Paralegal Program
102 Vasey Hall, 800 Lancaster Avenue
Villanova, PA 19085
Phone: (610) 519-4304
Fax: (610) 519-7910

Pennsylvania College of Technology
Legal Assistant Program
One College Avenue
Williamsport, PA 17701
Phone: (717) 327-4517
Fax: (717) 327-4529

Rhode Island

Roger Williams University
Paralegal Department
One Old Ferry Road
Bristol, RI 02809
Phone: (401) 254-3172
Fax: (401) 254-3431

South Carolina

Trident Technical College
Legal Assistant/Paralegal Program
P.O. Box 118067, 66 Columbus Street
Charleston, SC 29403
Phone: (803) 722-5526
Fax: (803) 722-5545

Columbia Junior College
Professional Center for Paralegal Studies
1207 Lincoln Street
Columbia, SC 29201
Phone: (803) 254-6065
Fax: (803) 779-5009

Midlands Technical College
Legal Assistant/Paralegal Program
Box 2408
Columbia, SC 29202
Phone: (803) 822-3312
Fax: (803) 882-3631

Florence-Darlington Technical College
Legal Assistant/Paralegal Program
P.O. Box 100548
Florence, SC 29501-0548

Phone: (803) 661-8047
Fax: (803) 661-8268
E-mail: fergusonf@flo.tec.sc.us

Greenville Technical College
Paralegal/Legal Assistant Program
P.O. Box 5616, Station B
Greenville, SC 29606-5616
Phone: (864) 250-8255
Fax: (864) 250-8455
E-mail: fisherrsf@gvltec.edu

South Dakota

National College
Paralegal Studies
321 Kansas City Street
Rapid City, SD 57701
Phone: (605) 394-4800
Fax: (605) 394-4871

Tennessee

Cleveland State Community College
Legal Assistant Program
P.O. Box 3570, Adkisson Drive
Cleveland, TN 37320-3570
Phone: (423) 472-7141 or (800) 604-2722
Fax: (423) 478-6255
E-mail: amccoin@clscc.cc.tn.us

Volunteer State Community College
Paralegal Studies
Nashville Pike
Gallatin, TN 37066
Phone: (615) 452-8600 ext. 300
Fax: (615) 230-3317

Knoxville Business College
Paralegal Program
720 N. Fifth Avenue
Knoxville, TN 37917
Phone: (423) 524-3043
Fax: (423) 637-0127

Pellissippi State Technical Community College
Legal Assistant Technology Program
10915 Hardin Valley Road, P.O. Box 22990
Knoxville, TN 37933-0990
Phone: (423) 971-5200
Fax: (423) 971-5221
E-mail: aballew@pstcc.cc.tn.us

State Technical Institute at Memphis
Legal Assistant Technology
5983 Macon Cove
Memphis, TN 38134-7693
Phone: (901) 383-4130
Fax: (901) 383-4377
E-mail: ghutton@stim.tec.tn.us

The University of Memphis
Paralegal Studies
University College, Johnson Hall, G-1
Memphis, TN 38152
Phone: (901) 678-2716
Fax: (901) 678-4913
E-mail: cdewitt@msuvx2.memphis.edu

Milligan College
Legal Assistant Studies
P.O. Box 500
Milligan College, TN 37682
Phone: (423) 461-8941
Fax: (423) 461-8716
E-mail: cchartier@kegley.milligan.milligan-college.tn.us

Southeastern Paralegal Institute
Legal Assistant Program
2416 21st Avenue South, Suite 300
Nashville, TN 37212
Phone: (615) 269-9900
Fax: (615) 383-4800

Texas

Del Mar College
Legal Assisting

101 Baldwin Boulevard
Corpus Christi, TX 78404-3897
Phone: (512) 886-1491
Fax: (512) 886-1524
E-mail: svanwie@davlin.net

El Centro College
Legal Assistant Program
Main and Lamar Streets, 5th Floor
Dallas, TX 75202
Phone: (214) 746-2429
Fax: (214) 746-2268

Southeastern Paralegal Institute
Paralegal Program
5440 Harvest Hill, Suite 200
Dallas, TX 75230
Phone: (214) 385-1446
Fax: (214) 385-0641
E-mail: skstoner@cyberramp.net

Texas Woman's University
Government Degree with Paralegal Emphasis
P.O. Box 425889
Denton, TX 76204-5889
Phone: (817) 898-2148
Fax: (817) 898-2130
E-mail: f_robb@twu.edu

Center for Advanced Legal Studies
Paralegal Program
3910 Kirby Drive, Suite 200
Houston, TX 77098
Phone: (713) 529-2778
Fax: (713) 523-2715

Southwestern Paralegal Institute
Legal Assistant Studies
4888 Loop Central Drive, Suite 800
Houston, TX 77081
Phone: (713) 666-7600
Fax: (713) 666-2030

Collin County Community College
Legal Assistant Program

2200 W. University Drive
McKinney, TX 75070
Phone: (214) 548-6823
Fax: (214) 548-6801

Midland College
Legal Assistant Program
3600 N. Garfield
Midland, TX 79705
Phone: (915) 685-4666
Fax: (915) 685-4761
E-mail: nlhtex@aol.com

Stephen F. Austin State University
Legal Assistant Program
Department of Criminal Justice
Box 13064 SFA
Nacogdoches, TX 75962-3064
Phone: (409) 468-4408
E-mail: crimj@sfasu.edu

Southwest Texas State University
Lawyer's Assistant Program
601 University Drive, Political Science
Department
San Marcos, TX 78666
Phone: (512) 245-2233
Fax: (512) 245-7815

Utah

Westminster College of Salt Lake City
Legal Assistant Certificate Program
1840 South 1300 East
Salt Lake City, UT 84105
Phone: (801) 488-4159
Fax: (801) 487-9507
E-mail: k-dehill@whitewater.wcslc.edu

Vermont

Champlain College
Legal Assistant Program
163 South Willard Street

Burlington, VT 05402-0670
Phone: (802) 658-0800
Fax: (802) 860-2750
E-mail: stgeorge@champlain.edu

Woodbury College
Paralegal Studies
660 Elm Street
Montpelier, VT 05602
Phone: (802) 229-0516
Fax: (802) 229-2141
E-mail: buckles@sover.net

Virginia

Marymount University
Paralegal Studies/MA in Legal Administration
2807 North Glebe Road
Arlington, VA 22207-4299
Phone: (703) 284-5910
Fax: (703) 527-3830

Virginia Intermont College
Paralegal Studies Program
1013 Moore Street
Bristol, VA 24201
Phone: (540) 669-6101
Fax: (540) 669-5763

Christopher Newport University
Legal Studies
50 Shoe Lane
Newport News, VA 23606
Phone: (804) 594-7820
Fax: (804) 594-7481
E-mail: hgreenle@powhatan.cc.cnu.edu

J. Sargeant Reynolds Community College
Legal Assisting Program
P.O. Box 85622
Richmond, VA 23285-5622
Phone: (804) 371-3265
Fax: (804) 371-3588

Washington

Edmonds Community College
Legal Assistant Program
20000 68th Avenue West
Lynnwood, WA 98036-5999
Phone: (206) 640-1658
Fax: (206) 771-3366
E-mail: mfitch@edcc.ctc.edu

Skagit Valley College
Paralegal Program
2405 E. College Way
Mount Vernon, WA 98273
Phone: (360) 428-1278
Fax: (360) 428-1186
E-mail: tmaloney@ctc.ctc.edu

Pierce College
Paralegal Studies
9401 Farwest Drive SW
Tacoma, WA 98498-1999
Phone: (206) 964-6638
Fax: (206) 964-6318

West Virginia

Marshall University Community & Technical College
Legal Assistant Program
400 Hal Greer Boulevard
Huntington, WV 25755-2700
Phone: (304) 696-3646
Fax: (304) 696-3013

Wisconsin

Lakeshore Technical College
Paralegal Program
1290 North Avenue
Cleveland, WI 53015
Phone: (414) 458-4183 ext. 202
Fax: (414) 457-6211

Chippewa Valley Technical College
Paralegal Program
620 West Clairemont Avenue
Eau Claire, WI 54701-6162
Phone: (715) 833-6355
Fax: (715) 833-6470

Northeast Wisconsin Technical College
Paralegal Program
2740 W. Mason Street
Green Bay, WI 54307
Phone: (414) 498-6277
Fax: (414) 498-6811

Concordia University Wisconsin
Paralegal Program

12800 North Lake Shore Drive
Mequon, WI 53097
Phone: (414) 243-5700
Fax: (414) 243-4351
E-mail: <jarratt>@bach.cuw.edu

Wyoming
Casper College
Legal Assistant Program
125 College Drive
Casper, WY 82601
Phone: (307) 268-2618
Fax: (307) 268-2224

C

Associations and Organizations You'll Need to Know

PARALEGAL ASSOCIATIONS

National Association of Legal Assistants

The following paralegal associations are affiliated with the National Association of Legal Assistants. For current addresses, telephone numbers, and contact names for these associations, please get in touch with NALA at

516 S. Boston, #200
Tulsa, OK 74119
(918) 587-6828
www.nala.org

This list was current as of the date of publication of this book. If you do not see an association listed in your area, contact NALA for information on new affiliated members that may not appear on this list.

Alabama
Alabama Association of Legal Assistants
Legal Assistant Society of Southern Institute
Samford University Paralegal Association

Alaska
Fairbanks Association of Legal Assistants

Arizona
Arizona Paralegal Association
Legal Assistants of Metropolitan Phoenix
Tucson Association of Legal Assistants

Arkansas
Arkansas Association of Legal Assistants

California
Legal Assistants Association of Santa Barbara
Los Angeles Paralegal Association
Orange County Paralegal Association
Paralegal Association of Santa Clara County
San Joaquin Association of Legal Assistants
Ventura County Association of Legal Assistants

Colorado
Association of Legal Assistants of Colorado

Florida
Dade Association of Legal Assistants
Florida Legal Assistants, Inc.
Gainesville Association of Legal Assistants
Jacksonville Legal Assistants
Pensacola Legal Assistants
Phi Lambda Alpha Legal Assisting Society of Southwest Florida
Tampa College–Brandon Student Association
Volusia Association of Legal Assistants

Georgia
Georgia Legal Assistants
Professional Paralegals of Georgia
South Georgia Association of Legal Assistants
Southeastern Association of Legal Assistants of Georgia

Idaho
Gem State Association of Legal Assistants

Illinois
Central Illinois Paralegal Association
Heart of Illinois Paralegal Association

Indiana
Indiana Legal Assistants

Iowa
Iowa Association of Legal Assistants

Kansas
Kansas Association of Legal Assistants

Kentucky
Western Kentucky Paralegals

Louisiana
Louisiana State Paralegal Association

Maine
Maine State Association of Legal Assistants

Michigan
Legal Assistants Association of Michigan

Mississippi
Mississippi Association of Legal Assistants
University of Southern Mississippi Society for Paralegal Studies

Missouri
St. Louis Association of Legal Assistants

Montana
Montana Association of Legal Assistants

Nebraska
Nebraska Association of Legal Assistants

Nevada
Clark County Organization of Legal Assistants

New Hampshire
Paralegal Association of New Hampshire

New Jersey
Legal Assistants Association of New Jersey

New Mexico
Southwestern Association of Legal Assistants

North Carolina
Coastal Carolina Paralegal Club
Metrolina Paralegal Association
North Carolina Paralegal Association

North Dakota
Red River Valley Legal Assistants
Western Dakota Association of Legal Assistants

Ohio
Toledo Association of Legal Assistants

Oklahoma
Oklahoma Paralegal Association
Rogers State College Association of Legal Assistants
Rose State Paralegal Association
TCC Student Association of Legal Assistants
Tulsa Association of Legal Assistants

Oregon
Pacific Northwest Legal Assistants

Pennsylvania
Keystone Legal Assistant Association

South Carolina
Central Carolina Technical College Paralegal Association
Charleston Association of Legal Assistants
Grand Stand Paralegal Association
Greenville Association of Legal Assistants
Paralegal Association of Beaufort County South Carolina
Tri-County Paralegal Association

South Dakota
South Dakota Legal Assistants Association
National College Student Association of Legal Assistants

Tennessee
Greater Memphis Legal Assistants, Inc.
Tennessee Paralegal Association

Texas
Capital Area Paralegal Association
El Paso Association of Legal Assistants
Legal Assistants Association/Permian Basin
Northeast Texas Association of Legal Assistants
Nueces County Association of Legal Assistants
Southeast Texas Association of Legal Assistants
Texas Panhandle Association of Legal Assistants
Tyler Area Association of Legal Assistants
West Texas Association of Legal Assistants
Wichita County Student Association

Utah
Legal Assistants Association of Utah

Virgin Islands
Virgin Islands Paralegal Association

Virginia
Peninsula Legal Assistants, Inc.
Richmond Association of Legal Assistants
Tidewater Association of Legal Assistants

Washington
Association of Paralegals and Legal Assistants of Washington State
Columbia Basin Paralegal Association

West Virginia
Legal Assistants of West Virginia

Wisconsin
Madison Area Legal Assistants Association

Wyoming
Legal Assistants of Wyoming

National Federation of Paralegal Associations

The following paralegal associations are affiliates of the National Federation of Paralegal Associations. Addresses, telephone numbers, and Web site addresses were current as of the time of the publication of this book. For more current information, contact NFPA at

P.O. Box 33108
Kansas City, MO 33108
(816) 941-4000
www.paralegals.org

Alaska

Alaska Association of Legal Assistants
P.O. Box 101956
Anchorage, AK 99510-1956
Web site: Alaska@paralegals.org

Arizona

Arizona Association of Professional
Paralegals, Inc.
P.O. Box 430
Phoenix, AZ 85001
Web site: Arizona@paralegals.org

California

Sacramento Association of Legal Assistants
P.O. Box 453
Sacramento, CA 95812-0453
Phone: (916) 763-7851
Web site: Sacramento@paralegals.org

San Diego Paralegal Association
P.O. Box 87449
San Diego, CA 92138-7449
Web site: SanDiego@paralegals.org

San Francisco Paralegal Association
P.O. Box 2110
San Francisco, CA 94126-2110
Phone: (415) 777-2390
Web site: SanFrancisco@paralegals.org

Colorado

Rocky Mountain Paralegal Association
P.O. Box 481864
Denver, CO 80248-1834
Phone: (303) 369-1606
Web site: RockyMountain@paralegals.org

Connecticut

Central Connecticut Paralegal
Association, Inc.
P.O. Box 230594
Hartford, CT 06123-0594
Web site: CentralConnecticut@paralegals.org

Connecticut Association of Paralegals, Inc.
P.O. Box 134
Bridgeport, CT 06601-0134
Web site: Connecticut@paralegals.org

New Haven County Association of Paralegals, Inc.
P.O. Box 862
New Haven, CT 06504-0862
Web site: NewHaven@paralegals.org

Delaware

Delaware Paralegal Association
P.O. Box 1362
Wilmington, DE 19899
Web site: Delaware@paralegals.org

District of Columbia

National Capitol Area Paralegal Association
P.O. Box 27607
Washington, D.C. 20038-7607
Phone: (202) 659-0243
Web site: NationalCapitol@paralegals.org

Georgia

Georgia Association of Paralegals, Inc.
1199 Euclid Avenue, N.E.
Atlanta, GA 30307
Phone: (404) 522-1457
Web site: Georgia@paralegals.org

Hawaii

Hawaii Paralegal Association
P.O. Box 674
Honolulu, HI 96809
Web site: Hawaii@paralegals.org

Illinois

Illinois Paralegal Association
P.O. Box 8089
Bartlett, IL 60103-8089
Phone: (630) 837-8088
Web site: Illinois@paralegals.com

Indiana

Indiana Paralegal Association
Federal Station
P.O. Box 44518
Indianapolis, IN 46204
Web site: Indiana@paralegals.com

Michiana Paralegal Association
P.O. Box 11458
South Bend, IN 46634
Web site: Michiana@paralegals.org

Northeast Indiana Paralegal Association, Inc.
P.O. Box 13646
Fort Wayne, IN 46865
Web site: NortheastIndiana@paralegals.org

Kansas

Kansas City Paralegal Association
8826 Santa Fe Drive, Suite 208

Overland Park, KS 66212
Phone: (913) 381-4458
Web site: KansasCity@paralegals.org

Kansas Paralegal Association
P.O. Box 1675
Topeka, KS 66601
Web site: Kansas@paralegals.org

Kentucky

Greater Lexington Paralegal Association, Inc.
P.O. Box 574
Lexington, KY 40586
Web site: Lexington@paralegals.org

Louisiana

New Orleans Paralegal Association
P.O. Box 30604
New Orleans, LA 70190
Phone: (504) 467-3136
Web site: NewOrleans@paralegals.org

Maryland

Maryland Association of Paralegals
P.O. Box 13244
Baltimore, MD 21203
Phone: (410) 576-2252
Web site: Maryland@paralegals.org

Massachusetts

Central Massachusetts Paralegal Association
P.O. Box 444
Worcester, MA 01614
Web site: CentralMassachusetts@
paralegals.org

Massachusetts Paralegal Association
19 Harrison Street
Framingham, MA 01702
Phone: (508) 879-4001
Web site: Massachusetts@paralegals.org

Western Massachusetts Paralegal Association
P.O. Box 30005
Springfield, MA 01103

Minnesota
Minnesota Paralegal Association
1711 W. County Road B, #300N
Roseville, MN 55113
Phone: (612) 633-2778
Web site: Minnesota@paralegals.org

New Jersey
Prudential Insurance Company of
America–Paralegal Council
751 Broad St.
Newark, NY 07102
Web site: Prudential@paralegals.org

South Jersey Paralegal Association
P.O. Box 355
Haddonfield, NJ 08033
Web site: SouthJersey@paralegals.org

New York
Long Island Paralegal Association
1877 Bly Road
East Meadow, NY 11554-1158

Manhattan Paralegal Association, Inc.
521 Fifth Avenue, 17th Floor
New York, NY 10175
Phone: (212) 330-8213
Web site: Manhattan@paralegals.org

Paralegal Association of Rochester
P.O. Box 40567
Rochester, NY 14604
Phone: (716) 234-5923
Web site: Rochester@paralegals.org

Southern Tier Paralegal Association
P.O. Box 2555
Binghampton, NY 13902
Web site: SouthernTier@paralegals.org

Western New York Paralegal Association
P.O. Box 207, Niagara Square Station
Buffalo, NY 14202
Phone: (716) 635-8250
Web site: WesternNewYork@paralegals.org

West/Rock Paralegal Association
P.O. Box 668
New City, NY 10956
Web site: WestRock@paralegals.org

Ohio
Cincinnati Paralegal Association
P.O. Box 1515
Cincinnati, OH 45201
Phone: (513) 244-1266
Web site: Cincinnati@www.paralegals.org

Cleveland Association of Paralegals
P.O. Box 5496
Cleveland, OH 44101
Phone: (216) 556-5437

Greater Dayton Paralegal Association
P.O. Box 515, Mid-City Station
Dayton, OH 45402
Web site: Dayton@paralegals.org

Northeastern Ohio Paralegal Association
P.O. Box 80068
Akron, OH 44308-0068
Web site: NorthEasternOhio@paralegals.org

Paralegal Association of Central Ohio
P.O. Box 15182
Columbus, OH 43215-0182
Phone: (614) 224-9700
Web site: CentralOhio@paralegals.org

Oregon
Oregon Paralegal Association
P.O. Box 8523
Portland, OR 97207
Phone: (503) 796-1671
Web site: Oregon@paralegals.org

Pennsylvania

Central Pennsylvania Paralegal Association
P.O. Box 11814
Harrisburg, PA 17108
Web site: CentralPennsylvania@paralegals.org

Chester County Paralegal Association
P.O. Box 295
West Chester, PA 19381-0295

Lycoming County Paralegal Association
P.O. Box 991
Williamsport, PA 17701

Philadelphia Association of Paralegals
P.O. Box 177
Lafayette, PA 19144
Phone: (610) 825-6504
Web site: Philadelphia@paralegals.org

Pittsburgh Paralegal Association
P.O. Box 2845
Pittsburgh, PA 15230
Phone: (412) 344-3904
Web site: Pittsburgh@paralegals.org

Rhode Island

Rhode Island Paralegal Association
P.O. Box 1003
Providence, RI 02901
Web site: RhodeIsland@paralegals.org

South Carolina

Palmetto Paralegal Association
P.O. Box 11634

Columbia, SC 29211-1634
Web site: Palmetto@paralegals.org

Tennessee

Memphis Paralegal Association
P.O. Box 3646
Memphis, TN 38173-0646
Web site: Memphis@paralegals.org

Texas

Dallas Area Paralegal Association
P.O. Box 12533
Dallas, TX 75225-0533
Phone: (972) 991-0853
Web site: Dallas@paralegals.org

Vermont

Vermont Paralegal Association
P.O. Box 6238
Rutland, VT 05702

Washington

Washington State Paralegal Association
P.O. Box 48153
Seattle, WA 98148
Phone: (800) 288-WSPA
Web site: Washington@paralegals.org

Wisconsin

Paralegal Association of Wisconsin, Inc.
P.O. Box 92882
Milwaukee, WI 53202
Phone: (414) 272-7168
Web site: Wisconsin@paralegals.org

Other Paralegal Associations

There are many state, regional and local paralegal associations that are not members of NALA or NFPA. To find a paralegal association in your area, contact your local county bar or paralegal school, or call a nearby paralegal association listed above.

LAW-RELATED ORGANIZATIONS

Academy of Family Mediators
4 Militia Drive
Lexington, MA 02173
Phone: (617) 674-2663
http://www.igc.apc/afm/

American Academy of Healthcare Attorneys
c/o American Hospital Association
1 North Franklin
Chicago, IL 60606
Phone: (312) 422-3700
http://www.aaha.org

American Arbitration Association
140 West 51st Street
New York, NY 10020
Phone: (212) 484-4000
http://www.adr.org

American Association for Paralegal
Education (AAfPE)
2965 Flowers Road So. #105
Atlanta, GA 30341
Phone: (770) 457-7746

American Association of Attorney-CPA's
24196 Alicia Parkway Suite K
Mission Viejo, CA 92691

American Association of Legal Nurse
Consultants (AALNC)
4700 Westlake Avenue
Glenview, IL 60025
Phone: (847) 375-4713

American Association of Nurse-Attorneys
3525 Ellicott Mills Drive #10
Ellicott City, MD 21043
Phone: (410) 418-4800

American Bar Association (ABA)
Standing Committee on Legal Assistants

750 North Lake Shore Drive
Chicago, IL 60611
Phone: (312) 988-5000

American Civil Liberties Union (ACLU)
132 W. 43rd Street
New York, NY 10036
Phone: (212) 944-9800

American Corporate Counsel Association
1225 Connecticut Avenue NW, Suite 302
Washington, DC 20036
Phone: (202) 296-4522

An organization of 11,000 corporate law department attorneys with 41 chapters nationwide. Publishes a monthly newsletter and quarterly magazine. Here's a great networking resource.

American Society of International Law
2223 Massachusetts Avenue NW
Washington, DC 20008
Phone: (202) 939-6000
http://www.asil.org

Association of Attorney-Mediators
One Galleria Tower
13355 Noel Road, Suite 500
Dallas, TX 75240
Phone: (972) 869-1183

Association of Defense Trial Attorneys
600 Bank One Building
124 SW Adams
Peoria, IL 61602
Phone: (309) 676-0400

Association of Legal Administrators (ALA)
175 East Hawthorn Parkway, Suite 325
Vernon Hills, IL 60061-1428
Phone: (708) 816-1212

Maintains a 24-hour job bank for members.

Association of Trial Lawyers of America (ATLA)
National Offices: 1050 31st Street NW
Washington, DC 20007
Phone: (202) 965-3500

Computer Law Association
3028 Javier Road,
Suite 402
Fairfax, VA 22031
Phone: (703) 560-7747
http://cl.org

Currently posts job openings on Web site; blind listings of availability for employment may be posted by members. Maintains a resume bank for members.

Council of School Attorneys
National School Boards Association
1680 Duke Street
Alexandria, VA 22314
Phone: (703) 838-6722

More than 3,000 members nationwide, primarily representing school districts.

CPR Institute for Dispute Resolution
366 Madison Avenue 14th Floor
New York, NY 10017
Phone: (212) 949-6490

International Alliance of Holistic Lawyers
P.O. Box 753
Middlebury, VT 05753
Phone: (802) 388-7478

J.A.M.S. Endispute
1920 Main Street, Suite 300
Irvine, CA 92714
Phone: (714) 224-1810

Legal Assistant Management
Association (LAMA)
2965 Flowers Road So. #105
Atlanta, GA 30341
Phone: (770) 457-7746

National Academy of Elder Law Attorneys
1604 N. Country Club Rd.
Tucson, AZ 85716
Phone: (520) 881-4005
http://www.naela.com/elderlaw

National Association for Public Interest Law
1118 22nd Street NW
Washington, DC 20037
Phone: (202) 466-3686
http://www.napil.org

Publishes *Guide to Public Interest Career Resources.* $20

National Association of Bond Lawyers
1761 S. Naperville Road
Wheaton, IL 60187
Phone: (630) 690-1135
http://www.nabl.org/nabl

National Association of College and
University Attorneys
One DuPont Circle Suite 620
Washington, DC 20036
Phone: (202) 833-8390
http://www.nacua.org

Represents about 1,200 colleges and more than 600 universities.

National Association of Criminal Defense Lawyers
1627 K Street NW
12th Floor
Washington, DC 20006
Phone: (202) 872-8688
http://www.criminaljustice.org

National Association of Law Placement
1666 Connecticut Avenue, Suite 325
Washington, DC 20009
Phone: (202) 667-1666

Bingo! Here's the association of law firm recruiting coordinators. Also publishes the *Survey of Legal Recruitment & Attorney Management Personnel* consisting of job descriptions and salaries of legal recruitment administrators and personnel directors.

National Association of Legal
Assistants, Inc. (NALA)
1516 Boston Avenue, Suite 200
Tulsa, OK 74119
Phone: (918) 587-6828
Fax: (918) 582-6772

National Conference of Bar Foundations
American Bar Association
Division for Bar Services,
541 N. Fairbanks Court, 14th Floor
Chicago, IL 60611
Phone: (312) 988-5354

For a membership fee of $25, you will receive frequent announcements of job openings at bar foundations nationwide.

National Employment Lawyers Association
600 Harrison Street Suite 535
San Francisco, CA 94107
Phone: (415) 227-4655
www.nela.org

More than 3,000 lawyers belong to this organization, which represents employees in actions against their employers.

National Federation of Paralegal
Associations (NFPA)
PO Box 33108
Kansas City, MO 64114
Phone: (816) 941-4000

Many state and local paralegal associations belong to this umbrella group. Also publishes *Directory of Paralegal Training Programs.*

National Health Lawyers Association
1120 Connecticut Avenue NW, Suite 950
Washington, DC 20036
Phone: (202) 833-1100

National Law Firm Marketing
Association (NLFMA)
401 N. Michigan Avenue, Suite 2200
Chicago, IL 60611
Phone: (312) 245-1592

Software Publishers Association
1730 M Street NW, Suite 700
Washington, DC 20036-4510
http://www.spa.org

For software publishers and developers. Also includes membership for law firms that represent software companies.

Transportation Lawyers Association
P.O. Box 15122
Lenexa, KS 66285-5122
Phone: (913) 541-9077

Volunteer Lawyers for the Arts
1 East 53rd Street, 6th Floor
New York, NY 10022
Phone: (212) 319-2787

Has 42 affiliated groups.

LAW-RELATED RESOURCES

Air Force Attorney Recruiting Office
Phone: (800) 524-8723

Altman Weil Pensa
Offices in Newtown Square, PA; Westport, CT;
and Bellevue, WA.

Management consulting to the legal profession. Call (610) 359-9900 to obtain a complete list of their law firm consulting services and publications.

Army Civilian Attorney Program
Recruiting Office
Phone: (703) 695-1353

Army JAG Corps
Recruiting Office
Phone: (800) 336-3315

Aspen Law & Business, Publishers
7201 McKinney Circle
Frederick, MD 21704
Phone: (301) 417-7500

Consider a staff position with a publisher.

The Estrin Organization
Professional Legal Staffing and Training
1901 Avenue of the Stars, Suite 350
Los Angeles, CA 90067
Phone: (310) 284-8585
www.estrin.com
Fax: (310) 284-5733

Hildebrandt, Inc. Management Consultants
Offices in Somerville, NJ; Chicago; Shaker
Heights, OH; Dallas; Naples, FL;
and San Francisco.

One of the largest management consulting organizations to law firms and in-house legal departments. Call (908) 725-1600.

Lexis/Nexis
P.O. Box 933
Dayton, OH 45401
Phone: (800) 528-1891
http://www.lexis.com

Hires sales and training positions in large cities nationwide.

Marine JAG
Recruiting Office
Phone: (703) 614-1242

Matthew-Bender & Co.
11 Penn Plaza
New York, NY 10001
Phone: (212) 967-7707
www.bender.com

The Michie Company, Publishers
P.O. Box 7587
Charlottesville, VA 22906
Phone: (804) 972-7600

Send your resume to Human Resources, and you will be sent an application.

Navy JAG
Recruiting Office
Phone: (703) 325-9830

The Thomson Corporation: Publishers
Corporate Offices
Metro Center, One Station Place, 6th Floor
North Stamford, CT 06902
www.thomson.com

Owns Clark Boardman Callaghan; Bancroft Whitney; and Lawyer's Cooperative.

West Information Publishing Group
610 Opperman Drive
Eagan, MN 55123
Phone: (612) 687-7000 (ask for human resources)
www.westpub.com

Tends to hire law school grads as regional sales reps and has been known to hire paralegals as trainers for Westlaw.

GENERAL RESOURCES

American Staffing Association
119 St. Asaph St.
Alexandria, VA 22314
Phone: (703) 549-6287
http://www.natss.com/staffing

Call to find a staffing organization in your city.

D

Paralegal Specialties

Trying to decide what area of the law to specialize in or to change to can be a daunting task. There are so many possibilities. Following is a general list of specialty practice areas for paralegals, along with brief descriptions of the types of work done by paralegals who practice those specialties:[1]

- Alternative Dispute Resolution (ADR)
- Appellate
  - Case Management
  - Record on Appeal
  - Preparing the Appeal
- Asbestos Litigation
  - General Case Work
  - National/Regional Counsel Tasks
  - FELA Asbestos
- Bankruptcy
  - Performed for Debtor
  - Performed for Creditor
  - Performed for Debtor and Creditor
- Business/Corporate
  - Formation of Corporate Entities
  - Maintenance of Corporate Entities
  - Formation and Maintenance of Partnerships and Limited Companies
  - Transactional (loan documentation; securities transactions)
  - Franchising
  - Blue Sky
  - Venture Capital Financing

- Collections
  - Preliminary Investigations
  - Commencement of Formal Action
  - Postjudgment Activities
- Commercial Litigation and Collection
  - Handling Suits for Monies Due
  - Investigating Claims
  - Collecting Judgments
- Computerized Litigation Support
  - General Duties
  - Management Level
- Construction
  - Construction Defect
  - Contract Administration
- Criminal
  - White-Collar Crime
- Domestic Relations/Family Law
- Employee Benefits
  - Compliance
  - Executive Compensation
  - Fiduciary Responsibility
  - Prohibited Transaction
  - ERISA

---

[1] Reprinted with permission by the National Federation of Paralegal Associations.

- Entertainment Law
  - Music
  - Film
  - Television
  - Stage
  - Publishing
- Environmental Law
  - Audits
  - Notice of Violation (NOV) Penalties
  - Parallel Disciplines
  - Real Estate Concerns
  - Rule/Regulation Tracking
  - State and Federal: Regulatory/Permitting
  - Superfund-Waste Allocation
- Foreclosure
- Health Care
- Holocaust Survivor Rights
- Homeowners Associations
- Immigration
- Insurance
  - Coverage
  - Bad Faith
  - General Tort
- Intellectual Property (with multidisciplinary business law practice)
  - General Duties
  - Biotechnology and Pharmaceuticals
  - Chemical
  - Consumer and Industrial Products
  - Electrical and Electronic Technologies
  - Litigation and Dispute Resolution
  - Trademarks
  - Patents

- Copyrights
- Technology (Computer software and hardware)
- International Law
- Labor/Employment
- Landlord/Tenant
- Litigation
  - General Duties
  - Preliminary Investigation
  - Initiation of Action
  - Discovery
  - Document Production
  - Depositions
  - Briefing
  - Settlement
  - Trial
  - Post-trial
- Malpractice
  - Medical
  - Legal
  - Professional
- Native American Rights
- Personal Injury
- Probate and Estate Administration
  - Trusts
  - Guardianships
  - Estate Administration
- Products Liability
- Public Finance
  - Municipal Bonds
- Real Property
  - Acquisition Responsibilities
  - Due Diligence Responsibilities
  - Closing Matters
  - Foreclosures
  - Purchase Money Loan
  - Post-Closing
  - Tax-Related Matters

- Transactional
- Leases
- Zoning
- Miscellaneous
- Regulatory
  - Compliance
- Schools/Education
- Sports
- Tax
  - Joint Ventures
  - IRS Matters

- Income Tax Planning
- International Financial Products
- Finance Leasing Transactions
- Investment Funds
- Securitizations
- Telecommunications
- Tort
- Travel/Hospitality Industry
- Workers' Compensation

Reality Check

All specialties are tied to the economy, region of the country, unemployment rates, trends, and supply and demand. Before you choose, check it out!

For more information on practice areas and task descriptions, you may order the following publications:

Paralegal Responsibilities
Published by the National Federation of Paralegal Associations
Phone: (816) 941-4000

Handbook on Paralegal Utilization
Published by the California Alliance of Paralegal Associations
P.O. Box 2234
San Francisco, CA 94126

E

Salary Surveys

One of the ways that paralegals can compare how they are faring in both salaries and benefits as compared with other paralegals in the same region or across the whole country is to review one of the three nationwide surveys that are done on a regular basis. These surveys—National Federation of Paralegal Associations (biannually), National Association of Legal Assistants (biannually), and *Legal Assistant Today* (annually)—compare a wide range of data on salaries, such as comparisons by years of experience, by practice area, by geographic location and by level of education. Some of the surveys also compare other non-compensation data, such as availability of private secretaries, office areas, and billable-hour requirements.

Following are summaries of the three most recent surveys available at the time this book was published. For more information on the NALA and NFPA surveys, see Appendix C for contact information for those organizations. For more information on the Legal Assistant Today survey, contact the magazine at P.O. Box 25202, Santa Ana, CA 92799-5202, (800) 394-2626.

NFPA 1997 PARALEGAL COMPENSATION AND BENEFITS REPORT

In July through September 1997, the National Federation of Paralegal Associations conducted its 1997 Survey of Paralegal Compensation and Benefits. On behalf of the NFPA, Hangley Management Service, Inc., distributed survey questionnaires to paralegals across the continental United States, Hawaii, and Alaska. Distribution was made through direct mailing to 41,000 persons, including 17,000 of its members, and by a publication on NFPA's Internet home page at paralegals.org. NFPA received 4,129 responses, which form the basis for this report. The response rate by city is a direct result of the local association's publicizing the survey and should not be construed as a basis of determining paralegal population.

The purpose of the report is twofold. Its primary function is to provide a basis for understanding the demographics, compensation, and benefits of the paralegal profession. Its second purpose is to measure those aspects in the work environment that affect the satisfaction level of paralegals.

The survey questionnaire asked respondents to provide their current salary as of July 1, 1997, salary increases during 1996 and 1997, and bonus information. A variety of information was requested on education, experience, type of employer, significant activities, satisfaction levels, hours worked, hours billed, and benefits.

Some caveats exist in virtually any statistical study. Although the methodology used in this survey is standard, the results must be considered and interpreted in perspective with the design. For example, some of the statistics reported may be based on a limited sample size. This is is particularly true for statistics related to population groups where relatively few responded to the survey instrument or exist in the sample frame (e.g., those relating to race). Accordingly, statistics reported on a national or regional level are generally representative of the applicable cross sections. Other data presented are actual survey results and may not be representative of the related cross section as a whole.

This is the fourth report prepared for and sponsored by NFPA. The first, in 1991, had 7,786 respondents. The second, in 1993, had 3,542 respondents. The lower response rate in 1995 of 1,431 can be attributed to using something other than the direct-mail method of delivery used in previous surveys.

Executive Summary

The NFPA survey collected information from members of various paralegal associations across the country regarding demographics, education, compensation, benefits, satisfaction levels, employer types, and other topics of interest. The following table presents the average responses concerning the important aspects of a paralegal's job and characteristics of members of the paralegal profession.

Characteristic	Average Response	1997 Percentage or Average of Population with Characteristic	1995 Percentage or Average of Population with Characteristic	1993 Percentage or Average of Population with Characteristic	1991 Percentage or Average of Population with Characteristic
Gender	Female	92%	94%	93%	94%
Race	Caucasian	91%	95%	94%	95%
Age	National average	38	38	37	36
Education— College	Bachelor degree	53%	54%	55%	52%
Education— Paralegal	Paralegal studies	85%	85%	n/a	81%
	ABA approved	64%	64%	n/a	65%

Characteristic	Average Response	1997 Percentage or Average of Population with Characteristic	1995 Percentage or Average of Population with Characteristic	1993 Percentage or Average of Population with Characteristic	1991 Percentage or Average of Population with Characteristic
Employer Type	Law firm	71%	71%	71%	78%
Time Employed as Paralegal	National average	7–10 years	7–10 years	3–10 years	6 years
Billing Rate	$41–80/hour	66%	74%	75%	n/a
Salary	National average	$34,514	$32,875	$31,021	$29,607
Bonus	National average bonus	$2,094	$1,869	$1,620	$1,565
	Percent receiving a bonus	64%	63%	68%	65%

From the 1997 NFPA Survey. Reprinted with permission.

LEGAL ASSISTANT TODAY'S 1997–98 SALARY SURVEY RESULTS[1]

Where do you stand among your fellow paralegals? Are you making the going rate for a professional with your credentials, and where can you expect to go from here? Where do the more lucrative opportunities lie, both in terms of specialty and geography?

Hopefully the results of our 1997–98 Salary Survey will be able to provide those answers for you. We've broken the paralegal field into subsections based on experience, education, practice area, type of employer and geographic region. We've also examined those other benefits which can be as important to you as the size of your paycheck.

To obtain these results, a compensation questionnaire was included in the November/December 1997 issue of *Legal Assistant Today.* From the questionnaires received, we extrapolated a random sampling of 420 responses, from which the following data was compiled. This data was then compared to results obtain in *Legal Assistant Today's* 1995 and 1996 Salary Surveys.

---

[1]Copyright 1998 James Publishing, Inc. Reprinted courtesy of *Legal Assistant Today* magazine. For subscription information, call (800) 394-2626.

National

Average salary: $34,002

Percent change from previous years: 1996—$32,415 +4.9%
1995—$31,503 +7.9%

Average salary by region:
60%   Metro $35,466
2%   Other $29,707
9%   Rural $28,338
29%   Urban $32,966

Average salary by employer:
20%   Corporate $39,442
6%   Government $32,155
74%   Law Firm $32,939

Do you think you are fairly paid?
52%   Yes $37,077   (average salary)
48%   No $30,655   (average salary)

Billing statistics:
Average billing rate $70
Hours expected (week)   38.3
Hours actual (week)   42.4
Minimum annual billable hour requirement   1,522

Average 1997 raise: 5.45%
Received bonus: 66%
Average bonus amount: $1,947

Paralegal positions at firm/department:
(Percent change from previous years)
34% increase
57% same
10% decrease

Average salary by gender:
93%   Female $33,923
7%   Male $34,487

Salary based on years of experience:

Years	Salary	Difference from 1996
Less than 1	$25,985	2.2% Decrease
1–3	$28,309	8.5% Increase
3–5	$31,625	2.3% Increase

5–7	$33,935	7.6% Increase
7–10	$35,277	4.5% Increase
10–15	$37,967	6.1% Increase
15–20	$44,504	10.4% Increase
20 Plus	$50,294	22.9% Increase

Specialty Average Salary:

Intellectual Property	$41,211
Corporate	$38,330
Real Estate	$37,499
Environmental	$37,077
Defense Litigation	$34,997
Plaintiff Litigation	$33,552
Workers' Compensation	$33,500
Employment	$32,968
Estate/Probate	$31,448
Criminal	$30,909
Insurance	$29,037
Family	$28,191
Personal Injury	$28,091
Bankruptcy	$28,060

Specialty Average Raise:

Intellectual Property	3.89%
Corporate	3.41%
Real Estate	4.59%
Environmental	6.0%
Defense Litigation	6.26%
Plaintiff Litigation	5.67%
Workers' Compensation	13.67%
Employment	5.38%
Estate/Probate	5.52%
Criminal	5.5%
Insurance	3.86%
Family	3.93%
Personal Injury	7.5%
Bankruptcy	5.0%

Regional

Northeast

Average 1997 raise:	5.48%
Received bonus:	61.6%
Average bonus amount:	$1,801

Average salary: $33,488
Percent change from previous years: 1996—$32,826 +2.0%
                                         1995—$32,454 +3.2%

Salary by employer:
27%   Corporate $39,686
 7%   Government $30,190
57%   Law Firm $31,958

Paralegal positions at firm/department:
(Percent change from previous years)
35%   Increase
52%   Same
12%   Decrease

Do you think you are fairly paid?
56%   Yes $36,964 (average salary)
44%   No $29,097 (average salary)

Salary by state:
Vermont* $23,840
Maine* $26,037
New Hampshire* $27,250
Rhode Island* $27,660
Maryland* $30,250
Pennsylvania $31,124
Connecticut $31,893
District of Columbia* $33,100
New York $35,319
Massachusetts $36,122
New Jersey $37,230

South
Average 1997 raise: 5.37%
Received bonus: 72%
Average bonus amount: $1,634
Average salary: $32,726
Percent change from previous years: 1996—$31,329 +4.4%
                                         1995—$29,799 +9.8%

---

*Note: Based on less than ten verifiable submissions and, as with all results, may not be representative of the salaries for your state, area, or city.

Salary by employer:

17%	Corporate	$37,050
5%	Government	$27,992
73%	Law Firm	$32,026

Paralegal positions at firm/department:
(Percent change from previous years)

50%	Increase
47%	Same
8%	Decrease

Do you think you are fairly paid?

49%	Yes	$34,894 (average salary)
51%	No	$30,636 (average salary)

Salary by state:

Alabama*	$23,680
Oklahoma*	$24,603
Kentucky	$28,258
Mississippi*	$28,500
Tennessee	$28,520
Louisiana*	$29,082
Arkansas*	$29,500
West Virginia*	$29,800
Virginia	$30,450
Texas	$32,267
South Carolina	$33,750
North Carolina	$34,106
Florida	$35,251
Georgia	$36,270

Midwest

Average 1997 raise:	5.09%
Received bonus:	58%
Average bonus amount:	$1,848
Average salary:	$31,354

Percent change from previous years: 1996—$30,772 +1.8
1995—$30,089 +4.2%

---

*Note: Based on less than ten verifiable submissions and, as with all results, may not be representative of the salaries for your state, area, or city.

Salary by employer:

21%	Corporate	$37,138
5%	Government	$29,727
66%	Law Firm	$29,622

Paralegal positions at firm/department:
(Percent change from previous years)

18%	Increase
70%	Same
12%	Decrease

Do you think you are fairly paid?

43%	Yes	$34,534 (average salary)
57%	No	$28,957 (average salary)

Salary by state:

Iowa	$25,982
South Dakota*	$25,500
North Dakota*	$26,000
Ohio	$28,322
Indiana*	$28,390
Kansas*	$28,525
Missouri	$29,316
Wisconsin	$31,277
Michigan	$33,542
Nebraska*	$34,412
Illinois	$35,538
Minnesota	$36,318

West

Average 1997 raise:	5.8%	
Received bonus:	70%	
Average bonus amount:	$2,533	
Average salary:	$38,323	
Percent change from previous years:	1996—$36,158 +5.9%	
	1995—$34,439 +11.2%	

Salary by employer:

11%	Corporate	$46,969
7%	Government	$39,142
80%	Law Firm	$37,025

*Note: Based on less than ten verifiable submissions and, as with all results, may not be representative of the salaries for your state, area, or city.

Paralegal positions at firm/department:
(Percent change from previous years)
37%   Increase
55%   Same
 8%   Decrease

Do you think you are fairly paid?
61% Yes $40,821 (average salary)
39% No $34,486 (average salary)

Salary by state:

State	Salary
Montana*	$28,441
Colorado	$31,316
Wyoming*	$31,520
Idaho*	$32,000
Oregon	$32,025
Washington	$33,500
New Mexico*	$33,650
Alaska*	$37,300
Utah*	$38,100
Hawaii*	$38,500
Nevada*	$38,736
Arizona	$40,173
California	$41,761

Education
Salary by Degree

20.5%	No degree	$34,422	+3.4%
22%	Associates	$31,318	+3.0%
49%	Bachelors	$34,519	+5.2%
7.8%	Masters	$36,352	+7.9%

By Region
Northeast

No degree	19%	$33,329
Associates	22%	$29,717
Bachelors	49%	$34,669
Masters	12%	$34,456

---

*Note: Based on less than ten verifiable submissions and, as with all results, may not be representative of the salaries for your state, area, or city.

South

No degree	26%	$33,036
Associates	25%	$28,654
Bachelors	43%	$33,823
Masters	7%	$31,969

Midwest

No degree	16%	$29,641
Associates	26%	$31,089
Bachelors	54%	$31,844
Masters	4%	$33,319

West

No degree	20%	$37,704
Associates	17%	$37,171
Bachelors	53%	$38,745
Masters	10%	$42,780

Paralegal Certificate

General   (average salary)

71%	Yes	$34,614
29%	No	$32,480

No Degree

49%	Yes	$35,333
51%	No	$33,893

Associates

67%	Yes	$31,860
33%	No	$30,215

Bachelors

80%	Yes	$34,831
20%	No	$33,394

Masters

87%	Yes	$36,803
13%	No	$33,312

First Year Class

Education	(Average salary)	
No degree	8%	$21,333
Associates	31%	$25,125
Bachelors	48%	$25,740
Masters	13%	$27,305

Paralegal Certificate

73.2%	Yes	$25,745
26.8%	No	$24,505

CLA Designation

4.8%	Yes	$29,900
95.2%	No	$25,180

Benefits Received from Employer

Benefit	Percent Received	Difference from 1996
Child care	3.24%	1% increase
Continuing education fees	62.84%	2% increase
Dental insurance	55.36%	5% increase
Disability insurance	51.12%	0% same
Flex-time	37.9%	5% increase
Free legal representation	28.43%	10% increase
Health insurance	90.02%	2% increase
Life insurance	63.84%	3% decrease
Paid maternity leave	43.14%	5% decrease
Paid parking	39.40%	3% increase
Paid personal days	54.36%	3% increase
Private office	63.52%	7% decrease
Professional dues	60.09%	5% decrease
Vision	29.67%	4% increase

F

Resources: Directories, Guides, Newsletters and a Whole Lot More

JOB SEARCH RESOURCES

AALS Placement Bulletin   Association of American Law Schools listings of faculty and administrative job openings at U.S. law schools. Published 3× per year. Association of American Law Schools, 1201 Connecticut Avenue NW, Suite 800, Washington, DC 20036; (202) 296-8851.

ABA Directory   American Bar Association. Available in most libraries. More than 1,000 pages of organizations, See *ABA Journal*.

ABA Guide to Foreign Law Firms   American Bar Association. Law firms in more than 90 foreign jurisdictions. 1993 edition. $40 plus $4.95 shipping.

ABA Journal   The monthly magazine published by the American Bar Association, P.O. Box 10892, Chicago, IL 60611; (312) 285-2221.

American Association for Paralegal Education   2965 Flowers Rd. So. #105, Atlanta, GA 30341; (913) 381-4458. Publishes a list of member paralegal schools, pamphlets regarding paralegal utilization, and annual directory available to nonmembers.

Antitrust   The ABA's Antitrust Law Section magazine.

Biographical Directory of Legal Administration Professionals   Altman Weil Pensa Publication. $139.

The Bottom-Line   Law Practice Management & Technology Section, State Bar of California, 555 Franklin Street, San Francisco, CA 94102; (415) 561-8820.

Careers in Entertainment Law   William Henslee. What to expect as an entertainment lawyer. Apply paralegal descriptions accordingly. American Bar Association, 1990.

Careers in Intellectual Property Law   American Bar Association. Free.

Careers in International Law   Mark W. Janis. American Bar Association, 1993.

Communications Lawyer   American Bar Association.

Directory of Corporate Counsel   Aspen Law & Business. A two-volume listing of in-house legal departments for major corporations, nonprofit organizations, and universities nationwide.

Directory of Environmental Attorneys   Aspen Law & Business. 1995.

Directory of Legal Aid and Defender Offices in the U.S.   National Legal Aid & Defender Association, 1625 K Street NW, Suite 800, Washington, DC 20006; (202) 452-0620. Employment opportunities listed in the newsletter.

Directory of Legal Employers   Directory of more than 1,000 private, government, and not for profit legal employers. Published yearly by the National Association for Law Placement. Contact Harcourt Brace at (800) 787-8717. $49.95.

Directory of Minority Partners in Majority/Corporate Law Firms   American Bar Association, 1995. More than 125 law firms in 25 specialties. $125.

Directory of Opportunities in International Law   John Bassett Moore Society of International Law, University of Virginia School of Law, Charlottesville, VA 22901; (804) 924-3087.

Directory of U.S. Labor Organizations   Bureau of National Affairs. 200 unions engaged in labor representation.

The Entertainment and Sports Lawyer   ABA Entertainment and Sports Industries Forum. $40 annually from American Bar Association.

Environmental Law Careers Directory   Law firms, not for profit organizations, and government agencies. Ecology Law Quarterly, 493 Simon Hall, Boalt Hall, University of California, Berkeley, CA 94720; (510) 642-0457.

Everything You Need to Know About Being a Legal Assistant   Chere B. Estrin. A lively book compiling this author's articles about the paralegal career. Quick reading, informative, and fun. Available through West Publishing or any bookstore, Amazon.com, or Barnes & Noble.com.

Federal Law Related Careers   More than 140 careers requiring a legal background. Explains hiring procedures for leading federal agency employers. More than 1,000 federal recruiting offices listed. 1994 edition. Federal Reports, Inc., 1010 Vermont Avenue, NW, Suite 408, Washington, DC 20005; (800) 296-9611.

Hot Docs and Smoking Guns: Document Productions   Co-author Stacey Hunt and Rhonda Gregory. Clark Boardman Callaghan. A step-by-step guide to the paralegal's role in document productions. From indexing to pleadings to handling difficult attorneys. Available also through Amazon.com.

Guerilla Tactics for Getting the Legal Job of Your Dreams   Kimm Alayne Walton. Harcourt Brace, 1996. $24.95.

Job Descriptions for Law Firms and Corporate Law Departments   Altman Weil Publications. P.O. Box 625, Newtown Square, PA 19073; (610) 359-9900. $155.

Law and Legal Information Directory   Gale Research. More than 30,000 law-related institutions, services and facilities, including legal periodicals, bar associations, and more.

Law Practice Management   American Bar Association. Available in most libraries.

The Lawyers Guide for JobSurfing on the Net   Career Education Institute, P.O. Box 11171, Winston-Salem, NC 27116; (910) 768-2999. $10 plus $2 shipping.

The Legal Job Interview   Clifford Ennico. Biennix Corporation, 1992. $17.95.

Legal Newsletter in Print   Infosources Publishing, 140 Norma Road, Teaneck, NJ 07666; (201) 836-7072.

Martindale-Hubbell Dispute Resolution Directory   Martindale-Hubbell, DRD Department, 121 Chanlon Road, New Providence, NJ 07974; (800) 526-4902.

Martindale-Hubbell Law Directory   More than 700,000 lawyers, law firms, and corporate legal departments. Extensive biographical information. Also published in CD-ROM. Available in most law libraries.

National Association for Public Interest Law   1118 22nd Street, NW, Washington, DC 20037; (202) 466-3686. The newsletter contains job openings and is available to nonmembers for $25.

NLJ Client List   The National Law Journal listing of 250 industrial companies featuring both numbers of outside counsel and in-house legal departments.

Now Hiring: Government Jobs for Lawyers   Annual directory prepared by the ABA Law Student Division for law students or entry-levels in executive, legislative and judicial branches of federal government. $19.95, American Bar Association.

Paralegal Career Guide, Third Edition (Prentice-Hall)   Chere B. Estrin. An entertaining and informative guide to the paralegal career. Great insider information on how to succeed in this field. For entry or experienced level professionals.

PIES: Public Interest Employment Services Job Alert!   Job listings for public interest law issued twice monthly. Public Interest Clearinghouse, 100 McAllister Street, San Francisco, CA 94102-4929.

Position Reports   Weekly compilation of 500+ job listings for lawyers in law firms, corporations, and government sector. (800) 962-4947.

Probate and Property   American Bar Association.

G

Suggested Reading Materials

The range of books available to today's paralegal is enormous. The legal publishing market realized that paralegals are professionals who continuously improve and expand on their skills through books and magazines. There are books on practically every practice area for paralegals. Following is a list of books and publications of general interest to paralegals:

BOOKS

Paralegal Career Guide, Third Edition (Prentice-Hall)
Estrin, Chere B.
(2001)

Essentials of Paralegalism
Statsky, William P.
West Thomson Learning (1997)

Everything You Need to Know About Being a Legal Assistant
Estrin, Chere B.
West Thomson Learning (1995)

Guide for Legal Assistants: Roles, Responsibilities, Specializations
Gowen, Michele C.
(1991)

How to Find a Job as a Paralegal: A Step by Step Job Search Guide
Kisiel, Marie, Ph.D
West Publishing (1996)

How to Survive in a Law Firm: Client Relations
Pulsifer, Nancy, et al
Paralegal Practice Library–Estrin Series
Aspen Law & Business (1993)

Introduction to Legal Assisting
Garrett, Vena
Legal Studies Series (1992)

Legal Analysis and Writing for Paralegals
Putnam, William H.
West Thomson Learning (1997)

Legal Ethics for Paralegals and the Law Office
Morrison, Laura L.
West Thomson Learning (1995)

Life Outside the Law Firm: Non-Traditional Careers for Paralegals
Treffinger, Karen
West Thomson Learning (1995)

Manual for Legal Assistants
National Association of Legal Assistants, Inc.
(1998)

Opportunities in Paralegal Careers
Fins, Alice
VGM Career Book Series (1990)

Paralegal Ethics and Regulation
Statsky, William P.
West Publishing Paralegal Series (1992)

Paralegal Practice and Procedure: A Practical Guide for Legal Assistants
Larbalestrier, Deborah E.
Prentice Hall
(1994)

Paralegal Drafting Guide
McClellan, Dorien Smith
Paralegal Law Library
Aspen Law & Business (1993)

Paralegal Management Handbook
Brophy, Maureen
Pressley, Patsy
Paralegal Practice Library
Aspen Law & Business (1993 & 1997 Supp.)

The Paralegal's Guide to U.S. Government Jobs: How to Land a Job in 140 Law-Related Careers
Federal Reports, Inc., Washington, DC (1996)

The Paralegal's Role at Trial
Feeney, Kerri W.
Paralegal Litigation Library–Estrin Series
Aspen Law & Business (1993)

The Professional Paralegal Job Search: A Guide for Launching Your Legal Career
French, Christofer Ulmont
Aspen Law & Business (1995)

Starting and Managing Your Own Business:
A Freelancing Guide for Paralegals
Secol, Dorothy
Paralegal Career Series
Aspen Law & Business (1996)

West's Paralegal Today: The Essentials: The Legal Team at Work
Miller, Roger Leroy
Urisko, Mary S.
West Thomson Learning (1995)

What Color Is Your Parachute?
Bolles, Richard
Ten Speed Press (1998)
Now a multimedia event on CD-ROM
with excellent links to the Web.

PERIODICALS

Most state and local paralegal associations publish their own journals and newsletters to keep their members informed on issues affecting paralegals, to update them on changes in the law, to inform them of job openings in the area, and to advertise continuing education seminars and association meetings.

Facts and Findings: The Journal for Legal Assistants
Published quarterly by
National Association of Legal Assistants
1516 S. Boston, Suite 200
Tulsa, OK 74119
(918) 587-6828

Legal Assistant Today
Published six times per year by
James Publishing, Inc.
3505 Cadillac Avenue, Suite H
Costa Mesa, CA 92626
(800) 394-2626

Legal Assistants Update
Published annually by American Bar Association
Standing Committee on Legal Assistants
750 North Lake Shore Drive
Chicago, IL 60611
(312) 988-5000
Web site: www.abanet.org
Paralegals are welcome to join the ABA as associate members.

National Paralegal Reporter
Published five times per year by
National Federation of Paralegal Associations
P.O. Box 33108
Kansas City, MO 64114-0108
(816) 941-4000

Federal Reports, Inc.
1010 Vermont Avenue, NW, Suite 408
Washington, DC 20005
(202) 393-3311
Web site: www.attorneyjobs.com

RECOMMENDED FOR GENERAL JOB SEARCH TECHNIQUES

Negotiate to Close: How to Make More Successful Deals
Karrass, Gary
Fireside/Simon & Schuster (1987)

Negotiate Your Job Offer
Simon, Mary B.
John Wiley & Sons (1998)

Don't Stop with the Want Ads: Conducting a Successful Job Search
McCarty, Mary
AMI/American Management How-to-Series (1998)

Temp: How to Survive & Thrive in the World of Temporary Employment
Smith, Deborhann
Shambhala (1994)

H

NFPA Model Code of Ethics and Responsibility*

PREAMBLE

The National Federation of Paralegal Associations (NFPA) is a professional organization comprised of paralegal associations throughout the United States. Members of NFPA have varying types of backgrounds, experience, education, and job responsibilities which reflect the diversity of the paralegal profession. NFPA promotes the growth, development and recognition of the paralegal professional as an integral partner in the delivery of legal services.

NFPA recognizes that the creation of guidelines and standards for professional conduct are important for the development and expansion of the paralegal profession. In May 1993, NFPA adopted this Model Code of Ethics and Professional Responsibility ("Model Code") to delineate the principles for ethics and conduct to which every paralegal should aspire. The Model Code expresses NFPA's commitment to increasing the quality and efficiency of legal services and recognizes the profession's responsibilities to the public, the legal community, and colleagues.

Canon 1.
A paralegal shall achieve and maintain a high level of competence.

EC–1.1 A paralegal shall achieve competency through education, training, and work experience.

EC–1.2 A paralegal shall participate in continuing education to keep informed of current legal, technical, and general developments.

EC–1.3 A paralegal shall perform all assignments promptly and efficiently.

---

*Reprinted with the permission of the National Federation of Paralegal Associations, Inc.

Canon 2.
A paralegal shall maintain a high level of personal and professional integrity.

EC–2.1   A paralegal shall not engage in any ex parte communications involving the courts or any other adjudicatory body in an attempt to exert undue influence or to obtain advantage for the benefit of only one party.

EC–2.2   A paralegal shall not communicate, or cause another to communicate, with a party the paralegal knows to be represented by a lawyer in a pending matter without the prior consent of the lawyer representing such other party.

EC–2.3   A paralegal shall be scrupulous, thorough, and honest in the identification and maintenance of all funds, securities, and other assets of a client and shall provide accurate accountings as appropriate.

EC–2.4   A paralegal shall ensure that all timekeeping and billing records prepared by the paralegal are thorough, accurate, and honest.

EC–2.5   A paralegal shall advise the proper authority of any dishonest or fraudulent acts by any person pertaining to the handling of the funds, securities, or other assets of a client.

Canon 3.
A paralegal shall maintain a high standard of professional conduct.

EC–3.1   A paralegal shall refrain from engaging in any conduct that offends the dignity and decorum of proceedings before a court or other adjudicatory body and shall be respectful of all rules and procedures.

EC–3.2   A paralegal shall advise the proper authority of any action of another legal professional which clearly demonstrates fraud, deceit, dishonesty, or misrepresentation.

EC–3.3   A paralegal shall avoid impropriety and the appearance of impropriety.

Canon 4.
A paralegal shall serve the public interest by contributing to the delivery of quality legal services and the improvement of the legal system.

EC–4.1   A paralegal shall be sensitive to the legal needs of the public and shall promote the development and implementation of programs that address those needs.

EC–4.2   A paralegal shall support bona fide efforts to meet the need for legal services by those unable to pay reasonable or customary fees; for example, participation in pro bono projects and volunteer work.

EC–4.3   A paralegal shall support efforts to improve the legal system and shall assist in making changes.

Canon 5.
A paralegal shall preserve all confidential information provided by the client or acquired from other sources before, during, and after the course of the professional relationship.

EC–5.1   A paralegal shall be aware of and abide by all legal authority governing confidential information.

EC–5.2   A paralegal shall not use confidential information to the disadvantage of the client.

EC–5.3   A paralegal shall not use confidential information to the advantage of the paralegal or of a third person.

EC–5.4   A paralegal may reveal confidential information only after full disclosure and with the client's written consent; or, when required by law or court order; or, when necessary to prevent the client from committing an act which could result in death or serious bodily harm.

EC–5.5   A paralegal shall keep those individuals responsible for the legal representation of a client fully informed of any confidential information the paralegal may have pertaining to that client.

EC–5.6   A paralegal shall not engage in any indiscreet communications concerning clients.

Canon 6.
A paralegal's title shall be fully disclosed.

EC–6.1   A paralegal's title shall clearly indicate the individual's status and shall be disclosed in all business and professional communications to avoid misunderstandings and misconceptions about the paralegal's role and responsibilities.

EC–6.2   A paralegal's title shall be included if the paralegal's name appears on business cards, letterhead, brochures, directories, and advertisements.

Canon 7.
A paralegal shall not engage in the unauthorized practice of law.

    EC–7.1   A paralegal shall comply with the applicable legal authority governing the unauthorized practice of law.

Canon 8.
A paralegal shall avoid conflicts of interest and shall disclose any possible conflict to the employer or client, as well as to the prospective employers or clients.

    EC–8.1   A paralegal shall act within the bounds of the law, solely for the benefit of the client, and shall be free of compromising influences and loyalties. Neither the paralegal's personal or business interest, nor those of other clients or third persons, should compromise the paralegal's professional judgment and loyalty to the client.

    EC–8.2   A paralegal shall avoid conflicts of interest which may arise from previous assignments whether for a present or past employer or client.

    EC–8.3   A paralegal shall avoid conflicts of interest which may arise from family relationships and from personal and business interests.

    EC–8.4   A paralegal shall create and maintain an effective record-keeping system that identifies clients, matters, and parties with which the paralegal has worked, to be able to determine whether an actual or potential conflict of interest exists.

    EC–8.5   A paralegal shall reveal sufficient non-confidential information about a client or former client to reasonably ascertain if an actual or potential conflict of interest exists.

    EC–8.6   A paralegal shall not participate in or conduct work on any matter where a conflict of interest has been identified.

    EC–8.7   In matters where a conflict of interest has been identified and the client consents to continued representation, a paralegal shall comply fully with the implementation and maintenance of an Ethical Wall.

I

Free Resume Critique

Send this form along with your resume and self-addressed, stamped envelope to:

Resume Critique
The Estrin Organization
1901 Avenue of the Stars, Suite 350
Los Angeles, CA 90067[1]

or e-mail to estrin@estrin.com. We're sorry, but we cannot give phone consultations. Please visit our Web site at *www.estrin.com.*

Please provide the following information:

Name: _____

Years of paralegal experience: _____

Years in the workforce: _____

Are you seeking your first paralegal job?

____ Yes   ____ No

Specialty: _____

What kind of position are you seeking? _____

Would you like to be included in our mailing list?

____ Yes   ____ No thanks

---

[1]You must send a self-addressed, stamped envelope in order for your resume to be reviewed and returned.

We will give our opinion about your resume in the following areas:

(A five-star rating is the highest.)

☆☆☆☆☆ ☆☆☆☆ ☆☆☆ ☆☆ ☆

I. Readability
  1. Easy to read
  2. Inviting
  3. Professional

II. Appearance
  1. Good format
  2. Acceptable length
  3. Readable font
  4. Type size
  5. Margins
  6. Paper quality
  7. Paper color
  8. Line spacing
  9. Lack of typos

III. Content
  1. Brevity
  2. Clarity
  3. Directed
  4. Sentence length
  5. Logical
  6. Vocabulary
  7. Clear skill set
  8. Length of job
     descriptions

Index